Helion & Company Limited
Unit 8 Amherst Business Centre
Budbrooke Road
Warwick
CV34 5WE
England
Tel. 01926 499 619
Email: info@helion.co.uk
Website: www.helion.co.uk
Twitter: @helionbooks
https://helionbooks.wordpress.com/

Illustrations are reproduced under the Creative Commons license, or derive from the author's personal collection.

Cover: U.S. Military personnel assigned to the 4th Psychological Operations Group, 193rd Special Operations Wing, Pennsylvania Air Nation Guard (ANG) broadcast television and radio programming from onboard an ANG EC-130J Hercules Commando Solo aircraft, in support of Operation Iraqi Freedom. (Defense Visual Information Center)

Designed and typeset by Mach 3 Solutions (www.mach3solutions.co.uk)
Cover design Paul Hewitt, Battlefield Design (www.battlefield-design.co.uk)

ISBN: 978-1-804518-80-9

British Library Cataloguing-in-Publication Data
A catalogue record for this book is available from the British Library

CONTENTS

Note: In order to simplify the use of this book, all names, locations and geographic designations are as provided in *The Times World Atlas*, or other traditionally accepted major sources of reference, as of the time of described events.

ABBREVIATIONS AND ACRONYMS

AIVD	General Intelligence and Security Service (Netherlands)
ANA	Afghan National Army
ANC	African National Congress
ANSF	Afghan National Security Forces
AP	Associated Press
CENTCOM	Central Command (US)
CIA	Central Intelligence Agency (US)
DoD	Department of Defense (US)
EU	European Union
EU INTCEN	EU Intelligence and Situation Centre
FSA	Free Syrian Army
GAO	Government Accountability Office (US)
HIG	Hezb-e Islami of Gulbuddin Hekmatyar
Hybrid CoE	European Centre of Excellence for Countering Hybrid Threats
IED	improvised explosive device
ISAF	International Security Assistance Force
ISI	Pakistani Inter-services Intelligence agency (Pakistan)
IUEF	International University Exchange Fund
NATO	North Atlantic Treaty Organization
NCTV	National Coordinator for Security and Counterterrorism (Netherlands)
NGO	non-government organizations
OCG	organized crime group
PKK	Kurdistan Workers' Party
PMC	private military company
PR	public relations
REE	rare earth elements
RFE	Radio Free Europe
RL	Radio Liberty
SDN	software-defined networking

INTRODUCTION

This book describes hybrid threats to national security, and how to deploy them as weapons against an adversary. Designed to be difficult to detect or attribute, hybrid threats constitute a twenty-first-century concept which enables, often with the help of advanced technology, the use of military and non-military means under conditions of plausible deniability.

This book also describes how to identify and define hybrid threats, when used by an aggressor against us. Hybrid threats are currently used by both state and non-state actors.

The concept of hybrid threats has in recent years become an integral part of the security and national security policies adopted by the European Union (EU), North Atlantic Treaty Organization (NATO), and indeed most Western countries. We will see that the concept also frequently appears in headline news. Yet, military intelligence services and security services seem unable to agree on how to define the phenomenon, or on how to take efficient countermeasures against them.

When the Cold War ended with the dissolution of the Soviet Union in 1991, the United States and the Western world felt triumphant. Global society was no longer bipolar, as it had been during the Cold War, but had become unipolar under American hegemony, they claimed. The American political scientist Francis Fukuyama went so far as to argue, in his book *The End of History and the Last Man* (1992), that the Western world's global victory and the introduction of liberal democracy and free-market capitalism of the Western style to the rest of the planet signified the final stage of humanity's sociocultural evolution and would become the final form of human government.

The book made Fukuyama a celebrity, but the euphoria did not last long. Old problems, including terrorism and nationalism, rapidly re-emerged, and the Western world soon felt beset by what looked like new threats, or at least threats of a new order of magnitude. The 9/11 2001 Al-Qaida terrorist attacks against the United States and the American 2003 invasion of Iraq launched a new period of feelings of vulnerability.

The world had not seen the end of history, after all. Instead, new poles of power emerged to threaten the Western-dominated world order. While the perceived threats often were quite similar, or even identical, to those in the past, there was a qualitative difference. This was largely the effect of the two major trends of the 1990s. Globalization, and yet more importantly, digitalization had changed the world since 1991. Together, these two trends caused a dramatic increase in connectivity. Henceforth, trends and opinions rapidly spanned the globe, which provided vastly enhanced leverage for opportunistic action by hostile actors.

It was the new technological developments of the information age, ranging from digitalization, information technology, the internet, and cyberspace to social media networks, that made global connectivity possible in the first place. However, these innovations also produced an interconnectedness of information technology that opened up a Pandora's box of unanticipated dangers. Suddenly, it was possible for a small group or even a single individual to carry out cyber-attacks that disabled critical infrastructure on the other side of the world, or to influence global public opinion in detrimental directions.

Governments quickly realized the danger. Yet, while everybody understood that cyberspace played a special role in the new threat landscape, everything else remained very vague. Who was responsible, and had the mandate, for addressing the new threats? Could the new threats even be defined, not to mention identified? Global society entered an age of undefined yet still lethal threats – the world of hybrid threats.

At present, little remains of the jubilation of the supposedly global victory of the West. Instead, news headlines describe in particular Russian and Chinese activities in terms of hybrid threats against the Western world. These actions range from specific information and cyber operations here and now to what is vaguely labelled clear and present threats to the security of billions of civilians and indeed all future generations.

In April 2024, Vice-Admiral Didier Maleterre, the deputy commander of NATO's Allied Maritime Command (Marcom), said that Russian undersea hybrid warfare threatened the security of 'nearly 1 billion Nato-nation civilians'.[1]

In May, the news agency Reuters reported that 'NATO says Russian hybrid attack intensify on members' territories'. NATO had announced that its members were 'deeply concerned' about recent attacks on the Czech Republic, Estonia, Germany, Latvia, Lithuania, Poland, and the United Kingdom all of which they attributed to Russia.[2] Was this a prelude to war, or had war already begun?

Days afterwards, the Jamestown Foundation argued that 'Russian attacks on Ukrainian critical infrastructure become hybrid threat to Europe'. The Western world must act, the Foundation claimed, because '[t]he environmental impacts of Russian bombings extend beyond Ukraine to ecosystems across Europe, requiring urgent action to protect future generations'.[3]

In July, a U.S. Army report claimed that henceforth, 'adversaries will have conventional, hybrid and irregular capabilities to conduct operations against the Homeland' and that 'China, Russia, and other adversaries are investing heavily in hybrid and irregular capabilities, such as information and cyber operations, to attack soft targets and systems within the territory of the United States and its Allies'.[4] Expectedly, the press picked up and amplified the report's findings, warning that the U.S. mainland was 'ultra-vulnerable to China, Russia hybrid attacks'.[5]

Beyond Russia and China, other dangers lurked. In August 2024 South Korea's President Yoon Suk Yeol urged preparedness against North Korea's hybrid warfare, including 'nonkinetic operations, such as public opinion warfare, cyberattacks and the spread of fake news'.[6]

Even the reinsurance industry issued warnings. 'Reinsurers grapple with hybrid cyber threat complexity', *Reinsurance Business* noted in November the same year. The report warned that 'hybrid threats blur lines between crime and warfare', for instance with regard to criminal ransomware tactics, and that '[n]ation-state cyber activity is complicating the risk landscape, with actors from Russia, Iran, North Korea, and China targeting critical sectors like energy, transportation, and public services for strategic objectives'.[7]

This was only a small sample of news headlines about hybrid threats. Many more appear in print every week. Besides, the conclusions to be drawn from such news reports and warnings have translated into a large number of articles and books about hybrid threats. These tend to reiterate a number of often-heard, but which we will see patently faulty, notions, namely:

1. Hybrid threats is a new phenomenon.
2. Hybrid threats is something that only authoritarian (or 'evil') states and their likeminded supporters engage in.
3. Hybrid threats is related to hybrid warfare, and thereby a form of war that must be under the control of the Armed Forces.

Already during a 2022 seminar at the European Centre of Excellence for Countering Hybrid Threats (Hybrid CoE) in Helsinki, a senior representative of the Centre concluded that '[h]ybrid threats only emanate from authoritarian states and authoritarian organisations. When democratic states use non-state actors to undermine authoritarian states, it is not at all the same thing, because our goals are good and our intentions pure, while their goals and intentions are evil'.[8]

To gain a proper understanding of the nature of hybrid threats, such notions need to be refuted, since they encourage fuzzy and highly politicized thinking. To the contrary, a serious examination of the subject will show that hybrid threats is not a new phenomenon, it is not something that only authoritarian states engage in, and hybrid threats take place in times of peace, not war – hence, the phenomenon is not the same as hybrid warfare (which, as will be shown, still remains a phenomenon that is difficult, if not impossible, to define in a practical manner).

All too often the hybrid threats label is added to any incident behind which we wish to see the hands of an adversary. Much of the present writing on hybrid threats is propagandistic in nature. It is far too easy to shift the blame for incidents that derive from human error and our own lack of planning to the adversary by labelling the incident as a hybrid threat.

Yet, the concept of hybrid threats is very real. While the nature of the threat, despite the hype, may not be new, the increased interconnectedness and vulnerabilities in modern society means that governments, security organizations, and armed forces presently need to pay significantly higher attention to such threats. This book will show why, and how.

Some hybrid threats operations are overt. Most are covert, or at least include covert elements. We will see that attacks typically come from unexpected directions. Deception always plays a major role, if only to keep the particulars of the operation out of the public eye. In hybrid threats operations, nothing is what it seems.

1

THE CONCEPT

New Vulnerabilities

The background to the increased interconnectedness and vulnerabilities of modern society can be found in technological innovations that were made during the Cold War but only became omnipresent from the 1990s onwards.

But let us begin with a brief re-examination of state power, and particularly military power, since the application of such power is what really defines military conflict.

Until the end of the Cold War, most conflicts could be described in deceptively simple terms. They would involve a state or alliance of states which applied all or most of its instruments of power (primarily military, but also financial, diplomatic, and media powers, among others) against another state or alliance of states. When states deployed military power, that is, employed possibly mass-casualty violence, the conflict turned into an armed conflict, hence a war.

Even before the twentieth century, war was most often total, that is, a type of warfare that mobilizes all of the resources of a society to fight the war, includes any and all (including civilian-associated) resources and infrastructure under the control of a militarized administration that aims to maximize military capabilities, and gives priority to warfare over non-combatant needs. The largest possible number of people is mobilized to participate in the war, as soldiers on the one hand and as part of the production of weapons and supplies on the other. The main purpose of total war is the deployment of maximum military force to defeat the adversary or to eliminate him physically. Hence, the enemy's non-combatant population, civilian infrastructure, and means of production are regarded as legitimate military targets. While military and legal theorists might argue about the details and validity of generally-agreed laws of war, the fundamental facts of war and the supremacy of the state were not questioned.

Besides, in a war between states the enemy was clearly defined and identified. There was little ambiguity. In the Cold War, two ideologically opposed blocs confronted one another, each attempting to dominate the other in military and political terms.

However, the development of nuclear weapons systems during the Cold War, in particular long-range strategic bombers and intercontinental ballistic missiles that were likely to penetrate the defender's air defences, meant that the actual application of military power against the adversary became increasingly fraught with peril. Until then, wars between states had mostly been conventional, particularly when defined as fighting in an open battle against another state's armed forces.

The new weapons systems brought in the doctrine of military strategy and national security policy eloquently called mutually assured destruction (MAD). The doctrine posited that a full-scale use of nuclear weapons by an attacker on a nuclear-armed defender with second-strike capabilities would result in the complete annihilation of both the attacker and the defender.

Previously, empires had often managed to prevent war between each other by maintaining a relative balance of power (military, economic, and diplomatic). This did not always work. When the relative balance between two empires changed, the risk of war increased. In comparison, the introduction of nuclear weapons in sufficient numbers to bring in mutually assured destruction by necessity made the balance of power more efficient. With increasing reluctance to go to open war, the balance of power henceforth began to be referred to as the balance of terror. It became not only too costly, but also too dangerous, for the opposed blocs actually to engage each other directly in open battle.

As a result, the two blocs shifted to what became known as a policy of proxy wars. A proxy war is a conflict in which one or more state or nonstate belligerents receive direct or indirect external support by a third party, which typically was one of the two opposing superpowers or blocs. A belligerent with such external support is a proxy of the principal, which can make use of the proxy to influence the outcome of the conflict and thereby to advance its own strategic interests or undermine those of its opponents – but without risking a direct confrontation with the other superpower. Although proxy wars had taken place in earlier centuries, in the Cold War they become typical of how superpowers engaged each other in Third World countries. One such example was when the United States and its NATO allies armed and financed Afghan Islamic extremist

On 3 July 1979, U.S. President Jimmy Carter in a secret presidential finding ordered the provision of clandestine aid (cash, radios, medical supplies) to Afghan Islamic extremist opponents of the pro-Soviet Afghan government. On the very same day, Carter's National Security Adviser, Zbigniew Brzezinski, wrote a note to the president in which he explained that the aid would trigger a Soviet military intervention in Afghanistan. According to Brzezinski's own statement several years later, his intention was to draw the Soviets into their own Vietnam War. After the subsequent Soviet intervention, the United States vastly increased its support, which henceforth included large supplies of military weaponry. The photograph shows Afghan irregulars who were chosen to receive medical treatment in the United States at Norton Air Force Base, California. (Photo: T.Sgt. Bob Simons, U.S. Department of Defense)

President Ronald Reagan meeting with Afghan insurgent leaders, 2 February 1983. From left to right: Gul Muhammad, Mir Niamatullah, Ronald Reagan, Michael A. Barry, Muhammad Umar Babrakzai, Muhammad Ghafoor Yousefzai, Habib-ur-Rehman Hashemi, and Farida Ahmadi. (U.S. National Archives and Records Administration)

groups in the hope that they would kill so many Soviet soldiers that their actions over time would reduce the threat from the Soviet Armed Forces. In addition to military supplies and funding, media propaganda activities played a prominent role in presenting the proxy war in terms of 'good versus evil'. So did U.S. President Ronald Reagan who in a famous speech tinged with religious references on 8 March 1983 referred to the Soviet Union as the 'evil empire'.

Both the balance of terror and the proxy wars were fundamentally symmetric. The conflicts can be explained as state against state, and weapon system against weapon system. Both sides were broadly equal, or symmetric, in the training of their armed forces, the technologies employed, the tactics applied, and the legal definitions employed with regard to state power and the distinction between combatants and non-combatants as legitimate targets. It did not matter that the proxies typically consisted of irregular soldiers. Practitioners knew, and had known for centuries, that asymmetric means of war (variously known as the small war, guerrilla warfare, and partisan warfare) could be devastatingly effective. However, since the superpowers and their respective blocs themselves were broadly symmetric, there was but little theoretical discussion on the possible repercussions brought along from asymmetric proxy wars, or what were the implications of asymmetry in warfare.[1]

However, the situation began to change already in the years immediately after the Cold War. New technologies had emerged, and from this point they reached civilian markets. The first

One of the beneficiaries of the U.S. policy decision to fund and support Islamic extremists in Afghanistan was a young and wealthy Saudi known as Usamah bin Ladin, who later would go on to found the terrorist group Al-Qaida. (Photo: Hamid Mir, 1997–1998)

Cyber-attacks are difficult to attribute, not least because they can be carried out with minimal investments. The workspace of hackers from Anarchist Village at Hackers on Planet Earth (HOPE) conference, 20 July 2018. (Photo: Rek2)

introduction of the Internet to the public in 1989, and in particular the first web browser in 1991, coincided with the end of the Cold War. Henceforth, information and communication technologies, along with social media networks, provided states with additional means and space in which to act in order to project power against other states.

Importantly, the new technologies enabled an increased concealed use of state power projection. Suddenly, there were many ways to strike at an adversary without having to escalate the conflict into open warfare, over which still loomed the half-forgotten menace of mutually assured destruction. Cyber-attacks are notoriously difficult to attribute, which allows an adversary plausible deniability. The aggressor can carry out his objective of inflicting harm on or influencing the other state in his own interest without being recognized as an aggressor. This allows the aggressor to retain a positive international image, and even opens up the possibility of shifting blame for an aggressive act onto another state, or the adversary itself. Such activities can be observed particularly in the field of cyber-attacks, but the practice is common elsewhere as well, including in the sabotage of unguarded pipelines and similar critical infrastructure.

The developments within information and communication technologies, along with the ubiquitous use of online social media and their ancillary social networks, facilitated the rapid rise of globalization. The technological developments took place accompanied by a global population boom.

Popular expectations boomed, too. There was an exponential escalation in demand to be satisfied, ranging from lifestyle improvements to additional resources for consumption. National economies were pushed into escalating competition over ever-scarcer raw materials. The demand for some natural resources were amplified by the developments in technology. Certain types of chips, batteries, electric motors, and numerous other modern manufactured goods need particular raw materials, in particular rare earth elements (REEs). Demand for lithium is growing rapidly with the introduction of environmentally friendly technologies.

Meanwhile, information, opinions, and capital circulate worldwide with practically no delay. Networked global media and the possibility of permanent communication by means of information and communications technologies (ICT) brought the potential, whether deliberately or inadvertently, to influence international as well as domestic audiences. Everybody could see for themselves the differing standards of living in different regions, which enabled the ability of choosing freely between different societies. The result of this comparison and the resultant freedom of choice became one key drive for flows of mass migration, particularly to Western Europe with its fully-developed social welfare systems but also to some extent to the United States with its opportunities for self-made men. The new trends challenged territorially-defined concepts such as sovereignty and national defence.

The changed circumstances produced a complex, interconnected world. Individuals, markets, and societies tend to network when opportunities arise, and they did. The increasingly interconnected world made states both more powerful and more vulnerable. New vulnerabilities arose in supply chains, power supply grids and other forms of critical infrastructure. The emergence in some countries of fundamentally cashless societies based on smooth, instantaneous, and secure systems for electronic payment produced its own set of vulnerabilities with regard to infrastructure that now was regarded as critical even though it previously had not existed. Critical infrastructure is defined as those assets, systems, and networks that provide functions necessary for daily life. These includes physical infrastructure such as highways, bridges, tunnels, and railways, but also utilities such as water and electric energy and virtual infrastructure such as those for electronic payments, all of which are necessary to maintain normalcy in daily life. These vital systems, on which transportation and commerce rely, are no longer distinct and separated but have become a system of systems.

If any component of the system becomes functionally compromised, it may produce severe negative effects on, individuals, markets, and societies, which in turn might seriously weaken state powers.

Hence, the welfare of individuals, the wellbeing of societies, and the security and stability of states depend on the integrity and functional efficiency of complex, interconnected systems which mostly have been in existence for only a few years.

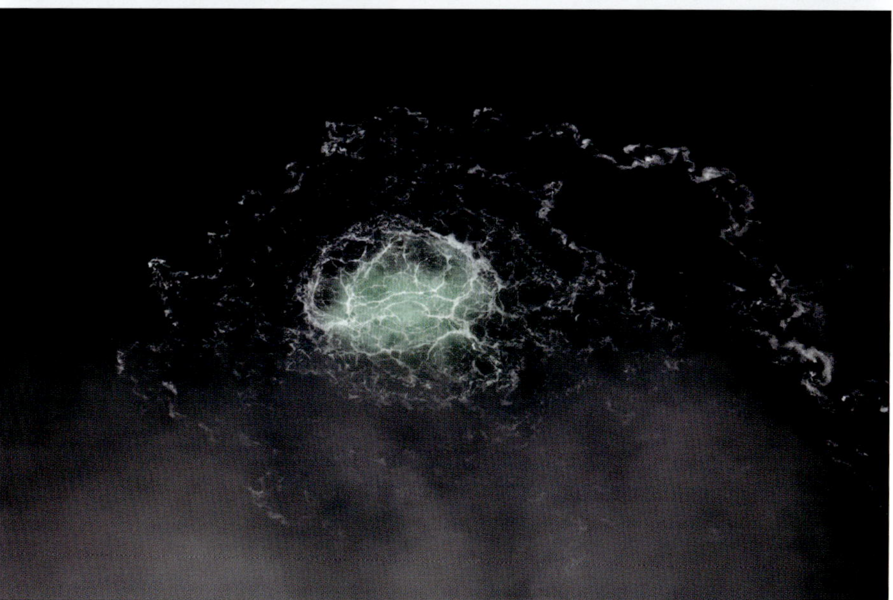

When the underwater Nord Stream gas pipeline, owned by an international consortium in which a Russian company was the majority owner, was blown up on 26 September 2022, much of the Western press and many political leaders immediately laid the blame on Russia, which was claimed to have sabotaged its own pipeline as part of a general campaign intended to damage the West. However, in June 2024, the German authorities issued a European arrest warrant for a Ukrainian national living near Warsaw suspected of having used the yacht *Andromeda* together with two others to sabotage the Nord Stream pipeline in an operation under the control of the Ukrainian government. (Photo: Free Malaysia Today)

An interconnected, networked society is a dependent society. Modern societies are less self-reliant than past societies. It is against this background that we must assess the risk that adversary state or non-state actors take advantage of the technological developments to influence states and societies by exercising hybrid power. This is particularly important, since there are three interwoven elements of critical infrastructure, namely, physical, cyber, and human elements. Either element may be vulnerable to an adversary wishing to compromise the function of the system.

Asymmetric Warfare

The first attempts to define how the Armed Forces might best react to the new circumstances were made in the mid-1990s. Soon, focus was turned to what became known as asymmetric warfare.

Explicit mention of asymmetry and asymmetric warfare in the United States first appeared in the 1995 Joint Publication 1, *Joint Warfare of the Armed Forces of the United States*. This publication used the concept in a simplistic, narrow sense devoted to conventional warfare.[2] This simplistic view was soon understood as being of little practical utility. The 1995 National Military Strategy described the asymmetric warfare phenomenon more broadly, and took pains to include terrorism, usage or threat of usage of weapons of mass destruction, and information warfare in its list of asymmetric challenges. Yet, the phenomenon only received greater attention in 1997, with the *Report of the Quadrennial Defense Review*, which concluded that:

> US dominance in the conventional military arena may encourage adversaries to … use asymmetric means to attack our forces and interests overseas and Americans at home.[3]

The asymmetric warfare phenomenon was finally detailed in the 1999 *Joint Strategy Review, Asymmetric Approaches to Warfare*. It provided a conceptual framework and gave recommendations:

> Asymmetric approaches are attempts to circumvent or undermine US strengths while exploiting US weaknesses

Arrival of migrants in Dobova, Slovenia, on 22 October 2015. Slovenian police and Armed Forces attempt to maintain order. The 2015 European migrant crisis, a direct result of the U.S. military interventions in the Middle East and Afghanistan, saw significantly increased movement of migrants into Europe primarily from Syria but also from Afghanistan, Pakistan, Iraq, Nigeria, Eritrea, and the Balkans. (Photo: Government of Slovenia)

> using methods that differ significantly from the United States' expected method of operations… . [Asymmetric approaches] generally seek a major psychological impact, such as shock or confusion, that affects an opponent's initiative, freedom of action or will. Asymmetric methods require an appreciation of an opponent's vulnerabilities. Asymmetric approaches often employ innovative, nontraditional tactics, weapons or technologies and can be applied at all levels of warfare – strategic, operational and tactical – and across the spectrum of military operations.[4]

Soon, the concept was criticized for primarily dealing with what an opponent might do to the United States rather than how U.S. Armed Forces might use asymmetric methods against its adversaries. A key assumption of asymmetric warfare was indeed that the concept was focused on the adversary, not own forces. Moreover, it was assumed that the adversary would be militarily inferior. In short, the concept of asymmetric warfare was seen as characterised by diverse groups of actors, ranging from conventional (but inferior) armed forces through paramilitary forces and private military companies to organized crime and terrorists. The aggressor employing asymmetric means would direct his attacks only against those physical and virtual areas in which there was a significant imbalance of power and resources in his favour.

Since the concept was adversary-focused, it was assumed that actors employing asymmetric means would be transnational in nature, and likely carry out attacks on U.S. soil. The distinction between combatant and non-combatant and between frontline and hinterland accordingly became blurred. If technological means enabled a local superiority, the aggressor would use them.

Since the U.S. Armed Forces already had weapons of mass destruction and means for cyberwars and information warfare of its own, perceptive observers like Lieutenant Colonel (ret.) Timothy L. Thomas, a specialist in Soviet/Russian and Chinese affairs, pointed out that it was only a terrorist attack that truly would be asymmetric, and that asymmetry in any case was a concept that was interpreted differently in different cultures, and occasionally used as a catch-all phrase in Western militaries for non-Western adversaries 'not fighting fair'.[5] The Armed Forces did realize that modern technology and globalization had changed strategic geography, that future adversaries would have the means to go on the offensive against the U.S. homeland with missiles, information attacks, and terrorism, and that an important 'future task' was to seal the seams between homeland defence agencies since gaps might create vulnerabilities that an adversary might exploit.[6]

Yet, the US discussions and definitions of asymmetric warfare mostly remained focused on the Armed Forces, specifically within the realm and jurisdiction of the Department of Defense (DoD). As behoves the term asymmetric warfare, there was little or no discussion on what asymmetry might mean in times of peace and away from the battlefield. It thus appears highly symbolic that Al-Qaida's 9/11 terrorist attacks on U.S. airliners, the Pentagon, and the World Trade Center in New York took place within weeks of these discussions.

Explosion following the aircraft impact into the South Tower of the World Trade Center, New York. (Photo: U.S. Federal Government)

Hybrid Warfare

In the light of the subsequent invasions of Afghanistan in 2001 and Iraq in 2003, some argued that the concept of asymmetric warfare was too limited to non-state actors and must be superseded by a concept called hybrid warfare. The wars in Afghanistan and Iraq had both been characterized by, first, a conventional phase against formed enemy units (a very brief phase in Afghanistan, a slightly longer one in Iraq), and then, second, a protracted phase of fighting against irregular forces that also included counterterrorist operations. This made it painfully obvious that it was far too simplistic to classify armed conflicts as either 'large-scale and conventional' or 'small-scale and irregular'. Modern conflicts, especially those fought by early twenty-first-century Western forces in the arc of instability, or Greater Middle East, that reached from North Africa to Central Asia, contained elements of both. Moreover, while non-state actors may mostly employ irregular forms of warfare, they would certainly inspire, support, and participate in conventional conflicts if it served their goals. Besides, adversary state actors might be equally likely to engage in irregular conflict in addition to conventional types of warfare to achieve their objectives (and we will see that at least one military practitioner and theorist, Colonel Roger Trinquier, had argued this already in the 1950s and 1960s in what he termed 'modern warfare').

Based on the U.S. experiences in Iraq, Lieutenant Colonel (ret.) Frank G. Hoffman, a key proponent of the new, combined way of looking at modern conflict, noted that hybrid warfare will 'blend the lethality of state conflict with the fanatical and protracted fervor of irregular warfare.'[7]

The hybridity of hybrid warfare, Hoffman argued, was the nature and means of the adversary, who henceforth simultaneously used both conventional and irregular organizational forms, tactics, and weapons systems. He elaborated:

> The term "Hybrid" captures both their organization and their means. Organizationally, they may have a hierarchical political structure, coupled with decentralized cells or networked tactical units. Their means will also be hybrid in form and application. In such conflicts, future adversaries (states, state-sponsored groups, or self-funded actors) will exploit access to modern military capabilities including encrypted command systems, man-portable air to surface missiles, and other modern lethal systems, as well as promote protracted insurgencies that employ ambushes, improvised explosive devices (IEDs), and coercive assassinations. This could include states blending high-tech capabilities, like anti-satellite weapons, with terrorism and cyber-warfare directed against financial targets. Conflicts will include hybrid organizations like Hezbollah and Hamas, employing a diverse set of capabilities. Additionally, states can shift their conventional units to irregular formations and adopt new tactics, as Iraq's *Fedayeen* did in 2003.[8]

Hoffman correctly argued that already the U.S. National Defense Strategy (NDS) of 2005 emphasized the new normality of hybrid warfare, which he described as 'a broadening number of challenges' including 'traditional, irregular, terrorist and disruptive threats.'[9] Two years later, Hoffman modified his expression into the more pertinent 'a broadening range of challenges including traditional, irregular, terrorist, and disruptive threats.'[10] While Hoffman interpreted the NDS 2005 correctly, and noted that the United States faced a range, not only a number, of challenges, the NDS did not actually use the term hybrid warfare. Nonetheless, it is worthwhile to read the deduction drawn in the strategy. The NDS 2005 determined that

> An array of *traditional*, *irregular*, *catastrophic*, and *disruptive* capabilities and methods threaten U.S. interests:
>
> - **Traditional** challenges are posed by states employing recognized military capabilities and forces in well-understood forms of military competition and conflict.
> - **Irregular** challenges come from those employing "unconventional" methods to counter the *traditional* advantages of stronger opponents.
> - **Catastrophic** challenges involve the acquisition, possession, and use of WMD or methods producing WMD-like effects.
> - **Disruptive** challenges may come from adversaries who develop and use breakthrough technologies to negate current U.S. advantages in key operational domains.
>
> These categories overlap. Actors proficient in one can be expected to try to reinforce their position with methods and capabilities drawn from others.[11]

Hoffman defined hybrid threats and pointed out that they were employed by both states and a variety of non-state actors:

> Hybrid threats incorporate a full range of different modes of warfare including conventional capabilities, irregular tactics and formations, terrorist acts including indiscriminate violence and coercion, and criminal disorder.[12]

Looking into the future, Hoffman forecast that

> Our greatest challenge will not come from a state that selects one approach, but from states or groups that select from the whole menu of tactics and technologies to meet their own strategic culture and geography.[13]

In 2010, the U.S. Government Accountability Office (GAO) noted that senior military officials recently had testified before Congress that current and future adversaries were likely to use hybrid warfare tactics, which they regarded as a 'blending of conventional and irregular approaches across the full spectrum of conflict'. U.S. troops, accordingly, would be confronted by threats

> from non-state- and state-sponsored adversaries, including computer network and satellite attacks; portable surface-to-air missiles; improvised explosive devices; information and media manipulation; and chemical, biological, radiological, nuclear, and high-yield explosive devices.[14]

Yet, the DoD had not agreed upon any official definition of a hybrid warfare and 'has no plans to do so because DOD does not consider it a new form of warfare.'[15] Moreover, GAO reported, the various organizations under the DoD defined the concept in different ways:

> For example, according to Air Force officials, hybrid warfare is a potent, complex variation of irregular warfare. U.S. Special Operations Command officials, though, do not use the term hybrid warfare, stating that current doctrine on traditional and irregular warfare is sufficient to describe the current and future operational environment.[16]

To exemplify further:

> Air Force officials stated that the conflicts in Iraq and Afghanistan are irregular warfare and hybrid, while Army and Navy officials both considered Afghanistan irregular warfare and Iraq initially conventional warfare and then later, irregular warfare. [Meanwhile,] U.S. Special Operations Command and Army officials characterized the Russia-Georgia conflict as conventional warfare, while Air Force officials considered it a hybrid conflict.[17]

In addition to hybrid warfare, GAO also noted that various policies also mentioned the idea of hybrid threats. Again, the DoD had no common definition of what this meant, so GAO listed the definitions that had been found in military concept and briefing documents:

> **Hybrid Threat**-An adversary that simultaneously and adaptively employs some fused combination of (1) political, military, economic, social and information means and (2) conventional, irregular, terrorism and disruptive/criminal conflict methods. It may include a combination of state and non-state actors. (Working definition derived by U.S. Joint Forces Command, Joint Irregular Warfare Center, 2008-2009)
>
> **Hybrid Threat**-A threat that simultaneously employs regular and irregular forces, including terrorist and criminal elements to achieve their objectives using an ever-changing variety of conventional and unconventional tactics to create multiple dilemmas. (U.S. Army Training and Doctrine Command's Operational Environment, 2009-2025)[18]

Meanwhile, NATO introduced a definition in 2010, approved by the NATO Military Working Group (Strategic Planning & Concepts):

> A hybrid threat is one posed by any current or potential adversary, including state, non-state and terrorists, with the ability, whether demonstrated or likely, to simultaneously employ conventional and non conventional means adaptively, in pursuit of their objectives.[19]

Unsurprisingly, U.S. Armed Forces, and for this reason also NATO, defined hybrid threats similarly to its previous definition of asymmetric warfare, that is, as something that primarily was linked to military conflict. While some definitions mentioned the economic, social, and information domains as means of the hybrid threats arena, these were always seen in a military, not societal, context.

This only began to change in 2011, when NATO Allied Command Transformation (NATO ACT) brought together some 100 experts drawn from both the private sector and NATO for a one-week workshop with the theme 'Countering Hybrid Threats'. The workshop was the first in a NATO context which displayed the change in direction from hybrid warfare to hybrid threats.

Taking into account diplomacy, political communications, media campaigns, social pressure, economic development, and humanitarian aid, together with the deployment of military force, NATO identified hybrid threats as those 'those posed by adversaries, with the ability to simultaneously employ conventional and non-conventional means adaptively in pursuit of their objectives.'[20]

Personnel from A Company, Task Force 1st Battalion, 35th Armor Regiment, 2nd Brigade Combat Team, 1st Armored Division, pose for a photo in their M1A1 Abrams MBT (Main Battle Tank) under the Victory Arch in Ceremony Square, Baghdad, on 13 November 2003. The conventional phase of the Iraq War was already over. (Photo: T.Sgt. John L. Houghton, Jr., U.S. Air Force)

As Coalition Forces respond to a car bombing in South Baghdad on 14 April 2005, a second car bomb is detonated, targeting those responding to the initial incident. The unconventional phase of war was far from over. (Photo: SPC Ronald Shaw Jr., U.S. Army)

The NATO workshop concluded that

> Admittedly, hybrid threat is an umbrella term encompassing a wide variety of existing adverse circumstances and actions, such as terrorism, migration, piracy, corruption, ethnic conflict, and so forth. What is new, however, is the possibility of NATO facing *the adaptive and systematic use of such means singularly and in combination by adversaries in pursuit of long-term political objectives*, as opposed to their more random occurrence, driven by coincidental factors. It is this possibility that merits a fresh and more conceptual approach from NATO's side as to how they can be countered. It is particularly important to note that hybrid threats are not exclusively a tool of asymmetric or nonstate actors, but can be applied by state and nonstate actors alike. The principal attraction of hybrid threats from the point of view of a state actor is that they can be largely nonattributable, and therefore applied in situations where more overt action is ruled out for any number of reasons.[21]

Indirect and Asymmetric Operations

While the concepts of asymmetric and hybrid warfare can be defined as American concepts, the next development allegedly took place in Russia. Asymmetric warfare primarily dealt with what nefarious, militarily inferior foreigners might do to us, and how the Armed Forces could handle the problem militarily. In contrast, the Russian concept, known to Westerners as the Gerasimov Doctrine, allegedly dealt with what nefarious, militarily superior foreigners might do to us, and how a large variety of state actors could be deployed to strike back.

The Gerasimov Doctrine, as it was explained in most media reports, purported to be a new Russian military doctrine that combined military, technological, information, diplomatic, economic, cultural, and other tactics, which were then deployed toward one set of strategic objectives. The doctrine was allegedly launched in 2013, when General Valeriy Gerasimov, Chief of the General Staff of the Armed Forces of Russia, published an article with the title 'The Value of Science in Foresight: New Challenges Demand Rethinking the Forms and Methods of Carrying out Combat Operations' in the journal *Voyenno-Promyshlennyy Kuryer* (*Military-Industrial Courier*).[22] The article led to Gerasimov's sudden rise to fame in the West, and from the following year, his alleged association with Russian hybrid warfare.[23]

The words 'alleged' and 'purported' are generously used in this book with regard to the Gerasimov Doctrine, because much, arguably most, analysis of what the General did took place in the West, by observers without actual knowledge of or insight into what happened inside the Russian General Staff. Yet, certain developments had taken place.

What General Gerasimov did was to add the concept of nonmilitary actions to Russian strategic thought. He observed that in the West's new way of conducting war, nonmilitary operations were used over military operations by a ratio of 4:1. Instead of overt military invasions

U.S. Marines assigned to the Hawai'i-based L Company, 3rd Battalion, 3rd Marine Regiment, 1st Marine Division, search a house for insurgents, weapons caches, and explosives during a patrol on 16 June 2006 in Barwana, Iraq. The unconventional phase of the war continued, and looked likely to continue as long as there were U.S. units in the country. (Photo: Sgt. Roe F. Seigle, U.S. Marine Corps)

General of the Army Valeriy Gerasimov, Chief of the General Staff of the Armed Forces of Russia since 2012. In addition to playing key roles in the Russian military intervention in Syria and, less successfully, the invasion of Ukraine, General Gerasimov made significant contributions to Russian military doctrine. His key adversary, General Valeriy Zaluzhnyy, then Commander-in-Chief of the Armed Forces of Ukraine, in an interview with *Time Magazine* in 2022 explained that 'I learned from Gerasimov. I read everything he ever wrote … He is the smartest of men, and my expectations of him were enormous.' (Photo: Government of Russia)

as in the past, attacks were now instigated by the instalment of and support to a political opposition in countries which supposedly were rivals to the West. In North Africa and the Middle East during the Arab Spring, technology and information networks were used to instigate revolts. Economic and political sanctions were imposed to combat the legitimate government. Eventually, military forces under the guise of peacekeepers could be employed to assume control over the territory. His conclusion was that henceforth, non-military methods were the key means used to achieve political and strategic goals.

However, Gerasimov formulated his findings more as an explanation of what the Western powers were doing against Russia and its former or present allies, including Georgia, Ukraine, and Syria, than what Russia was hoping to achieve for itself. Gerasimov was right in his conclusion that hybrid nonmilitary and military means were used to achieve political and strategic goals. He was also right in assessing that Western sources of funding and organization often were instrumental in fomenting protests against Russia's allies. Grievances might be genuine, but foreign support certainly helped when it came to overthrowing governments – that is, regime change.

The use of such means soon also began to be referred to as full spectrum warfare, which refers to its multi-dimensional aspect, and nonlinear warfare. The latter term, however, was particularly unfortunate, since it was popularized in the West in the mistaken belief that this was the official Russian term. The error resulted from the term's incidental use in a short story of fiction, published in 2014 and set in a dystopian future, by a certain Natan Dubovitskiy, which most now agree was the pen name of Vladislav Surkov, one of Russian President Vladimir Putin's political advisors.[24]

However, Russian doctrine does not employ terms such as full spectrum warfare or nonlinear warfare. Instead, from at least 2005 Russian officers described such actions as indirect and asymmetric operations.[25] The intellectual link to the U.S. concept of asymmetric warfare seems obvious. Since thoughts along these lines took hold within the Russian armed forces during the 1990s, when Russia was weak, the Western term was predominantly used to describe threats aimed at Russia, not Russian strategies toward other countries. Indeed, in March 2017 Gerasimov published an article titled 'World on the Brink of War'. In it he explicitly mentioned the concept of hybrid war, but in a discussion of U.S. actions in North Africa and the Middle East.[26]

Nonetheless, the Western term hybrid threats can be employed for what Russian strategic thought apparently still terms indirect and asymmetric strategies, as long that we do not fall into the analytical trap of believing that it was Russia which introduced this particular concept.

The concept of indirect and asymmetric operations also relate to what during the Cold War was known as active measures, a KGB concept designed for exerting influence on the foreign policy and the internal political situation of target countries, with the ultimate aim of weakening the positions of a perceived enemy and undermining its aggressive plans, in order to create conditions favourable to the successful implementation of Russia's foreign policy, to paraphrase the old KGB definition.[27] There is every reason to believe that non-military methods are being used to achieve the desired results, not because of Gerasimov's published articles but because such means were used by the KGB during the Cold War.

Hybrid Threats

While the Western world worried about the alleged Gerasimov Doctrine, a project at the National Defence Academy of Austria worked to understand, and find a scientifically valid definition of, the idea of hybrid threats. The following discussion derives from the work carried out by the project team at the National Defence Academy of Austria, of which the author formed a part, and which was subsequently developed further by Anton Dengg and Michael N. Schurian and published by the Academy.[28]

Work began in the years 2011 to 2012, when the Institute for Peace Support and Conflict Management of the Austrian National Defence Academy carried out the 'Strategies of Hybrid Power Projection Exemplified by the United States, Russia, China and India' (*Strategien hybrider Machtprojektion am Beispiel USA, Russland, China und Indien*) project.[29] While the Austrian project was not the first in which the term hybrid threats was mentioned, it was arguably the first which began to put the concept in a scientific framework. Moreover, the Austrian National Defence Academy followed up the project with the 'Hybrid Potential Threats and Resultant Security Policy Deductions for Small States' (*Hybride Bedrohungspotentiale und daraus resultierende sicherheitspolitische Ableitungen für Kleinstaaten*) project in 2013–2014.

The Austrians began planning for the hybrid threats project in early 2013, and in July the same year invited Sweden (among other countries) to participate.[30] The initial meeting of the Austrian working group took place in October 2013, and the author of this book took part. A series of workshops followed, which ultimately resulted in the book *Vernetzte Unsicherheit* (2015). Soon, an English-language edition was published, known as *Networked Insecurity* (2015).

The Austrian-led project advanced our understanding of hybrid threats in two key directions. Although roughly in agreement with previous research with regard to the nature of the threat, the Austrian-led project first put the definition on a sound scientific foundation by basing the application of hybrid threats on a number of powers or domains (more on which below). Then the project redefined the implication of hybridity in hybrid threats. Previously, the term 'hybrid' had mostly been a political catchphrase employed for whatever was not conventional warfare and hence a threat. The one who had come closest to formulating a viable definition had been Hoffman, who as we have seen had argued that the hybridity of hybrid warfare was the nature and means of the adversary, who henceforth simultaneously used both conventional and irregular organizational forms, tactics, and weapons systems.

However, was this really hybridity? Hoffman's definition was very similar to the combined arms approach to warfare, which seeks to integrate the different combat arms of a military force to achieve mutually complementary effects. For instance, hitting the enemy with two or more combat arms simultaneously in such a manner that the actions he must take to defend himself from one make him more vulnerable to the other. Similarly, hitting the enemy simultaneously with conventional and irregular tactics and weapons systems might make him more vulnerable to both.

Might there be more to hybridity than a mere political catchphrase?

Yes, there was. The term hybridity derives from biology, where a hybrid is the offspring resulting from combining the qualities of two organisms of different varieties, subspecies, species, or genera. The proverbial example is the mule, a cross between a horse and a donkey, which is bred so as to emphasize significant advantages of each respective animal species. Combining two or more originally independent elements allows something new to emerge, which in the hybrid threats environment means that the new configuration of existing forms of threats extends the threat spectrum into multiple dimensions (domains) well beyond that of the original forms.

In short, hybrid threats constitute a synthesis of threat scenarios previously mostly regarded as isolated. There is not a single hybrid threat as such. Hybrid threats should always be regarded in the plural. Hybrid threats consist of different actions that when combined, give rise to new threat scenarios and lines of attack. Most would be non-military. It follows that hybrid warfare is no more than a subset of the hybrid threats spectrum.

The Austrian-led project also developed a proper definition of hybrid threats:

> A hybrid threat is a threat to a state or an alliance that emanates from the capability and intention of an actor to use its potential in a focused and multi-dimensional manner in order to enforce its interests. To qualify as a hybrid threat, threat activities must be coordinated in time and occur in several dimensions or domains (political, economic, military, social, media, and so on). Moreover, threat activities must exceed a strategic threshold in order to count as a hybrid threat. The strategic threshold is exceeded if at least

two dimensions of government (domains) are affected by hybrid threats and accordingly at least two ministries or corresponding government functions must be involved in defending against them.[31]

What remains is the question of identifying a strategic threshold. The strategic threshold is exceeded if the hostile activity substantially impedes the attacked state's freedom to act or make decisions. The form this obstruction takes may differ from case to case and, depending on its effects, may be interpreted differently by each state. One approach would be: the threshold is exceeded if at least two dimensions or domains of power are affected by hybrid threats and accordingly at least two ministries must be involved in defending against them.

Hybrid threats are in this respect similar to the concept of total war. The aggressor will use multiple instruments of power (soft ones such as financial, diplomatic, and media but possibly also hard powers such as terrorism, cyber, and even military) to harm the target state. However, contrary to traditional definitions of total war, hybrid threats are not necessarily aimed at the destruction of the target state's population, government structures, or industrial capacity. Instead, hybrid threats will mostly aim to bring about overextension on various levels in multiple spheres that collectively may lead to institutional breakdown in the target state.

The Austrian-led project found that the types of power applied in hybrid threats campaigns correspond to what is perhaps best referred to as dimensions or domains of operations. These categories constitute a vital means of assessing hybrid threats, and are best divided into general categories based on the type of power employed (Table 1).[32]

Table 1: Common means employed in hybrid threats campaigns divided into categories of dimensions (domains) of operations based on the type of power employed.

Hard Power	Soft Power
State Power	Real Economic Power
Cyber Power	Financial Power
Privatized Power	Diplomatic Power
People's Power	Civil Power
Terrorist Power	Scientific & Technological Power
	Media Power

As seen in Table 1, the types of power employed in hybrid threats campaigns are the same as in other types of application of power in politics. They are first divided in hard and soft powers. Hard power is the use of military or paramilitary means to influence the behaviour of other political bodies such as states and organizations. This form of political power is typically aggressive, coercive, and is most immediately effective when imposed by one political body upon another of inferior corresponding powers.

Soft power, on the other side, is the ability to co-opt rather than coerce. Soft power is non-coercive, and relies on culture, political values, and foreign policies to enact change. In the ideal case, it can be described as shaping the preferences of others through appeal and attraction. However, there is a harsher side to soft power, in which powers of various non-military types are employed to persuade the other political body to accept demands instead of merely presenting an appealing surface.

Among the hard powers, the strongest and broadest is state power (defined as consisting of military, law enforcement, intelligence, and judicial actors). It includes military power, which involves the deployment of armies and special forces, but it also includes judicial power, in which legislation and the judicial apparatus is employed so as to disadvantage another state, its economy, or citizens. The enforcement of laws on individuals or companies as a means to exert political influence on another state has become known as 'lawfare', the strategy of using or misusing law as a weapon to achieve an operational objective in a merger of law and warfare. Finally, state power also includes intelligence power, in which state intelligence services are tasked to carry out assassinations, acts of sabotage, or blackmail, or manipulate information for propaganda purposes.

Intelligence services often have the capability to apply cyber power. This involves the carrying out of cyber-attacks of various types, up to and including direct attacks on critical infrastructure, but also suppression of web services, alteration of web site content, identity theft, data interception and manipulation, and much else.

Privatized power includes all types of hard power deployed by private military companies (that is, mercenaries, a term which for legal reasons seldom is used today), paramilitary security firms, paramilitary volunteer forces, warlord-led militias, organized crime groups, and specialized subsets of organized crime such as pirates.

People's power involves all types of hard power wielded by armed insurgents, professional revolutionaries, political or religious extremists, and indeed any armed and mobilized mass of malcontents and impoverished or marginalized groups who rally around a cause, which usually involves violence against those whom they consider more privileged. Wittingly or unwittingly, such groups often act on behalf of an actor with the capacity to arouse them.

Terrorist power (when not a part of state power, that is) is wielded by ideological or religious terrorist groups.

Soft power, as noted, involves the application of non-military and non-kinetic powers, but the disruptive effect may be equal to or exceed those of military-based hard power. For instance, real economic power includes, but is not limited to, the acquisition of strategic resources, infrastructure, and control over transportation routes, the imposition of monopolies and prices favourable to the stronger party, and the interruption of supplies of raw materials, fuels, and critical components as a means to raise prices or force compliance with other demands.

Likewise, financial power typically entails the imposition of trade barriers, financial sanctions (in particular punitive tariffs and embargoes, which often are employed in conjunction with diplomatic sanctions), and the manipulation of exchange rates for reasons of speculation or for inducing targeted indebtedness in states regarded as adversarial.

Diplomatic power customarily involves threats, sanctions, and the crafting and introduction of resolutions by international organizations over which the state has some lever of influence or in which it is able to find support from like-minded states. The purpose is commonly to isolate the target state from the international community in order to reduce its freedom of manoeuvre which translates into the reduction of its potential to carry out an independent policy or act as a threat.

Civil power is best described as the soft-power version of people's power. It is customarily deployed by non-governmental organizations (NGOs), charities, law firms and public relations (PR) agencies which operate on behalf of interested parties, and some international organizations. Civil power is typically deployed as protests, demonstrations, consumer boycotts, fundraisers, and the like.

Scientific and technological power relies on new technologies which can be used either as enablers or influencers.

Media power primarily deals with propaganda and disinformation and is most often deployed to direct and influence public opinion.

Notably, most of these powers are not military in nature. When the present author looked into the matter of hybrid threats on behalf of the Swedish Police Authority, it was found, to the dismay of many, that the legal context meant that any pre-war criminal activities that constituted hybrid threats fell under the jurisdiction of the police, not the Amed Forces. This was not what the police wanted, since they were busy with multiple other threats, and it was surely not what the Armed Forces wanted, since they argued that a hybrid threats campaign might change overnight into a military conflict. Yet, the legal mandate of the two respective authorities was clear. The police were dutybound and had the mandate to take action against criminal activities that constituted hybrid threats in times of peace. The Armed Forces had no such formal mandate or authority before war was declared. Legislation had not caught up with the new vulnerabilities of the twenty-first century. Similar conclusions were drawn in many other small and medium-sized states.

With all these powers available for hybrid threats campaigns, we should remember that most hybrid threats constitute the combination of an adversary's capabilities and intent with our own weakness. In its simplest form, the application of hybrid threats accordingly is a focused multi-dimensional campaign of, typically, the deployment by a state of political pressure, military power, and propaganda activities to enforce its interests vis-a-vis another state. The aggressor can threaten a target state in either a serial or parallel mode. In the former case, the aggressor will deploy each power in consecutive order, so that the effect of the first will amplify that of the second, which in turn will amplify that of the third, and so on (Table 2). In parallel mode, the aggressor instead deploys all power simultaneously, or near-simultaneously (Table 3).

Opportunism is a key factor for the successful deployment of hybrid threats power (a characteristic which, incidentally, hybrid threats deployment shares with that of intelligence operations and organized crime). Most commonly, this means that the aggressor will take advantage of any self-inflicted weakness on the part of the target state, such as political chaos or rampant corruption. However, the aggressor might also to take advantage of any natural disasters by adapting subsequent application of additional hybrid power projection in order to create greater destabilization of the target's state structures to his advantage. This capability to react rapidly depends critically on the aggressor's flexibility, preparedness, and capability to project power.

Unless the target state already at an early stage gives in to the multi-dimensional pressure and submits, the result is often a state of undeclared or declared war. The hybrid threats potential has then been transformed into a means for waging war, that is, hybrid warfare.

But the world is seldom that simple. Wars are costly, with regard to human and material losses as well as the potential loss of political prestige. The outcome is frequently unpredictable. Major states often prefer to attain their objectives without the need actually to engage in open warfare. It is for this reason that the use of non-state actors as proxies, although always present in inter-state conflict and commonplace during the Cold War, has grown yet more prevalent in the twenty-first century.

The EU Intelligence and Situation Centre (EU INTCEN)

In April 2016, the European Commission adopted a 'Joint Framework on Countering Hybrid Threats'. It was based on the English-language edition of the Austrian report, issued in the same year. The Joint Framework was intended as a rigorous response to the increasing hybridity of threat scenarios.[33]

The European Commission did not specifically reference the Austrian report which had formed the foundation of the Joint Framework. Perhaps the Commission found a reference undesirable because it wanted other member states to embrace the definition (something that we will see proved difficult). Besides, the Joint Framework in any case relied on a slight rewording of the definition of hybrid threats in the Austrian-led project. The Commission accordingly defined hybrid threats as:

> the mixture of coercive and subversive activity, conventional and unconventional methods (i.e. diplomatic, military, economic, technological), which can be used in a coordinated manner by state or non-state actors to achieves specific objectives while remaining below the threshold of formally declared warfare.[34]

The Joint Framework recommended improved information exchange and increased intelligence-sharing across sectors and between the European Union, its member states, and partners. Specifically, the Joint Framework projected an EU Hybrid Fusion Cell for the analysis of hybrid threats. The Hybrid Fusion Cell would be established within the EU Intelligence and Situation Centre (EU INTCEN) of the European External Action Service (EEAS). This Fusion Cell would receive, analyze, and share classified and open-source intelligence specifically relating to indicators and warnings concerning hybrid threats from different stakeholders within the EEAS, the Commission with EU agencies, and member states. The Fusion Cell would liaise with, among others, European Cybercrime Centre and Counter Terrorism Centre of the European Union Agency for Law Enforcement Cooperation (Europol), European Border and Coast Guard Agency (Frontex), EU Computer Emergency Response Team (CERT-EU), and similar bodies at national level. The plan was for the Fusion Cell to analyse external aspects of hybrid threats which affected the EU and its neighbourhood in order to rapidly assess relevant incidents and inform the EU's strategic decision-making processes. Member states were expected ('invited' in EU parlance) to establish National Contact Points connected to the EU Hybrid Fusion Cell. Finally, staff inside and outside the EU (including those deployed to EU delegations, operations, and missions) and in member states would be trained to recognize early signs of hybrid threats.

A little over a year later, in July 2017, the European Commission issued a Joint Report to the European Parliament and the Council on the implementation of the Joint Framework. The report noted that the EU Hybrid Fusion Cell was created in 2016 to provide all-source analysis on hybrid threats and was now fully operational:

> The EU Hybrid Fusion Cell has been established within the EU Intelligence and Situation Centre to receive and analyse classified and open source information from different stakeholders concerning hybrid threats. Analysis is then shared within the EU and amongst Member States and in turn informs the EU decision-making processes, including inputs to the security risk assessments carried out at EU level. The EU Military Staff Intelligence Directorate contributes to the Fusion Cell work with military analysis. To date, over 50 assessments and briefings on hybrid topics have been produced. Since January 2017, the Cell has produced a periodical "Hybrid Bulletin", analysing current threats and hybrid issues, shared directly within the EU institutions and bodies and national

Table 2: The serial mode of deploying hybrid threats (chain of attack). (Diagram by Tom Cooper based on information provided by author)

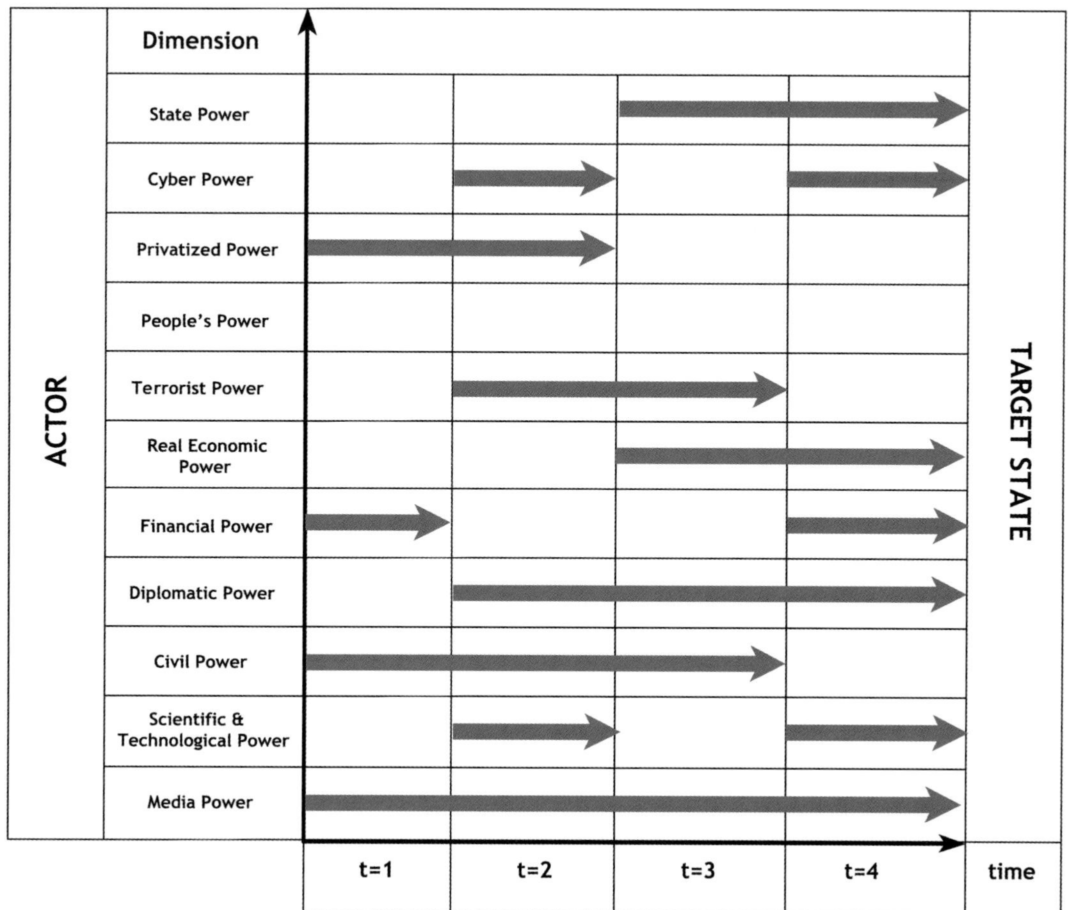

Table 3: The parallel mode of deploying hybrid threats (wave of attack). (Diagram by Tom Cooper based on information provided by author)

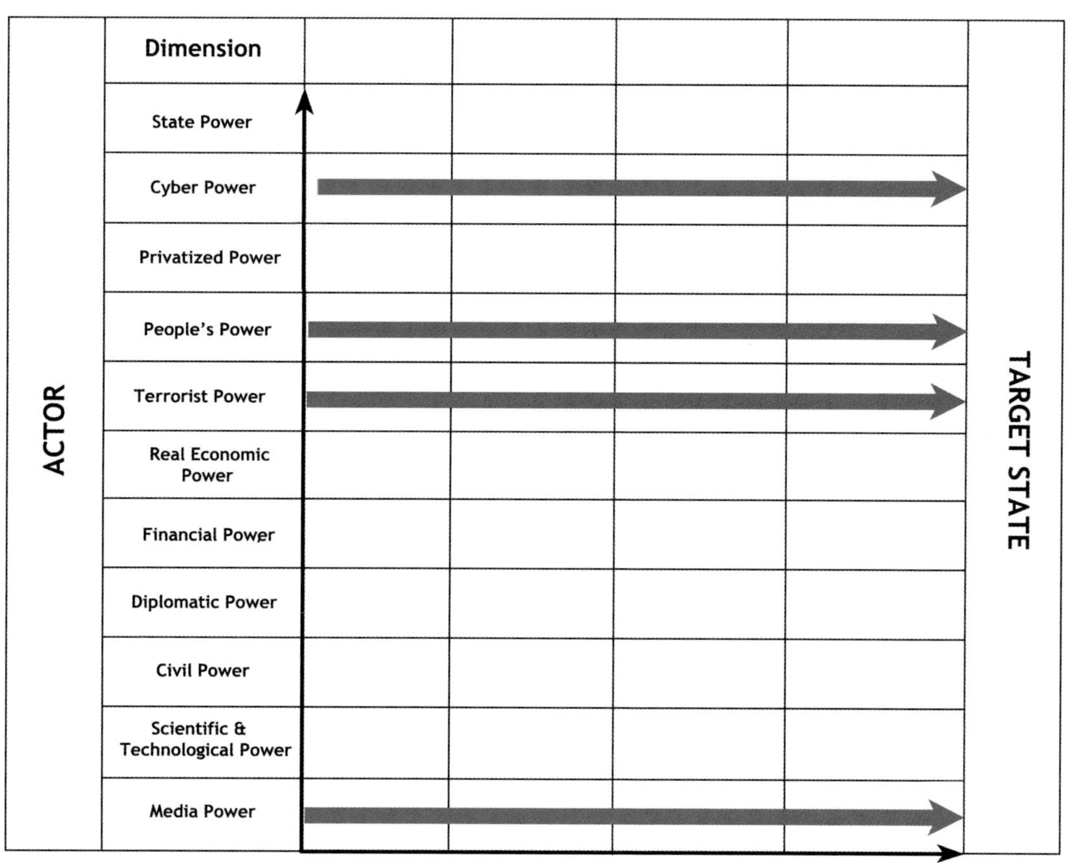

> points of contact. (Footnote: To date, 21 Member States have nominated national points of contact. These are individuals working in Member States capitals in a policy / resilience role). The Cell's Full Operating Capacity has been achieved, as planned, in May 2017. Finally, staff-to-staff engagement with NATO's nascent Hybrid Analysis Branch is ongoing, both in regard to sharing lessons learnt in the creation of the Fusion Cell and in sharing information (carried out in full respect of the EU rules on classified information exchange).[35]

This meant that 21 out of 27 member states had joined the effort. Not bad, but also not a full turnout. There was also a particular focus on cyber threats and propaganda, for which EU Internet Referral Unit at Europol played an important role.

Cooperation with non-member states also increased, with a pilot cybersecurity project in the former Yugoslav Republic of Macedonia, Kosovo, and Moldova concluded in 2016, and a new programme launched for the period 2017–2020 to enhance cyber resilience in Ukraine, Africa, and Asia.[36]

In July 2017, the EU also adopted an EU Playbook for countering hybrid threats.[37] The document details the procedure for an EU response to a hybrid threats incident, with the EU Hybrid Fusion Cell a critical component in initially identifying a threat before a full crisis arose.

So far, everything seemed fine.

The intelligence veteran Dr. Gerhard Conrad was Director of INTCEN at the time. In his memoirs he recalls that the creation of the Hybrid Fusion Cell was one of his central tasks and challenges.[38] The challenge was real, because not every member state was interested in cooperating with the fusion cell on hybrid threats.

Dr. Gerhard Conrad was an officer of the Federal Intelligence Service (*Bundesnachrichtendienst*, BND), Germany's foreign intelligence service. He was one of the service's foremost experts on Arab affairs. A fluent Arabic speaker, he for several years served as BND's station chief in Damascus. Dr. Conrad was Director of EU INTCEN from 2016 to 2019. (Photo: Tagesschau, 2022)

The reasons for this were complex and sometimes varied. Some member state intelligence services were not in the habit of making assessments of the type which INTCEN needed. The reason could be that they regarded themselves as agencies exclusively tasked with intelligence collection, that is, agencies that would hand over the collected intelligence to others for them to make their own assessments. Others, in particular the domestic security services of the various EU member states, typically regarded the preparation of assessments as outside of their mandate, often did not have a tradition or culture of sharing intelligence with other agencies, not with other national agencies and certainly not with a whole set of foreign ones in a fusion centre, and moreover, tended exclusively to deal with individual cases of terrorism or espionage that were of little interest to the EU as a whole.

Yet others, in particular those from the major EU member states, did not use the concept of hybrid threats but relied on alternative concepts and terminologies, such as the aforementioned asymmetric, full spectrum, or nonlinear warfare. Therefore, they did not see their mission objectives as aligning with those of the EU Hybrid Fusion Cell. Moreover, it soon became clear that the major states, that is, those that by 2016 already were interested in this phenomenon, did not really subscribe to the idea of employing a formal definition of hybrid threats. This had become clear during internal discussions before the establishment of the EU Hybrid Fusion Cell. As a result, already the 2016 Joint Framework included the words 'While definitions of hybrid threats vary and need to remain flexible to respond to their evolving nature ...'.[39] What this means was, frankly, that member states for reasons of political expediency wanted to feel free to define just about anything as hybrid threats, as long as it emanated from an adversary.

The EU Hybrid Fusion Cell could not overcome the resistance from some member states toward the standardization of definitions and sometime reluctance to share intelligence information. The resistance and the resulting lack of coordination had the effect of stalling the efforts at the EU level for standardizing the concept to avoid this very confusion.

This was fairly common for the EU, since few national agencies are willing to give up traditional missions and homegrown terminologies. Although, strictly speaking, this reluctance is more related to internal bureaucratic factors than national intelligence requirements, the agencies tend to receive the support of their respective national governments on this matter, since no member-state government is willing to give up its prerogative in national security.

For this reason, the INTCEN had to dilute existing definitions of hybrid threats so as not to antagonize any participating state or organization. While a pragmatic decision, it was also a decision which reduced the efficiency of INTCEN's work. Although some may argue otherwise, it is the present author's experience that a solid formal definition of what intelligence should look for improves both intelligence collection and analysis and operational countermeasures.

One of few instances when intelligence services (ultimately) made public their resistance to the evolving EU definition of and focus on hybrid threats was a report by the Dutch National Coordinator for Security and Counterterrorism (NCTV), in a report also endorsed by the General Intelligence and Security Service (AIVD) and the Defence Intelligence and Security Service (MIVD). Apparently unaware of the Austrian report (which the European Commission for pragmatic reasons had not referenced), the NCTV persuasively argued that since the term hybrid threats refers to 'threats that can assume various forms and impact on multiple national security interests simultaneously and thus pose a threat to national security', the adjective 'hybrid' did not add anything new. Hence, the NCTV proposed, it was better to speak of a 'threat to national security from hybrid conflict'. The point that the term hybrid threats was cumbersome and less well-chosen that one might have hoped for was valid. However, then the NCTV went on to argue that hybrid threats (or threats to national security from hybrid conflict) only related specifically to state actors, because 'it is highly improbable that non-state actors could meet the requirements for hybrid conflict (such as having strategic objectives or possessing sufficient state instruments to make the integrated deployment of such instruments possible).'[40] As will be shown, and as was already shown in the Austrian report, this conclusion greatly underestimated the powers and strategic objectives of some non-state actors.

Nonetheless, the EU Hybrid Fusion Cell became a model for the hybrid analysis branch which NATO a year later established within its Joint Intelligence and Security Division.[41] In part for this reason, the NATO definition of hybrid threats also became somewhat diluted:

> Hybrid threats combine military and non-military as well as covert and overt means, including disinformation, cyber attacks, economic pressure, deployment of irregular armed groups and use of regular forces. Hybrid methods are used to blur the lines between war and peace, and attempt to sow doubt in the minds of target populations. They aim to destabilise and undermine societies.[42]

By 2018, the European Commission had shortened its definition of hybrid threats. Even so, it retained the essence of the original definition including its focus on non-military operations:

> Hybrid campaigns are multidimensional, combining coercive and subversive measures, using both conventional and unconventional tools and tactics (diplomatic, military, economic, and technological) to destabilise the adversary. They are designed to be difficult to detect or attribute, and can be used by both state and non-state actors.[43]

The European Centre of Excellence for Countering Hybrid Threats (Hybrid CoE)

The 2016 Joint Framework on Countering Hybrid Threats also 'invited' the EU member states to establish a Centre of Excellence for addressing hybrid threats.

The Centre would focus on researching how hybrid strategies were applied, and would encourage the development of new concepts and technologies within the private sector and industry to help member states build resilience. Research at the Centre was expected to contribute to aligning EU and national policies, doctrines, and concepts, and to ensure that decision-making could take into account the complexities and ambiguities associated with hybrid threats. The Centre would rely on the expertise developed by its multinational and cross-sector participants from the civilian and military, private, and academic sectors, and work closely with existing EU and NATO centres of excellence in order to benefit from insights into hybrid threats that were gained from cyber defence, strategic communication, civilian-military cooperation, and energy and crisis response.

The result was the European Centre of Excellence for Countering Hybrid Threats (Hybrid CoE) in Helsinki, which Finland established in April 2017. Hybrid CoE was officially established on 11 April 2017 by the first nine participating states: Finland, Sweden, Britain, Latvia, Lithuania, Poland, France, Germany and the United States. Participation in the Centre's activities was open to all EU and NATO member states, and all ultimately joined the Centre.

Significantly, the Hybrid CoE was the first joint NATO/EU institution established for purposes of national security capacity-building. The initiative to establish the Centre was supported in the 'Common set of proposals for the implementation of the Joint EU/NATO Declaration', which was endorsed by the Council of the European Union and the North Atlantic Council already on 6 December 2016.[44]

The Centre's key task was to build capabilities to prevent and counter hybrid threats. This was achieved by sharing best practices, providing recommendations, as well as testing new ideas and approaches in hands-on exercises. The Centre also built the operational capacities of the participating states by training practitioners and conducting research in the nature, types, and implications of hybrid threats.

In most ways, the Hybrid CoE lived up to the initial hopes for such an institution. However, with the vastly increased membership brought in by NATO, political sensitivities sometimes hampered cooperation. The key issue then became how to assess hybrid threats operations carried out by one member state against another member state. Naturally, the only politically acceptable solution was to ignore this particular hybrid threats incident. The issue was not a minor one, because some Hybrid CoE member states did carry out frequent hybrid threats operations against partner states. The reader of this book may possibly infer some such activities in the case studies, but since this book is published in a NATO member state, neither the author nor publisher is in a position to suggest that NATO Allies intentionally carry out hybrid threats operations against each other.

Moreover, the Hybrid CoE, like INTCEN before it, had to dilute existing definitions of hybrid threats so as not to antagonize any member state. Ultimately, with the expansion of Hybrid CoE membership, yet another issue emerged, namely that the original definition of hybrid threats was seen as too scientifically objective and insufficiently adversary-focused. Hybrid CoE accordingly redefined hybrid threats, narrowing the concept down to something that only authoritarian states would do to democratic states. This was a later and more political decision than previous ones made by the services with regard to the INTCEN fusion cell,

The Hybrid CoE for this reason does not actually present a definition of hybrid threats but describes the issue as follows:

> Hybrid threats are harmful activities that are planned and carried out with malign intent. They aim to undermine a target, such as a state or an institution, through a variety of means, often combined. Such means include information manipulation, cyberattacks, economic influence or coercion, covert political manoeuvring, coercive diplomacy, or threats of military force. Hybrid threats describe a wide array of harmful activities with different goals, ranging from influence operations and interference all the way to hybrid warfare.
>
> Hybrid threats are used by authoritarian states and regimes, and by non-state actors (NSAs), which often act as proxies for authoritarian regimes. Examples of hybrid threat actors include Russia, China, and Iran. Non-state hybrid threat actors can include groups, movements or entities, which are used or co-opted to fulfil certain strategic objectives… .
>
> Authoritarian states aim to fulfil their strategic objectives, such as increased global influence and power, by means of interfering in and influencing other states. Hybrid threats are

a cost-efficient way to achieve these objectives and affect the processes and institutions of democratically governed states. Hybrid threat actors seek to avoid both accountability for, and countermeasures against, their hostile activities. Hence, hybrid threats are designed in such a way that detecting and defending against them is difficult. They are devised to remain under a threshold which could constitute or be perceived as (an act of) war against the attacked state.

…

Hybrid CoE characterizes hybrid threats as:

1. Coordinated and synchronized action that deliberately targets democratic states' and institutions' systemic vulnerabilities through a wide range of means.
2. Activities that exploit the thresholds of detection and attribution, as well as the different interfaces (war-peace, internal-external security, local-state, and national-international).
3. Activities aimed at influencing different forms of decision-making at the local (regional), state, or institutional level, and designed to further and/or fulfil the agent's strategic goals while undermining and/or hurting the target.[45]

Notably, the Centre's characterization of hybrid threats postulated that they were only used by authoritarian states against democratic states, and that Russia, China, and Iran were the primary hybrid threats actors. We will see that reality was somewhat more complex than this.

Proxies

Many hybrid threats campaigns are carried out by proxies, which usually are non-state actors. The use of non-state actors by states is ubiquitous, because it allows the concealed use of state power projection. By employing non-state actors, the state achieves an important, sometimes primary, objective in that it allows itself not to be recognised as an aggressor but rather to achieve the objective of influencing the other state in its own interest.

Non-state actors have existed since the formation of the first states. They appear in all forms of human endeavours. Among the earliest examples were insurgents and religious movements. Insurgents were those who for whatever reason directly opposed the state in which they emerged and for this reason regarded themselves as an alternative to the state, its ruling strata, or both. A well-known early example was the Spartacus uprising against the Roman Republic in the first century BC. As for religious movements, they might support or oppose the state in which they arose but in either case followed their own agenda. A well-known early example was the Christian Church in the Roman Empire in the first centuries AD. The same types of non-state actors – insurgents and religious movements – are as prevalent today as they were in ancient times.

Equally old is the employment of non-state actors by state actors as a means to gain levers of influence for foreign policy or national security objectives. In AD 348, the Gothic ruler Aoric expelled numerous Christian groups from his territory because he assessed (probably incorrectly) that they acted as agents of a foreign power, the Roman Empire. In AD 447, the Hunnic head of state Attila for reasons of national security demanded the extradition for punishment of all Hunnic exiles who had received sanctuary (asylum) in the Roman Empire, since he assessed (correctly) that the Romans tolerated their presence in order to use them against him.

State actors continued to employ non-state actors in later centuries as well, including those which today would be labelled organized crime groups (OCGs). In 1714, the pirate Samuel St. Léger offered to bring a fleet of 25 ships and 1,400 Madagascar pirates into Swedish service. Several high-ranking Swedish officials supported the plan, which included the stationing of the pirate fleet in a base south of Gothenburg. The Swedish objective was to gain a sorely needed paramilitary naval force, intimidate shipping, and attack merchant ships of enemy states, that is, commerce raiding, by employing the pirates as privateers, by which was meant legal, state-sponsored piracy. The plan constituted a hybrid threat, since it simultaneously involved the military, diplomatic, and economic domains.

These early examples show that hybrid threats posed by non-state actors do not constitute a new phenomenon. It was early on recognized that state actors used non-state actors as proxies. This was perhaps most eloquently put into words by the nineteenth-century founder of modern Afghanistan, Emir Abdur Rahman:

> Some Powers take new countries by the force of their strength and victories; others take them by treachery, fraud, and stirring up home quarrels between chiefs of the country, themselves keeping behind the curtain, and benefiting themselves at the expense of the folly of others. Such Powers are more difficult to deal with, and one ought to be more careful in dealing with them than with the Powers that attack openly.[46]

Abdur Rahman, writing in the final years of the nineteenth century, was suspicious of the British and Russian Empires, both of which had the will and capacity to employ hybrid threats against his rule as a means to avoid the need actually to invade Afghanistan. That he had these two empires in mind was unsurprising, since it predominantly is great powers which employ non-state actors for foreign policy or national security objectives. However, it will be shown that all states do it at least to some extent, including weak states which resort to the use of non-state actors since they have few other levers of influence at their disposal.

Colonel Roger Trinquier, an experienced French counterinsurgency and counterterrorism practitioner who served in Indochina, China, Algeria, and Congo before, during, and after the Second World War, recognized the opportunities in war by proxy. In Algeria, where France's chief adversary was the National Liberation Front (commonly known by its French acronym FLN), he was also involved in a disinformation campaign which arranged for the dissemination by subverted FLN agents of rumours of and even lists with names of supposed traitors within their own organization. The disinformation triggered widespread and lethal internal purges within the FLN, which significantly weakened its structures without further French intervention.

Based on his experiences in counterinsurgency and counterterrorism, in particular in Indochina and Algeria, Trinquier in 1961 developed a concept for what he termed 'modern warfare', which he defined as 'an interlocking system of actions – political, economic, psychological, military -that aims at the *overthrow of the established authority in a country and its replacement by another regime*'.[47]

The terms hybrid warfare and hybrid threats were not yet invented, but Trinquier was nonetheless a pioneer in the field. His concept of 'modern warfare' corresponds to much of what takes place within the field of hybrid threats. Trinquier explained:

> To achieve this end, the aggressor tries to exploit the internal tensions of the country attacked – ideological, social, religious,

> economic – any conflict liable to have a profound influence on the population to be conquered. Moreover, in view of the present-day interdependence of nations, any residual grievance within a population, no matter how localized and lacking in scope, will surely be brought by determined adversaries into the framework of the great world conflict. From a localized conflict of secondary origin and importance, they will always attempt sooner or later to bring about a generalized conflict.[48]

Trinquier noted that the adversary in modern warfare, that is, in both counterinsurgency and counterterrorism operations, was not a conventional armed force but a secret organization of small armed elements which hid within the civilian population, an armed clandestine organization.[49] The enemy was accordingly difficult to define, because the border between friend and enemy was not geographical but ideological, and cut straight through the civilian population.[50]

The adversary armed clandestine organization, Trinquier noted, engaged in forms of clandestine warfare that included terrorism as a tactic of war. The clandestine organization operated in guerrilla mode, terrorist mode, or both. Guerilla and terrorist modes functioned differently, since they operated in different types of terrain.[51] Since most successful insurgent and terrorist organizations had access to cross-border sanctuaries, Trinquier advocated a clandestine war against the state that supported the enemy organization. He urged that an armed group – a proxy – be established on this state's territory, tasked with striking at the enemy's base organization. Further, he advocated the application of political pressure against the state's government until its material support ceased.[52]

Emir Abdur Rahman, the founder of modern Afghanistan, knew that both the British and Russian Empires had the will and capacity to employ hybrid threats against him. (Public domain)

Colonel Roger Trinquier served in Indochina, China, Algeria, and Congo before, during, and after the Second World War. Based on his experiences in counterinsurgency and counterterrorism, he developed a concept for what he termed 'modern warfare'. Trinquier's methods, in particular the use of torture against terrorists (Trinquier, *Modern Warfare*, pp.16–18, 21–23), were long regarded as controversial. Regrettably, torture of terrorist suspects was in the early twenty-first century again deemed legitimate, if still publicly condemned, in many Western counterinsurgency and counterterrorism operations associated with the global War on Terror. (Public domain)

In short, the concept of hybrid threats has been known and understood for a considerable time, although different terminology was used. Yet, what has changed since previous centuries is the emergence of a whole array of new types of non-state actors, empowered by modern developments in fields such as information technology and financial services. Meanwhile, the traditional non-state actors (religious institutions, diaspora-based entities, extremist movements, OCGs, and the like) remain as prevalent as ever.

The relationship between any given non-state actor and the state that employs the non-state actor as a proxy may be complicated. Essentially, a non-state actor employed as a proxy might be an ally, non-aligned, or even a rival of the state which employs it. Moreover, the relationship between the non-state actor and the state might be either long-term or short-term, and it is equally possible that the relationship between the state and the proxy is one of temporary exploitation only. Likewise, the non-state actor and state may share goals, but it might also be a case in which the non-state actor is funded, hired, or even compelled by the state to act as a proxy. Some non-state actors are established by the state which employs them, and some may well be dependent on the state in question. We will see examples of all these types of relationships in the case studies which constitute the recognition guide of this book.

2

RECOGNITION GUIDE

Case Studies

Successfully addressing hybrid threats requires a common understanding by practitioners, academics, and policymakers of what constitutes a hybrid threats actor. This is particularly important because hybrid threats actors frequently do not belong to the traditional set of state actors (Armed Forces, intelligence, police, and so on). Instead, many are non-state actors. These come in a large variety of shapes and forms and, unlike many state actors, tend to be characterized by multiple and sometimes conflicting strategic objectives. The prevalence of non-state actors becomes obvious from the case studies in this book, since most, although not all, deal with non-state actors which act as proxies for state actors. While almost every non-state actor also acts on behalf of itself, following an agenda of its own making, these activities only seldom reach the strategic threshold that characterizes a hybrid threat.

Yet, this does not mean that non-state actors never turn into genuine hybrid threats. Under certain conditions some non-state actors do exceed the threshold. We will see that examples include organized crime groups in Colombia (Pablo Escobar and Los Extraditables, 1984), Sweden (PKK, 1984), Italy (Sicilian Mafia, 1993), Mexico (Los Zetas, 2009), and certain insurgent groups (Afghan Taliban movement, 2001–2014).[1] The Afghan Taliban movement is particularly interesting, because we will see that it succeeded in establishing a full-scale hybrid power capability of the type normally exclusively employed by states.

As we have seen, it was the EU, not NATO, that took the lead in devising policies to identify, understand, and counter hybrid threats. The journey began with the academic-practitioner approach of the National Defence Academy of Austria; progressed with the work carried out in the various affiliated meeting formats of the EU's politically independent executive arm, the European Commission in Brussels; continued with the ultimately not fully successful attempts of the EU Hybrid Fusion Cell at INTCEN to coordinate and streamline definitions; transformed at the Hybrid CoE in Helsinki; and finally became part of EU policy.

From all these efforts at identifying and understanding what is, and what is not, hybrid threats, the European Union finally reached an understanding of how to counter them. By 2022, the EU based its counter-hybrid threats policy on four lines of action:

Situational awareness is crucial for making Member States aware of the challenges, informing decision making and developing a common strategic culture.

Resilience – the EU's resilience concept includes our ability to prevent, withstand and recover from crises, including multifaceted hybrid attacks… .

Response options can range from diplomatic engagement, CSDP [Common Security and Defence Policy] and crisis response mechanisms, to rapid response teams and restrictive measures.

Cooperation – the EU is committed to working on countering hybrid threats with international partners and organisations as well as with other stakeholders from civil society.[2]

All this was fine, but to counter a hybrid threats campaign, it was first necessary to identify it. For this, we have to return to the academic-practitioner approach of the National Defence Academy of Austria, which identified hybrid threats activities according to categories of dimensions (domains) based on the type of power employed. Since hybrid threats can come in numerous shapes and guises, the identification of the dimensions (domains) in which the operation plays out is usually the best means to determine what is, and what is not, a hybrid threats campaign.

To assist in this process, this part of the book will give details from a large number of case studies, which when taken together functions as a recognition guide of hybrid threats. The case studies are based on evidence-based observations which adheres to academic standards. Evidence that only exists, or is assumed to exist, in classified intelligence reports will not be used. This should not be seen as a limiting factor, since the hybrid threats phenomenon has existed for a long time. While classified intelligence might add to our knowledge of particular cases, the inclusion of such data would not materially change our understanding of the characteristics that define hybrid threats.[3]

In previous conflicts, a recognition guide was typically a book or pamphlet that helped the user to recognize different types of military equipment, typically the aircraft and ships used by a potential adversary but also those used by friendly forces, in order to prevent friendly-fire incidents if war broke out. The aim of this book is similar.

By defining and illustrating the types of hybrid threats activities that commonly take place, and by giving real-life examples of their usage, the book aims to help the reader in recognizing potential and actual hybrid threats actors when they are encountered. Hopefully, countermeasures can then be put in place, before their detrimental capacity can be fully implemented.

State Power

State Power, defined as the powers deployed by military, intelligence, and judicial actors including law enforcement, is for obvious reasons the exclusive realm of state actors.

Military power can be deployed either overtly or covertly. The U.S. Department of Defense makes clear that both types of military power projection are on the table. U.S. policy also acknowledges clandestine application of military power. A clandestine operation differs from a covert operation in that emphasis is placed on concealment of the operation rather than on concealment of the identity of the sponsor. In special operations, an activity may be both covert and clandestine and may focus equally on operational considerations and intelligence-related activities. The different types of operations are defined as follows:

covert operation – An operation that is so planned and executed as to conceal the identity of or permit plausible denial by the sponsor.

overt operation – An operation conducted openly, without concealment.

clandestine operation – An operation sponsored or conducted by governmental departments or agencies in such a way as to assure secrecy or concealment.[4]

Power exerted by intelligence services primarily pertains to the collection of intelligence and information. Additionally, intelligence services are commonly used for the manipulation of information and creation and dissemination of propaganda. In times of conflict, they are also tasked to carry out sabotage operations and assassinations against the adversary. Such operations may take place in third countries. Western intelligence services generally do not disclose information about such measures, or of their existence.

Judicial power implies the employment of legislation and the judicial apparatus as means to disadvantage another state, its economy, or citizens. The enforcement of laws on individuals or companies as a means to exert political influence on another state has, as noted, become known as 'lawfare', the strategy of using or misusing law as a weapon to achieve an operational objective in a merger of law and warfare. Lawfare can be used in both defensive and offensive capacities.

Case Study: Little Green Men of Crimea, February-March 2014

For many, the archetypal application of military state power in a hybrid threats operation was the Russian Federation's deployment of 'little green men' in Crimea. Russia's Crimea operation was a hybrid threats operation, because it included elements of state military power (special forces and a naval blockade), civil power (parliamentary demands for a referendum and the vote that then took place), and media power (pro-Kremlin media) in a coordinated operation.

The direct impetus for the operation was the ouster of Ukrainian President Viktor Yanukovych in Kyiv on 22 February 2014 in a coup which introduced a new government with pro-Western policies. In response, Russian President Vladimir Putin during an all-night emergency meeting on 22–23 February mobilized several battalions of special forces and airborne forces. Russia had a naval base in Crimea, which hosted a special forces unit, so Russian soldiers were already present. Yet more special forces arrived in Crimea on 25 February. Meanwhile, Russia launched a surprise military exercise further north. Involving 150,000 troops from the Western Military District, the exercise on 26 February diverted attention away from Crimea, where special forces soon began seizing strategic locations.[5] Early in the morning of 27 February, Russian special forces and airborne units, playing the role of spontaneously formed local self-defence militias, assumed control of the Crimean Parliament building and raised the Russian flag. A pro-Russian government was installed, which promptly announced a referendum on Crimea's status.

The Russian soldiers carried regular-issue weapons and equipment, but were always masked and wore unmarked green military uniforms. Pro-Kremlin media soon began to refer to the Russian troops as 'little green men', a term that stuck and also was adopted abroad. The Russian soldiers met little resistance. They were well-mannered, kept to themselves, declined to give interviews to journalists, and mostly did not interfere with civilian life. As a result, they began to be called 'polite people' as an alternative to 'little green men'. Over the next few days, anonymous Russian special forces units expanded their control in Crimea, surrounding Sevastopol Belbek airport, seizing Simferopol airport, and closing Crimea's border crossings.[6]

Meanwhile, Russian naval units blockaded the Ukrainian navy vessels in Crimean ports. This was accompanied by an information operation to prompt Ukrainian servicemen and officers to switch sides. The ongoing situation, with a revolution and coup in the capital and increasing de facto Russian control in Crimea, meant that psychological pressure to switch sides grew rapidly. On 1 March, the acting supreme commander of the Ukrainian Navy Sergey Yeliseyev changed his allegiance to Russia. Yeliseyev's newly-appointed successor as Navy supreme commander, Denis Berezovskiy, ordered his men to lay down arms – for which the Ukrainian government promptly dismissed him early on the next day (2 March). Berezovskiy, too, then changed allegiance. Neither saw a future in Ukraine, and both men retained their ranks in the Russian Navy.

These actions were not unique. The little green men did their job. Ukrainian soldiers trapped inside bases on the Crimean Peninsula soon agreed to remain on base without escalating violence while the political battle was played out.

Meanwhile, Russian units sealed off Crimea. Troops at northern crossing points detached the peninsula physically from Ukraine. They also severed landline communications, jammed signals, and cut off electricity to some military bases as a means to apply further pressure.

On 6 March, Crimea's parliament voted for a referendum to decide the peninsula's status. The referendum was held 10 days later (16 March). Voters overwhelmingly voted to join Russia. On the next day (17 March), President Putin officially recognized Crimea as a sovereign independent state. And on the next day (18 March), he signed a bill to absorb Crimea into the Russian Federation. Crimea was formally annexed by the Russian Federation on 21 March.

Accepting realities on the ground, the Ukrainian government on 24 March ordered the full withdrawal of all of its armed forces from Crimea. The last Ukrainian military bases and Ukrainian navy vessels were seized by Russian troops on 26 March.

The little green men arrive and take up positions at Perevalne military base, 9 March 2014. Soon, the military base was secured. (Photo: Anton Holoborodko)

The little green men take up positions at Simferopol Airport, 3 March 2014. Russians constituted the majority population of Crimea. Many Crimeans supported the takeover, not least because the new, pro-Western Ukrainian government in Kyiv which had deposed the elected Ukrainian president was perceived, in its language policy, to discriminate against ethnic Russians. Hybrid threats operations have a greater impact if based on real grievances with solutions to which the target population is receptive. (Photo: Ilya Varlamov)

Russia did not regard the Crimea operation as a hybrid threats operation. Militarily, this assessment makes sense, since the operation was more a conventional military take-over than a hybrid threats operation. However, while Russian units were moving into Crimea, the Kremlin was also pursuing a comprehensive information operation targeted at the Russian public and Crimean residents.[7] The information operation had three objectives. The first objective was to discredit the new government in Ukraine as fascist, which in Russian eyes was easy since armed Ukrainian right-wing extremists from *Pravyy Sektor* ('Right Sector') played a prominent role in the coup that toppled President Yanukovych and also openly seized presidential administration buildings during the coup. The second objective was to emphasize the discrimination faced by ethnic Russians in Ukraine under the new government in Kyiv. This was easy, too, since the Ukrainian parliament immediately after the coup voted to revoke the Russian language's status as official language in areas with a substantial Russian population such as Crimea. The information operation's third objective was to assert the broad popular support for Crimea's return to Russia. Again, this objective was easily achieved since the majority population in the peninsula was ethnic Russian. In short, the Kremlin chose narratives all of which contained a seed of apparent truth, accuracy, or plausibility, which naturally helped to push the message to its audience. Most Western media outlets immediately, and without deliberation or fact-checking, denounced the claims asserted in the information operation, which in Russian eyes only served to discredit the Western narrative and emphasize the civilizational struggle between Russia and the West.

The information operation was deployed simultaneously and synchronized with the military operation. It helped that the special forces units appeared as anonymous little green men. Although most observers took for granted that they were Russian soldiers, Russia could still invoke plausible deniability. The appearance of unidentified but well-behaved soldiers raised the possibility that they were locals. Besides, Russia also deployed real paramilitary units and organizations during the Crimea operation. Crimean self-defence militia units raised from locals, Cossacks, and former special police units took part in the operation. Volunteers included army veterans, boxers and other athletes, and members of the biker gang Night Wolves, with which President Putin had a long history. Members of Night Wolves mobilized, they said, to ensure a free and fair referendum and to assist the local population in the struggle against Ukrainian fascism.

President Vladimir Putin of Russia with Aleksandr Zaldastanov, a.k.a. 'The Surgeon', President of Night Wolves Motorcycle Club, at the 14th International biker rally in Sevastopol, Crimea, 24 July 2010. Members of Night Wolves operated on behalf of the Russian government in the Crimea operation four years later. (Photo: Russian government)

A key reason for Russia's success in the Crimea operation was the presence of bases of the Russian Black Sea Fleet in the peninsula. This provided Russia with the necessary men, vehicles, and equipment, and greatly facilitated logistics throughout the operation. According to interstate agreements, Russia was allowed up to 25,000 servicemen for the Black Sea Fleet (although that many were not present). The centuries-long presence of the Black Sea Fleet in Crimea contributed to the local population's acceptance of Russian troops.

Moreover, no troops of the Ukrainian Army were stationed on the peninsula, only naval and coastal defence units armed with rocket artillery, as well as a tactical air force group and Interior Ministry units, both in poor operational shape. The Ukrainian coastal defence forces appear to have been superior to the Russian units in terms of both numbers and heavy weapons.[8] Yet, the revolution in Kyiv produced a grave leadership crisis within the Ukrainian Armed Forces. Many key military officers remained loyal to President Yanukovich. Others preferred to sit out the revolution to see what would happen.

Yet, the most important reason for Russia's success in the Crimea operation was the presence of a Russian majority population. While the ethnic Russians in Ukraine had a history of loyalty to Kyiv, the Ukrainian parliament's fiery condemnation of Russian minority rights was a spectacular own goal which alienated the Russian population and greatly facilitated the Russian operation in Crimea.

Comparable Cases

The multi-state NATO-led coalition which on 19 March 2011 began a military intervention in Libya to implement United Nations Security Council Resolution 1973 shared a key feature with the Russian Crimea operation: the deployment of special forces without military insignia well before the operation was supposed to take place. Officially, the intervention in Libya began two days after the Security Council adopted Resolution 1973 in response to widespread and systematic attacks against the civilian population that took place during the First Libyan Civil War.

The NATO military intervention was primarily an air operation, with participation of over 260 aircraft and 21 naval vessels.[9] In fact, the Security Council Resolution did not authorize a foreign occupation force of any form on any part of Libyan territory.[10] However, numerous media reports still make it clear that NATO member state special forces in essentially civilian dress were deployed in Libya in support of the insurgents and as spotters for the air operations.[11] Moreover, press reports suggested that 'hundreds' of British SAS troops, divided in two units and with attached signallers, engineers and medics, had already operated on the ground in Libya in support of insurgents for three weeks before Resolution 1973 was adopted.[12] Although primarily a military operation, the NATO mission also included a significant information operation, which suggests that the intervention carried some aspects of a hybrid threats operation.

The men of the special forces units were described as mostly wearing sand-coloured clothes, peaked caps, and cotton Arab scarves. However, the most senior of the group reportedly wore a pink, short-sleeved shirt.[13] Perhaps they should be referred to as the little pink men of Libya.

Cyber Power

Cyber power is deployed in a variety of forms, including cyber-attacks by hackers, identity theft by organized cybercrime groups (phishing), data interception and manipulation, alteration of website content for reasons of propaganda or sabotage, suppression of web services, and so on. Cyber power can also be deployed for the interception and surveillance of web-based communications, and for the manipulation and sabotage of critical infrastructure which relies on web-based services. Moreover, cyber power has the potential to take advantage of the new applications, processes, and business models in the financial services industry generally referred to as FinTech (Financial Technology). Non-state actors play a prominent role in the deployment of contemporary cyber power.

The challenge with cyber operations lies in attributing them. Even if the source of the cyber-attack can be traced, does this mean that this particular actor in fact is the initiator of the attack? It might well be that another, more sophisticated actor merely has hijacked somebody else's cyber infrastructure and toolkit. If the victim of the cyber-attack decides to retaliate, will the retaliation actually strike the responsible party? Governments all too frequently find it tempting to attribute blame to their regular geopolitical rivals, instead of clarifying who actually carried out the cyber-attack.

While the new information and communication technologies, along with social media networks, brought many positive aspects for society through the interconnectedness that suddenly became possible negative interdependencies emerged, too. The increased infrastructure vulnerabilities enabled the use of cascading attacks for the sabotage of critical infrastructure. A cascading attack is defined as a type of attack where corrupt data items lead to service disruption by causing a chain reaction of errors in a system, ultimately resulting in incorrect service delivery or system failure.

One of the first cyber-attacks on critical infrastructure, and for intelligence services possibly the archetypal cyber operation, was Stuxnet. This became the popular name of a malicious computer worm which targeted supervisory control and data acquisition (SCADA) systems in designated industrial processes. Stuxnet was first uncovered by a Belarusian antivirus company in 2010 but was assessed to have been in development since at least 2005. Most independent observers recognize Stuxnet as a cyber weapon built by the United States with the support of Israel in order to damage and delay Iran's nuclear programme. Neither country openly admitted responsibility, but initial damage seems to have been inflicted only on embargoed Siemens centrifuges procured clandestinely by Iran for uranium enrichment purposes without the manufacturer's knowledge.

Stuxnet functioned by first targeting any machines which used the Microsoft Windows operating system by taking advantage of several design flaws (so-called zero-day vulnerabilities) in the operating system. Then, Stuxnet sought out any Siemens Step7 software, which was used in the Iranian uranium enrichment programme. Next, Stuxnet compromised the programmable logic controllers (PLCs) in the Siemens equipment procured clandestinely by Iran with corrupt data. PLCs allow the automation of electromechanical processes such as those used to control machinery and industrial processes. The corrupt data caused the Siemens centrifuges to self-destruct by spinning too fast.

Ultimately, it was reported that the Dutch intelligence service AIVD had been instrumental in installing equipment infected with Stuxnet in Iran's underground nuclear complex at Natanz around 2008 on behalf of U.S. intelligence, which nonetheless reportedly kept crucial information a secret from the Netherlands. The Dutch agent, Erik van Sabben, died in a car incident in Sharjah in the United Arab Emirates soon afterwards.[14]

The Stuxnet was a deployment of state cyber power, but it was not a hybrid threats operation. The malware attack had a specific objective and was not coordinated with other offensive operations in other domains. For hybrid threats in the cyber power domain, we will have to look elsewhere.

The underground nuclear complex at Natanz, 2006. The complex was heavily guarded, including by the Samavat 35mm twin-cannon anti-aircraft system, an Iranian version of the Swiss Oerlikon 35mm twin cannon. (Photo Hamed Saber)

Stuxnet was designed to target the Siemens Simatic S7-300 PLC Central Processing Unit (CPU), here displayed with three attached I/O (input/output) modules. (Photo: Ulli1105)

Case Study: Mabna Institute, Iranian Hackers-for-Hire, 2013–2018

The Mabna Institute was founded in Tehran, Iran, in approximately 2013 as a private enterprise to assist Iranian universities and scientific and research organizations in gaining access to non-Iranian scientific resources. For this reason, the Mabna Institute employed, contracted, and affiliated itself with a number of hackers-for-hire to conduct cyber intrusions to steal academic data, intellectual property, email inboxes, and other proprietary data. In 2018, a grand jury in the U.S. District Court for the Southern District of New York indicted nine Iranian nationals for their alleged involvement in the Mabna Institute's cyber intrusions and other crimes. Based on an FBI investigation, the Court alleged that the Mabna Institute operated as a private government contractor which performed cyber intrusions for the Iranian government, at the behest of the Islamic Revolutionary Guard Corps (IRGC). The Court also alleged that the Mabna Institute targeted over a hundred thousand accounts of academics throughout the world, at 144 universities based in the United States and 176 universities located in foreign countries, including Australia, Britain, Canada, China, Denmark, Finland, Germany, Ireland, Israel, Italy, Japan, Malaysia, Netherlands, Norway, Poland, Singapore, South Korea, Spain, Sweden, Switzerland, and Turkey. Furthermore, the Mabna Institute conducted a computer hacking campaign against various governmental and non-governmental organizations within the United States, including the Department of Labor, the Federal Energy Regulatory Commission, the State of Hawai'i, the State of Indiana, the State of Indiana Department of Education, the United Nations, and the United Nations Children's Fund. Interestingly, in addition to targeting universities, the Mabna Institute targeted employee email accounts used by private companies, at least 36 based in the United States and at least 11 in Germany, Italy, Switzerland, Sweden, and the United Kingdom.[15]

The salient factor about the Mabna Institute was that it directed cyber operations simultaneously at targets of interest to the IRGC and targets which could provide data which could be sold on the open market. The focus on academics derived from the need for students and researchers at Iranian public universities to gain access to the online library systems of foreign universities, for which they had to pay the Mabna Institute a fee. In a manner of speaking, the Mabna Institute provided a public service to Iranian academe, although one which was illegally obtained. In short, the Mabna Institute combined the functions of a state-sponsored hacking operation and a hacker-for-hire. In its role as state-sponsored operation, it may have provided information that could be used in hybrid threats campaigns.

Comparable Cases

The Mabna Institute is best compared to some of the often-opaque groups of cybercrime organizations customarily known as advanced persistent threats (APTs). Perhaps the best comparable case is that of APT41, also known as Double Dragon or Cicada, which is generally assessed to be a Chinese state-sponsored group which engages in cyber espionage on behalf of the government while simultaneously carrying out financially motivated cybercrime for personal gain. The group's activities have been traced back to 2012, and Double Dragon operations are far more advanced than those achieved by the hackers of the Mabna Institute.[16] While the Mabna Institute functioned as a non-state actor which was hired by a state actor, Double Dragon is more likely a state actor the members of which simultaneously operate for non-state purposes.

State actors are deeply involved in the deployment of cyber power. As shown by the Stuxnet case, this goes well beyond hybrid threats. In 2014, a grand jury in the U.S. Western District of Pennsylvania indicted five Chinese military officers for alleged computer hacking, economic espionage, and other offenses directed at the U.S. nuclear power, metals, and solar products industries. The five officers allegedly belonged to Unit 61398, which is believed to operate under the Third Office of the Second Bureau of the People's Liberation Army General Staff Department Third Department, which is responsible for electronic warfare. Among cyber security professionals, the unit was called APT1, also known as Comment Crew, Comment Panda, GIF89a, and Byzantine Candor. Unlike the hackers of the Mabna Institute and Double Dragon, there was nothing to suggest that the officers of Unit 61398 in any way operated for personal gain. Unit 61398 was a military organization which worked office hours.[17]

The indictment marked the first time criminal charges were filed against known or suspected state actors for hacking. The indictment was followed by harsh political statements against China by a range of senior U.S. officials. FBI Executive Assistant Director Robert Anderson issued the following clear and present threat: 'If you are going to attack Americans – whether for criminal or national security purposes – we are going to hold you accountable. No matter what country you live in.'[18]

Privatized Power

Privatized power is, by definition, primarily associated with non-state actors. The non-state actors may be, in order of ascending respectability, OCGs (including the subcategories of pirates and terrorists who are in it for profit), insurgent groups and warlord-led militias, or private military companies (PMCs) and paramilitary security firms. Either way, their specialty involves the deployment of privatized force for the purpose of carrying out armed attacks, killings, hostage-takings, intimidation, extortion, blackmail, and/or other sometime illegal activities such as black-market trading and corruption. Even so, although OCGs may well be able to provide access to smuggling networks, for individuals, goods, and money, as well as safe houses, vehicles, weapons, and forged IDs, they constitute a blunt instrument. In short, they are violent but unskilled.

Case Study: D-Company, Indian Smugglers-for-Hire, 1986–2024

The perhaps most enduring relationship between state actors and an organized-crime non-state actor entity in modern times is the one between D-Company and the Pakistani Inter-services Intelligence agency (ISI). Sometime between 1984 and 1986, Dawood Ibrahim, a Bombay-based Indian Muslim smuggler, due to pressure from law enforcement as well as rival gangs fled to Dubai, United Arab Emirates. There his criminal organization grew into what became known as D-Company. His original, and no doubt primary, motivation was arguably crime for profit, yet this did not prevent him from allying with Pakistani intelligence and terrorist groups. One reason was sectarian, since he wanted to take revenge for anti-Muslim riots in India, and this resulted in a series of bombings in Bombay 1993, which killed hundreds. However, the Bombay attacks split D-Company along sectarian lines, and Ibrahim and his key lieutenants took refuge in Karachi, where they received the protection of the ISI. Ibrahim also forged links with *Lashkar-e Tayyiba* (LeT), a terrorist group loyal to the Pakistani state. In effect, Ibrahim's and D-Company's motivation was dual: to connect with Pakistani intelligence and terrorist groups for reasons of faith and to acquire sanctuary, a safe haven, as a pragmatic choice from which their regular criminal activities could be sustained. In return, he was quite willing to support and act on behalf of Pakistani intelligence and terrorist groups. The ISI's objective in the cooperation was to gain access to an experienced smuggling network and to acquire plausible deniability in criminal operations. Soon, D-Company began to employ the means of violent crime, intimidation, and acts of terrorism against the Indian population and Indian state institutions. Meanwhile, relationships within the Indian/Pakistani D-Company were held together by mutual interests and/or fear of punishment for insubordination, not a rigid command and control structure, and members were allowed to engage in opportunistic, private criminal activities on the side, as long as they remained loyal to the organization as a whole. This freedom to engage in other undertakings also helped to ensure that the organization's activities remained diversified. Furthermore, it protected the organization from collapsing in case of the loss of any top leader.[19]

CONSPIRACY TO COMMIT COMPUTER INTRUSIONS; CONSPIRACY TO COMMIT WIRE FRAUD; COMPUTER FRAUD - UNAUTHORIZED ACCESS FOR PRIVATE FINANCIAL GAIN; WIRE FRAUD; AGGRAVATED IDENTITY THEFT

Gholamreza Rafatnejad

Ehsan Mohammadi

Seyed Ali Mirkarimi

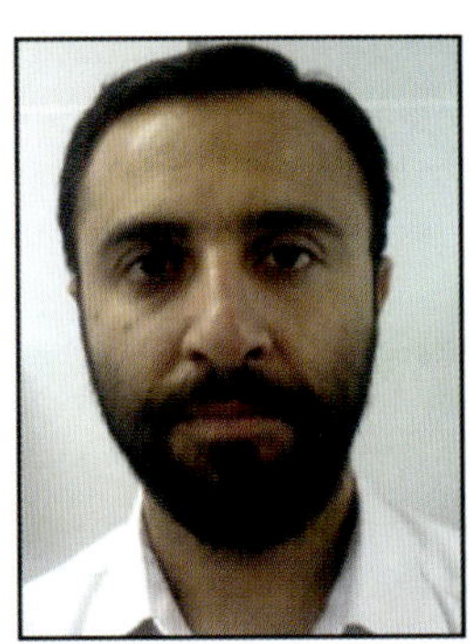
Abdollah Karima

Mostafa Sadeghi

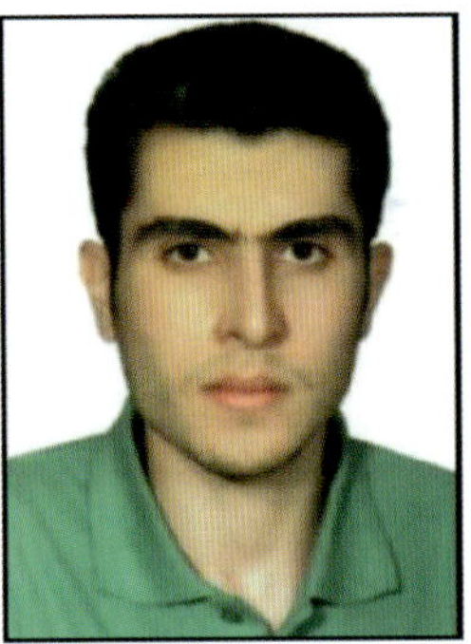
Sajjad Tahmasebi

Mohammed Reza Sabahi

Roozbeh Sabahi

Abuzar Gohari Moqadam

CAUTION

On February 7, 2018, a grand jury sitting in the United States District Court for the Southern District of New York, indicted nine Iranian nationals for their alleged involvement in computer intrusion, wire fraud, and aggravated identity theft offenses. As alleged in the indictment, the men were involved in a scheme to obtain unauthorized access to computer systems, steal proprietary data from those systems, and sell that stolen data to Iranian customers, including the Iranian government and Iranian universities. Each individual was a leader, contractor, associate, hacker for hire, or affiliate of the Mabna Institute, a private government contractor based in the Islamic Republic of Iran that performed this work for the Iranian government, at the behest of the Islamic Revolutionary Guard Corps. Victims of the scheme included approximately 144 universities in the United States, 176 foreign universities in 21 countries, five federal and state government agencies in the United States, 36 private companies in the United States, 11 foreign private companies, and two international non-governmental organizations.

THESE INDIVIDUALS SHOULD BE CONSIDERED AN INTERNATIONAL FLIGHT RISK

If you have any information concerning this case, please contact your local FBI office, or the nearest American Embassy or Consulate.

Field Office: New York

www.fbi.gov

Nine Iranian nationals wanted by the FBI for their alleged involvement in the Mabna Institute's cyber intrusions. (Photo: FBI)

The D-Company/ISI cooperation was a hybrid threat, since it involved privatized violence together with other means to gain the desired strategic objectives. Both parties in the cooperation were able to achieve their objectives, since they shared strategic goals.

Comparable Cases

A similar case but suggesting a less enduring relationship between state actor and non-state actor was the attempted assassination in February 2020 of Tumsu Abdurakhmanov, who lived in exile in Sweden where he was engaged in social media activities directed against the Chechen government. Both the subsequently prosecuted assailant, Ruslan Mamayev, and Abdurakhmanov himself alleged that the attempted murder resulted from a blood feud between Abdurakhmanov and an 'actor linked to the Chechen government'. In the ensuing trial, the court concluded that much indeed pointed in this direction, although neither motive nor the link between the attacker and the Chechen government could be decisively proven. The court also concluded that Mamayev, who admitted to links with organized crime actors, had been offered EUR 60,000 for the murder contract, in addition to his travel and accommodation expenses.[20] The case illustrates how a state actor may hire one or more actors in organized crime for the carrying-out of a single mission involving violence. The relationship is one of short-term interaction only and does not necessitate shared goals or similar

SUN KAILIANG

Conspiring to Commit Computer Fraud; Accessing a Computer Without Authorization for the Purpose of Commercial Advantage and Private Financial Gain; Damaging Computers Through the Transmission of Code and Commands; Aggravated Identity Theft; Economic Espionage; Theft of Trade Secrets

Aliases: Sun Kai Liang, Jack Sun

CAUTION

On May 1, 2014, a grand jury in the Western District of Pennsylvania indicted five members of the People's Liberation Army (PLA) of the People's Republic of China (PRC) for 31 criminal counts, including: conspiring to commit computer fraud; accessing a computer without authorization for the purpose of commercial advantage and private financial gain; damaging computers through the transmission of code and commands; aggravated identity theft; economic espionage; and theft of trade secrets.

The subjects, including Sun Kailiang, were officers of the PRC's Third Department of the General Staff Department of the People's Liberation Army (3PLA), Second Bureau, Third Office, Military Unit Cover Designator (MUCD) 61398, at some point during the investigation. The activities executed by each of these individuals allegedly involved in the conspiracy varied according to his specialties. Each provided his individual expertise to an alleged conspiracy to penetrate the computer networks of six American companies while those companies were engaged in negotiations or joint ventures or were pursuing legal action with, or against, state-owned enterprises in China. They then used their illegal access to allegedly steal proprietary information including, for instance, e-mail exchanges among company employees and trade secrets related to technical specifications for nuclear plant designs. Sun, who held the rank of captain during the early stages of the investigation, was observed both sending malicious e-mails and controlling victim computers.

If you have any information concerning this person, please contact your local FBI office or the nearest American Embassy or Consulate.

Field Office: Pittsburgh

In 2014, the United States took the highly unusual measure of indicting five serving Chinese military officers in China on charges of computer hacking, economic espionage, and other offenses directed at the U.S. nuclear power, metals, and solar products industries. This marked the first time criminal charges were filed against known or suspected state actors for hacking. The officers belonged to Unit 61398. Several were shown in uniform when the FBI published wanted posters for them, including Captain Sun Kailiang, depicted here. (Photo: FBI)

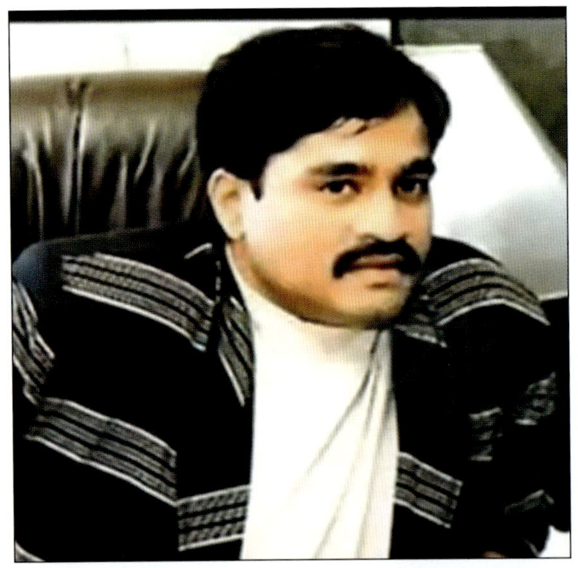

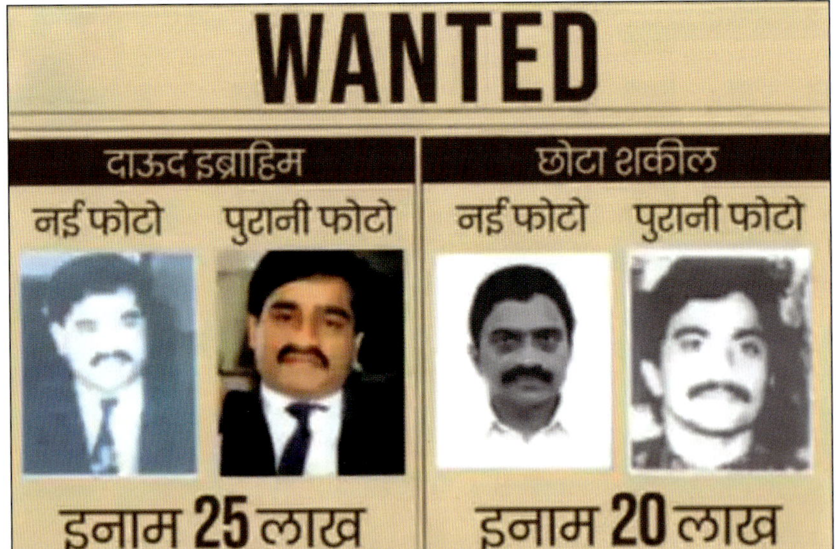

WANTED
दाऊद इब्राहिम
नई फोटो
पुरानी फोटो
इनाम 25 लाख
छोटा शकील
नई फोटो
पुरानी फोटो
इनाम 20 लाख

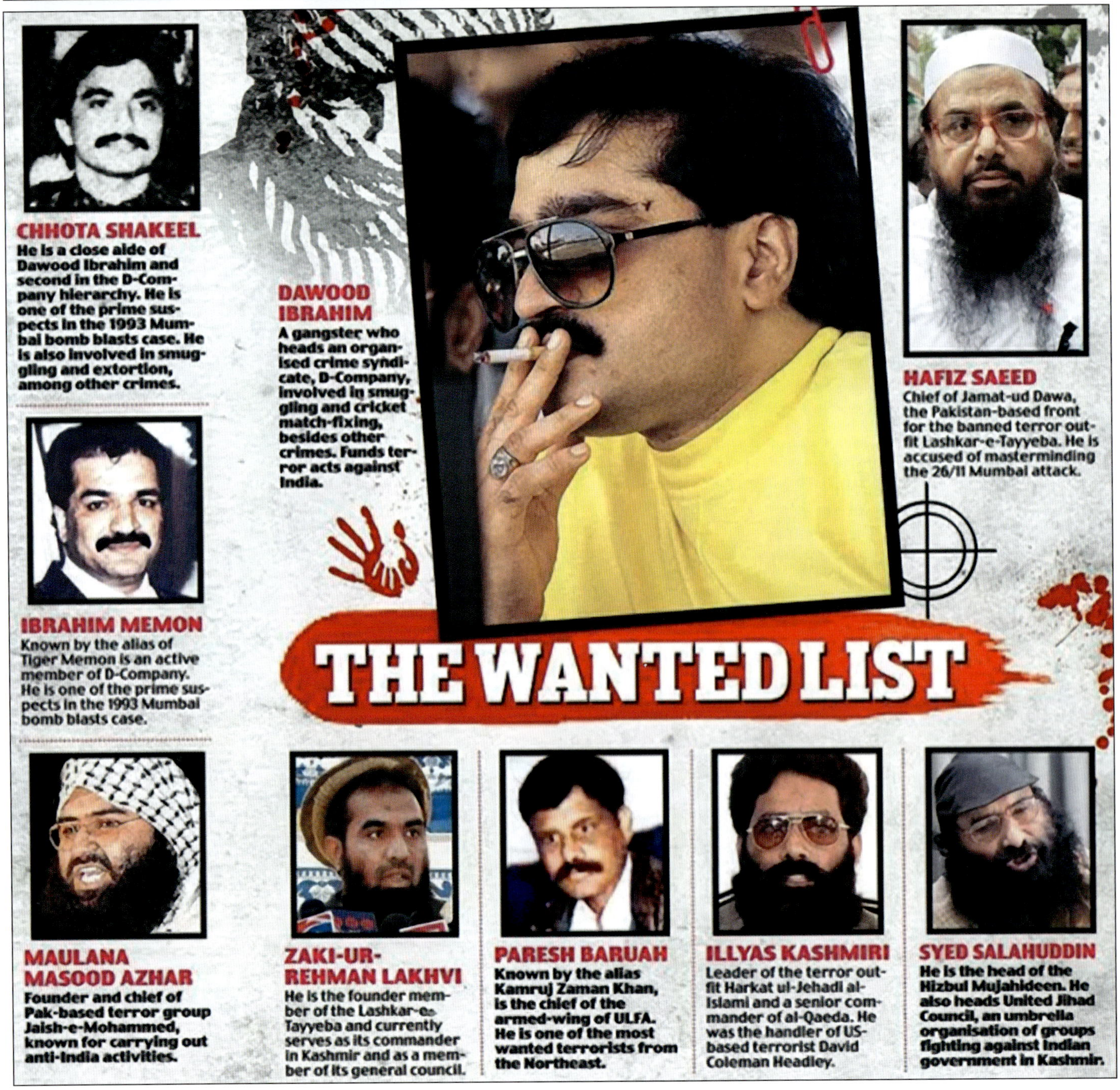
CHHOTA SHAKEEL
He is a close aide of Dawood Ibrahim and second in the D-Company hierarchy. He is one of the prime suspects in the 1993 Mumbai bomb blasts case. He is also involved in smuggling and extortion, among other crimes.
DAWOOD IBRAHIM
A gangster who heads an organised crime syndicate, D-Company, involved in smuggling and cricket match-fixing, besides other crimes. Funds terror acts against India.
HAFIZ SAEED
Chief of Jamat-ud Dawa, the Pakistan-based front for the banned terror outfit Lashkar-e-Tayyeba. He is accused of masterminding the 26/11 Mumbai attack.
IBRAHIM MEMON
Known by the alias of Tiger Memon is an active member of D-Company. He is one of the prime suspects in the 1993 Mumbai bomb blasts case.
THE WANTED LIST
MAULANA MASOOD AZHAR
Founder and chief of Pak-based terror group Jaish-e-Mohammed, known for carrying out anti-India activities.
ZAKI-UR-REHMAN LAKHVI
He is the founder member of the Lashkar-e-Tayyeba and currently serves as its commander in Kashmir and as a member of its general council.
PARESH BARUAH
Known by the alias Kamruj Zaman Khan, is the chief of the armed-wing of ULFA. He is one of the most wanted terrorists from the Northeast.
ILLYAS KASHMIRI
Leader of the terror outfit Harkat ul-Jehadi al-Islami and a senior commander of al-Qaeda. He was the handler of US-based terrorist David Coleman Headley.
SYED SALAHUDDIN
He is the head of the Hizbul Mujahideen. He also heads United Jihad Council, an umbrella organisation of groups fighting against Indian government in Kashmir.

Dawood Ibrahim, the most wanted leader of D-Company. (Photo: Author's collection)

circumstances. The non-state actor within organized crime is merely hired by the state actor to do a job. In the Mamayev case, he failed and was arrested. The case was a hybrid threat, since it involved the use of deniable privatized power to neutralize what was, according to Abdurakhmanov, a perceived media threat to actors linked to the Chechen government. Possibly, the assumption was that the assassination of Abdurakhmanov would stifle other criticism. Even so, it can be questioned whether the Mamayev operation, a stand-alone event, really reached the strategic threshold to qualify as a hybrid threat. However, if the attack had been carried out in conjunction with other threat activities, by state actors or non-state actors, then it might well have qualified as a hybrid threat.

Privatized power is not the exclusive domain of organized crime. PMCs can be utilized in similar ways. The employment of a PMC will allow some degree of plausible deniability, although commonly not to the same extent as when hiring a non-state actor within organized crime. Instead, a PMC generally operates within the law, which in itself insulates its activities from the principal. Moreover, PMCs are more commonly employed when a long-term relationship with the state actor is desirable. The relationship may be one of shared goals, or a more business-like relationship involving long-term funding. Either way, the leadership of the PMC tends to consist of former military or security officers of the state which employs the PMC. Typical examples of PMCs include South Africa's Executive Outcomes (in operation 1989–1998), Britain's Sandline International (in operation 1994–2004), and Russia's Wagner Group (in operation since 2014 and, in a slightly different form, into the present).[21]

People's Power

People's power is deployed by insurgents, extremists, and revolutionaries, but also by the mobilization of malcontents and impoverished or marginalized groups who, wittingly or unwittingly, act on behalf of an actor with the capacity to arouse them. Any large group of protesters on a street in a developing country, regardless of who aroused them, is likely to receive favourable attention from the Western press, as long as it commands social media and the crowd voices the customary demands for human rights and democracy. Demonstrations, riots, and violent unrest may be the result of genuine sentiments, but they are easily hijacked by demagogues, extremist groups, and – not least – state actors.

It is often difficult to distinguish between genuine popular discontent and hostile activities directed from abroad, since global links and events influence population segments in many countries, especially in diaspora groups. Not every hostile action is a hybrid threat. Yet, there are also cases of people's power actors who function as proxies in hybrid threat operations for hostile powers, or for foreign organizations.

Case Study: Free Syrian Army, Syrian Insurgents on a Retainer, 2011–2012

The Free Syrian Army (FSA) was established in Turkey in 2011.[22] Although the result of a popular uprising against the Syrian government and, for this reason, more of an umbrella organization for insurgent groups than a genuine army, the FSA soon became the proxy of several foreign states, in particular Turkey, Saudi Arabia, and Qatar, which desired a united Syrian national insurgency under their control.[23] For a while, these states used the FSA as a proxy for gaining territorial control through the FSA's capacity to mobilize segments of the Syrian population through the domain of people's power. The FSA was also employed as a proxy for gaining further international support for the campaign against the Syrian government. The FSA was accordingly used as a means to wield people's power, privatized power, and media power, with the additional hope of also being able to bring diplomatic power to bear. The non-state actor accordingly reached the strategic threshold to qualify as a hybrid threat.

However, while the outcome at first seemed favourable, the FSA never managed to gain the control over its constituent parts that was required for the organization to function as the command centre

FSA irregular loads an M2 Browning heavy machine gun on a technical in northern Aleppo, 1 November 2016. (Photo: Mada Media)

in exile of a national insurgency. Moreover, the FSA soon acquired a less than sterling reputation. In February 2015, a Swedish court sentenced Mouhannad Droubi, an FSA member who had received asylum in Sweden, to prison for torturing a captive in 2012. The case marked the first instance of a Syrian being prosecuted abroad for crimes against humanity committed during the Syrian conflict.[24] The case also caused protests among those opposing the Syrian government. Syrian opposition sources warned that 'Sweden must also be aware of the negative perceptions that these prosecutions might induce among Syrians' and concluded that 'Syrians have strongly criticized Droubi's prosecution, despite the clear evidence that he participated in torture. If foreign national courts disregard such perceptions, anger and frustration among anti-regime parties will only grow'.[25] The protests against the prosecution can themselves be labelled as a hybrid threats campaign, since the activities involved media power, diplomatic power, and even carried a faint suggestion of threat of terrorist power, in case Droubi was convicted.

Comparable Cases

The use of an armed exile group against an adversary constitutes the possibly oldest type of hybrid threats activity, as exemplified by the aforementioned conflict over exiles between ancient Imperial Rome and the Hunnic state. Comparable cases can be found in almost every conflict, from ancient times into the present. Strictly speaking, the group does not need to qualify as a pure exile group. In 1979, Iran formed two organizations purportedly out of Afghan exiles. The Sazman-e Nasr-e Islami-ye Afghanistan (Organization for Islamic Victory of Afghanistan) consisted of young Hazara radicals educated in Iran and inspired by the Iranian revolution. The Sepah-e Pasdaran (Army of the Guardians) was established as a branch of the IRGC among Shias from Afghanistan. Both organizations dispatched fighters into Afghanistan to fight the Kabul government and the Soviets, liberate traditional Shia regions in Afghanistan, and serve as Iran's proxies. Both included Afghan as well as Iranian members, and soon both also supplied troops to fight in Iran's then-ongoing war with Iraq, for which they were paid.[26] Although Iran benefited from the soldiers provided by these two organizations, their primary use was not military but to function as an extension of Iranian influence in the Shia regions of Afghanistan. Their purpose was to mould Afghan Shia culture, politics, and organizational structures into a copy of the Iranian model. To some extent, they succeeded (although at the cost of causing a civil war among the Afghan Hazaras). Hence, the activities of Sazman-e Nasr-e Islami-ye Afghanistan and Sepah-e Pasdaran constituted hybrid threats to both the government of Afghanistan and traditional Hazara society.

Terrorist Power

Terrorist power may be deployed by non-state actors or state actors. Either way, it involves the carrying-out of violent attacks, killings, and acts of sabotage. Attacks do not need to be simple; many terrorists are fascinated by CBRN agents and weapons of mass destruction, but few know how to deploy them. Some states actively support terrorists. However, more common is for the state to provide passive support to those terrorist organizations with which it shares goals, in so far that state actors tolerate and turn a blind eye on their activities as long as the bloodshed does not reach too blatant levels (for an example of the latter, see the section on civil power, below).

Case Study: Chatayev Group of the Caucasus Emirate, Chechen Jihadists-for-Hire, 2012

In April 2013, the Public Defender of Georgia issued a report revealing how the counterterrorism department of the Ministry of Internal Affairs from February 2012 onwards recruited about 120 primarily Chechens and a few other North Caucasians from Europe to conduct terror operations in Russia. The group included several veteran fighters. Georgia was then under the Saakashvili administration. The counterterrorism department picked up the fighters at Tbilisi airport. They were then armed and given driver's licenses and gun registration certificates, after which they were trained by Georgian personnel and Chechen veterans at Vaziani and Shavnabada military bases. Flats were rented for them in various parts of Tbilisi. The terrorist training program did not end well, however. The program was exposed by the so-called Lopota incident which took place in August 2012. This was a clash between some of the Chechens and Georgian government forces in Lopota, near the border with Daghestan in the Russian Federation. Several people died on each side. The Chechens involved in the Lopota incident had been tired of waiting for permission to cross the border into Russia, grew impatient, and decided to depart on their own – but had been refused passage and intercepted. The Ministry of Internal Affairs had then turned to Ahmed Chatayev (a.k.a David Mayer) to mediate. Chatayev was a Chechen 'authority' (the term for a senior leader in traditional organized crime) residing in Austria. However, the negotiations had failed, the Chechens and Georgian security forces had opened fire on one another, and Chatayev, wounded in the crossfire, ended up in custody, at which point the Public Defender got involved. The Ministry of Internal Affairs then arranged for the surviving Chechen fighters to leave for Turkey.[27]

In June 2013, the Chechen side of the story was presented. It was a report signed by Usman Ferzauli, a leader of a Chechen exile group known as the Chechen Republic of Ichkeriya (ChRI). The ChRI report fundamentally followed the facts as presented by the Public Defender of Georgia. The Georgian Ministry of Internal Affairs, with the approval of President Saakashvili, concluded an agreement with the Caucasus Emirate, the Chechen jihadist group which by then had assumed control over the former Chechen separatist movement. The Caucasus Emirate recruited, on behalf of Georgia, up to 200 fighters among Caucasus Emirate sympathizers from Belgium, France, Austria, Britain, Norway, Turkey, and Egypt. Many of them, including Chatayev, were already involved in organized crime unrelated to ideological activities. Upon arrival in Georgia, the recruits were given flats in Tbilisi and in the Pankisi Gorge, money, and necessary documents including driver's licenses. They also received military training at Vaziani and Shavnabada military bases. The operation was organized by Akhmad Umarov, the elder brother of the Caucasus Emirate's leader Doku Umarov. Chatayev, who was described as Doku Umarov's representative in Turkey, was called to Georgia to arrange matters further. The ChRI report confirmed that Chatayev was called in to negotiate at Lopota.[28]

In 2015, Chatayev departed for Syria, where he joined the terrorist group known as the Islamic State of Iraq and the Levant (ISIL). In June 2016, he masterminded the ISIL terrorist attack on Istanbul's Atatürk International Airport which left at least 42 people dead and more than 200 injured. In November 2017, Chatayev was killed in a gunfight with Georgian police officers during an anti-terrorist operation in Tbilisi.[29]

The Saakashvili administration's objective had been to undermine Russian security through acts of terrorism against the Russian state institutions and public under conditions of plausible deniability.

The operation qualifies as a hybrid threat, since it involved not only terrorist power but also military, judicial, and diplomatic means, among others. As far as is known, the cooperation was intended as a long-term relationship between the Saakashvili administration and the Caucasus Emirate, since both entities were hostile to Russia. However, ultimately it became a short-term interaction only, which (like the aforementioned Mamayev case) ended in failure.

Ahmed Chatayev in court, 2013. He had previously lost his right hand in combat. (Author's Collection)

Comparable Cases

State cooperation with terrorist non-state actor entities was quite widespread during the Cold War but due to the increasing risk of exposure, grew less ubiquitous afterwards. Even during the Cold War, cooperation was seldom as flagrant as in the Chatayev case. Yet, state links with terrorist entities were already then characterized by relationships of a hybrid nature. For instance, Poland in the 1970s and 1980s cooperated with the Abu Nidal Organization (ANO) as a means to receive intelligence but even more because brokers linked to the ANO assisted Polish state-owned companies engaged in arms export to Third World countries.[30]

Real Economic Power

Real economic power is mostly deployed by states. However, some multinational firms and conglomerates have similar resources at their disposal as small states, so non-state actors are active within this domain. While they frequently act as proxies for states, some may have agendas of their own. Real economic power projection displays itself in a variety of activities. These include, but are not limited to, the acquisition of strategic resources, infrastructure, and control over transportation routes, the imposition of monopolies and prices favourable to the stronger party, and the interruption of supply of raw materials, fuels, and critical components as a means to raise prices or force compliance with other demands.

Real economic power of this kind is increasing in importance. As noted, demand for certain natural resources was amplified by developments in technology. Certain types of chips, batteries, electric motors, and numerous other modern manufactured goods need particular raw materials. The near future may see shortages of rare earth elements (REEs) for magnets in electric car motors and more. The same goes for lithium and cobalt for batteries. Demand for lithium is expected to grow rapidly as demand grows for environmentally friendly technologies. Although some REEs are not really rare, extraction and refining are often concentrated to certain countries or regions. Besides, shortages and delays within the technology supply chains do not only involve raw materials. There are also supply chain problems for refined, processed, and purified materials. While low purity neon or silicon is plentiful, sources of ultrapure industrial-quality materials of these kinds are few, with Ukraine the source of about 50 per cent of semiconductor grade neon, and China the source of 80 per cent of global polysilicon. The same goes for manufactured specialty compounds, such as certain types of plastic, resin, or cleaning fluids.

Moreover, natural disasters such as earthquakes, typhoons, fires, floods, and pandemics may cause significant and enduring supply chain interruptions. Political decisions including embargoes and sanctions may bring the same effects. The deployment of real economic power may be straightforward with regard to intention but tends to involve large numbers of commercial and other entities and complex series of negotiated agreements.

Case Study: Nord Stream AG, International Consortium for Natural Gas Supplies, 2005–2009

By the turn of the century, Russia perceived difficulties in its reliance on the energy sector for export revenues. The nearest markets characterized by liquidity were located in western Europe. However, to reach them Russia depended on transit routes across other states. From Russia's perspective, transit dependence made Russia vulnerable not only to swings in business conditions but more importantly, to economic or political blackmail by foreign powers. These concerns were spelled out in the Russian energy strategy of 2003, which expressed key goals for Russia within the energy sector. The strategy singled out foreign threats (geopolitics, macroeconomics, and business conditions) to Russian security, and furthermore indicated the need to have export terminals not under the control of foreign powers.[31] Because of perceived problems in its relations with the transit states (primarily Poland, Ukraine, and Belarus), Russia was then in the process of developing a system of natural gas pipelines (one across the Baltic and another across the Black Sea) that would bypass them and instead deliver gas straight to the west European markets. By this means, Russia wanted to escape transit dependence. However, within the transit states, many regarded the pipeline projects as detrimental to their interests.

Several of them were not only transit states but also, in their turn, dependent on imported Russian energy.

In September 2005, Russian President Vladimir Putin and German Chancellor Gerhard Schröder met in Berlin. During the meeting, business representatives from the two countries signed an agreement in principle to construct a pipeline across the Baltic Sea. Both the Russian and German sides regarded as a key prerequisite of the project that natural gas delivery through the projected pipeline to the consumer would not be contingent on the political will of the transit countries. Nor would transit fees be paid as was required when moving natural gas through other countries. The decisions during the Schröder-Putin summit were strongly opposed by several neighbouring countries. Having been quite deliberately shut out of the project and at risk of losing both transit fees and political influence over the Russian gas trade with western Europe, Poland and Ukraine opposed the construction of the new pipeline. So did the Baltic states.[32] Nonetheless, in December 2005, construction work on the project began.[33] It was also announced that ex-Chancellor Schröder would become the future chair of the joint company to be established to manage the pipeline.[34] This caused additional controversy around what ultimately would become known as the Nord Stream project.

The Nord Stream project was the result of vulnerabilities which Russia perceived in the domain of real economic power, but simultaneously, the transit countries perceived the project as a threat to their security within the same domain. In light of their previous history, both sides were correct to see risks in their mutual relationship, so there was no way to find middle ground. As a result, the debate soon turned acrimonious. In 2006, several countries which opposed the pipeline project initiated counterstrategies based on, among others, the utilization of environmental concerns and directed media campaigns.[35] When faced with such opposition, Russia responded with its own multidimensional counter-counterstrategy. In effect, Russia used hybrid means to influence the media, society, and ministries of neighbouring states to gain permission for a favoured strategic industrial infrastructure project. A broad spectrum of actors was used to achieve the objective of building the pipeline, including several non-state actors. The Russian state-controlled commercial firm Gazprom handled project coordination, while the new commercial consortium Nord Stream AG handled pipeline construction and lobbying activities. Russian state media carried out several media campaigns. Yet, the most ingenious application of media power was in the employment of PR agencies which, in addition to general advertising, also recruited as consultants several policy makers in the countries opposed to the project. Already from the outset, when ex-Chancellor Schröder was appointed chair of the consortium, the venture had been keen to recruit influential lobbyists. Yet, far more strategic recruitments followed, on national as well as local level in the countries in whose waters pipeline construction would take place. In August 2008, for instance, Finland's former Prime Minister Paavo Lipponen was employed as a consultant for Nord Stream AG, with the task to assist in the application to Finland.[36]

Yet, as far as can be determined, most lobbying activities took place in Sweden, which was hostile to the project which would have to pass through the Swedish exclusive economic zone. Neither Sweden nor the other Baltic states could formally stop pipeline construction but they were involved in consultations which gave them the power to affect how quickly the project moved forward. In effect, they could obstruct and delay the project but not prevent it. According to international legislation, all states are entitled to lay submarine cables and pipelines on the continental shelf.[37] However, under the Espoo Convention of 1991, the state or enterprise which intended to lay such a pipeline first had to prepare an environmental impact assessment (EIA).[38] A pipeline project could accordingly be refused upon environmental grounds, until such a time that an acceptable EIA had been prepared.

When the commercial Swedish television station TV 4 in its investigative television show *Kalla fakta* ('Cold facts') investigated the lobbying activities of Nord Stream AG, it noted that many of these activities took place on the local level of government, in towns and local academic institutions. For instance, the television reporters alleged that a professor at Gotland University College who had criticized the pipeline project had changed his assessment after in June 2007 having been offered, and received, a research grant of SEK 5 million from Nord Stream AG. The reporters also alleged that politicians on Gotland who had criticized the pipeline had ceased their criticisms when it was decided that Nord Stream AG would renovate the local port-town of Slite.[39] In August 2007, months before the consortium even approached the Swedish government with its EIA, the Gotland port-town of Slite had accepted that the Nord Stream consortium used its facilities for logistics during the pipeline project construction, in exchange for the consortium providing approximately SEK 70 million to renovate the harbour.[40] A new quay was eventually constructed, since the old quay was too small, with work starting in December 2008, before the consultation period relating to the amended EIA was over.[41] In total, Gotland benefited from SEK 100 million which was spent on Slite port and various cultural research projects.[42]

On the national level in Sweden, Nord Stream AG in spring 2008, following Sweden's rejection of the first EIA application, hired the press secretary to the minister who had initiated the public debate in opposition to the project in 2006.[43] Then Nord Stream hired a close advisor of another minister as communications project manager.[44] Finally, Nord Stream hired former State Secretary Ulrica Schenström, who had been described as the right hand of Prime Minister Fredrik Reinfeldt and reportedly had enjoyed access to classified information about Swedish strategies with regard to the Nord Stream project.[45] By these recruitments, Nord Stream AG successfully hired key people from both the government and the leading opposition party who were well versed in how the Swedish government functioned and, at least in some cases, no doubt had insider knowledge of the government's views on the Nord Stream project.

In addition, Nord Stream AG spent considerable efforts and funds on public hearings in Stockholm and other Swedish cities and the distribution of information on the pipeline project. Between 2006 and 2008 the Nord Stream consortium claimed to have arranged or participated in more than a hundred public meetings and conferences in the countries around the Baltic Sea.[46] As lobbying intensified, this number rose to more than two hundred by late 2009.[47] Of these, a large share took place in Sweden. Nord Stream AG even sponsored a number of academic research projects, including marine archaeology research carried out off Gotland in 2007 and a book in Swedish on sixteenth-century naval warfare written by a Russian journalist.[48] The book described the Nordic Seven Years' War (1563–1570), which was chiefly fought between Sweden and Denmark. It was presumably a coincidence that the book described a war between Sweden, the government of which was against the Nord Stream project, and Denmark, which was in favour of it.

Finally, Nord Stream AG employed the renowned global public relations agency Hill and Knowlton to polish the image of the project. Hill and Knowlton described the firm's participation in the following terms: 'H+K Strategies' corporate communications and public

Medellín Cartel soldier, Colombia, 1984
Long before the term hybrid threats was invented, practitioners understood its implications. Colonel Roger Trinquier, an experienced French counterinsurgency and counterterrorism officer who served in Indochina, China, Algeria, and Congo before, during, and after the Second World War, in 1961 developed a concept for what he termed 'modern warfare'. By this, he meant fighting an adversary organization which engaged in clandestine warfare that included terrorism as a tactic of war, and operated in guerrilla mode, terrorist mode, or both simultaneously. Not long after, organized crime groups in Colombia began to exceed the threshold which turned them into genuine hybrid threats. Medellín Cartel leaders such as Pablo Escobar and Carlos Lehder initiated a terror campaign of indiscriminate violence against shopping malls, theatres, newspapers, and banks with the aim to coerce the government into refusing their extradition to the United States. Escobar and Lehder also aimed to build political support bases within the system. Escobar gathered supporters to be elected to Congress, while Lehder founded a nationalist political movement. Drug Cartel soldiers, unsurprisingly, wore civilian clothes and carried whatever weapons they could lay their hands on, in this case an AK-47 assault rifle. (Artwork by Renato Dalmaso)

Executive Outcomes soldier, Angola, 1992
With the end of the Cold War, Western governments realized that from now, public opinion and international law precluded the carrying out of too blatant armed interventions in foreign countries. The solution became the private military company (PMC), a mercenary company transformed into a corporate entity. Typical examples were South Africa's Executive Outcomes, in operation 1989–1998, and Britain's Sandline International, in operation 1994–2004. The PMC mostly operated within the legal system, which insulated the principal from its activities. Moreover, the leadership of the PMC tended to consist of former military or security officers of the state which employed the PMC. This Executive Outcomes soldier in Angola is armed with a PKM general purpose machine gun of Soviet/Russian origin. (Artwork by Renato Dalmaso)

UK Special Air Service operator, Libya, 2011
The 2001 War on Terror reinvigorated public and governmental support of direct military intervention in foreign countries that could be labelled terrorist or anti-Western. PMCs were no longer required. Special forces could do the job equally well or better, and they were much easier for the principal to control. When a NATO-led coalition was formed in 2011 to intervene in Libya to implement United Nations Security Council Resolution 1973, NATO special forces without military insignia deployed on the ground already before the Security Council adopted the Resolution. The men of the Special Forces units mostly wore sand-coloured garments, civilian shirts, peaked caps, and cotton Arab scarves. The dress and general appearance of this Special Air Service (SAS) operator is based on a series of photographs taken in Libya by an Al Jazeera Media Network photographer. He carries an L119A1 Special Forces Individual Weapon (SFIW), a carbine in widespread use within United Kingdom Special Forces (UKSF). (Artwork by Renato Dalmaso)

Russian 'Little Green Man', Crimea, 2014
Perhaps taking a cue from the Libya operation, Russia deployed special forces without military insignia when moving into Crimea in 2014. The Russian soldiers carried regular-issue weapons and equipment, but were masked and wore unmarked green military uniforms. Pro-Kremlin media soon began to refer to the Russian troops as 'little green men', a term that stuck and also was adopted abroad. The Russian soldiers were well-mannered, kept to themselves, declined to give interviews to journalists, and mostly did not interfere with civilian life. Russia's Crimea operation was a hybrid threats operation, because it included elements of state military power (special forces and a naval blockade), civil power (parliamentary demands for a referendum and the vote that then took place), and media power (pro-Kremlin media) in a coordinated operation. The information operation was deployed simultaneously and synchronized with the military operation. Although most observers took for granted that the anonymous little green men were Russian soldiers, Russia could still invoke plausible deniability. The appearance of unidentified but well-behaved soldiers raised the possibility that they were locals. The soldier wears the then-new Russian multifunctional battle dress *Ratnik* ('combatant'), a system which incorporates military/tactical 6B43 model ceramic hard armour plates (to chest and back) and tactical armour plate carriers (tactical vests). The 6B43 model plates reportedly consist of a titanium/boron carbide ceramic composite. (Artwork by Renato Dalmaso)

Free Syrian Army soldier, Syria, 2014
The Free Syrian Army (FSA) was established in Turkey in 2011. Although the result of a popular uprising against the Syrian government, the FSA soon became the proxy of several foreign states, in particular Turkey, Saudi Arabia, and Qatar, which desired a united Syrian national insurgency under their control. The FSA was also favoured by Western governments. American and British contractors were tasked to develop infrastructure for the production of propaganda to stimulate support in the West as well as in Syria for the insurgents, among which were groups such as the FSA. The contractors developed a network of opposition media activists inside Syria, flooded Syria with opposition propaganda, and yet more importantly, made sure that numerous articles and videos that sowed hatred toward the Assad government were planted in Western and Arab mass media, which then went on to amplify these materials. While many FSA units fought in the insurgency, the organization never became independent of its foreign sponsors and accordingly primarily played the role of proxy in a hybrid threats operation. This soldier is dressed in mixed civilian and military dress. FSA units carried a variety of weapons, depending on what they could scrounge on the battlefield or received from their sponsors. This man carries an AK-47 assault rifle, the street price of which was $25. (Artwork by Renato Dalmaso)

Afghan Taliban soldier, Afghanistan, 2021
The Afghan Taliban movement, after it had been forced out of Afghanistan, soon learnt the value of hybrid threats operations. Despite, or perhaps because, the movement was a dispossessed non-state actor, it quickly managed to deploy a full spectrum of powers and soon mastered the application of such methods. The Taliban movement developed significantly as a military force, too. This soldier carries a US-made M4 carbine, many of which unsurprisingly fell into Taliban hands when the United States pulled out of Afghanistan. Of greater interest is the professional level of his other equipment. By 2021, the Taliban were no longer the paramilitary, barely trained civilians they once had been. (Artwork by Renato Dalmaso)

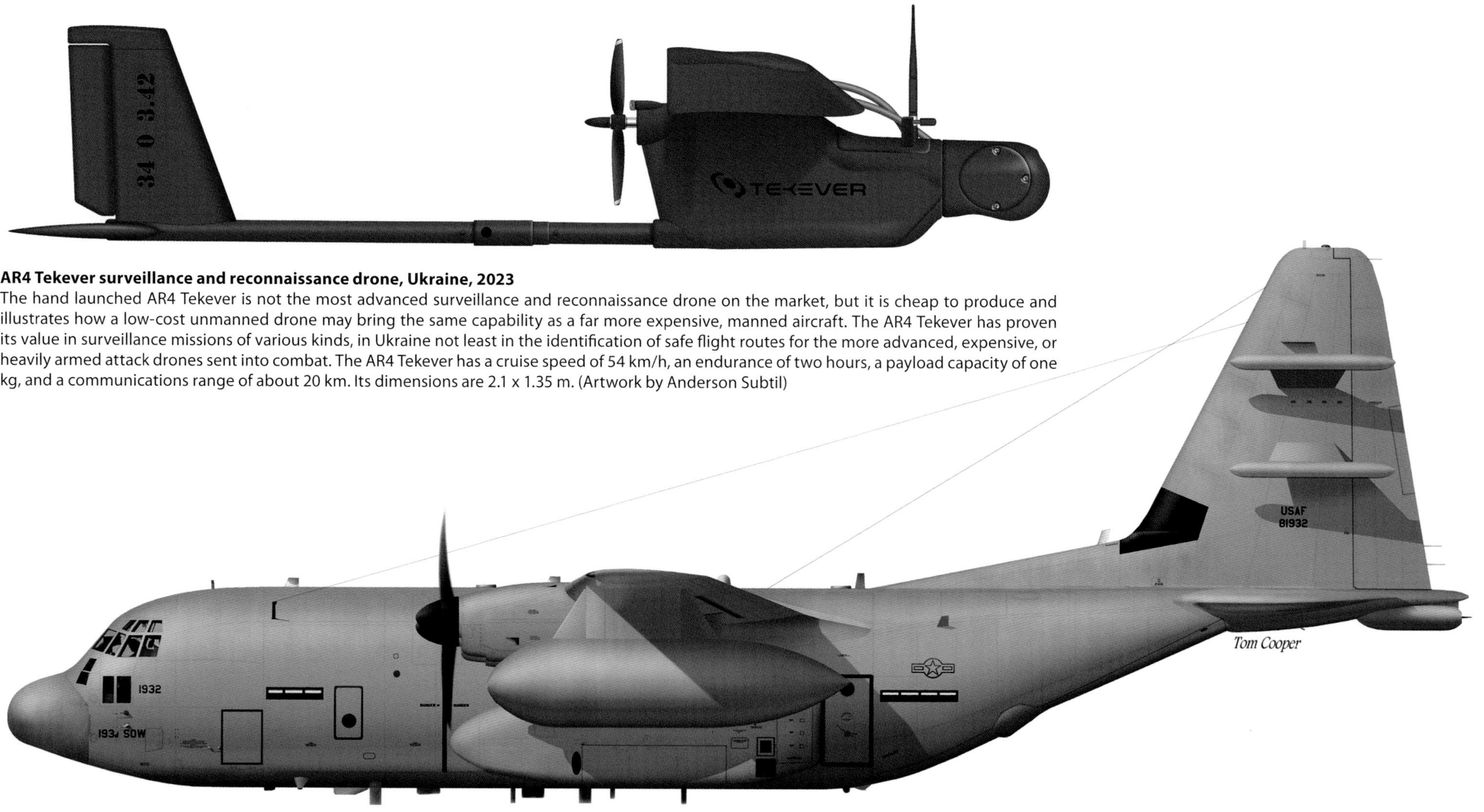

AR4 Tekever surveillance and reconnaissance drone, Ukraine, 2023
The hand launched AR4 Tekever is not the most advanced surveillance and reconnaissance drone on the market, but it is cheap to produce and illustrates how a low-cost unmanned drone may bring the same capability as a far more expensive, manned aircraft. The AR4 Tekever has proven its value in surveillance missions of various kinds, in Ukraine not least in the identification of safe flight routes for the more advanced, expensive, or heavily armed attack drones sent into combat. The AR4 Tekever has a cruise speed of 54 km/h, an endurance of two hours, a payload capacity of one kg, and a communications range of about 20 km. Its dimensions are 2.1 x 1.35 m. (Artwork by Anderson Subtil)

United States EC-130J Commando Solo PSYOP aircraft, Libya, 2011
The NATO intervention in Libya in 2011 included a significant information element, so carried some aspects of a hybrid threats operation. A key asset was the EC-130J Commando Solo, a modified C-130J Super Hercules, which was used for psychological operations (PSYOP) and airborne Information Operations missions via digital and analog radio and television broadcasts, either pre-recorded or live, in all the standard AM, FM, HF, TV, and military communications bands. The aircraft broadcast messages in Arabic, French, and English aimed at both military and civilian personnel. Messages were either generally pro-intervention or specifically invited Libyan military personnel to leave their positions and return to their families. Libyan ship crews were told that if they attempted to leave port, they would immediately be attacked and destroyed. The Commando Solo was operated by 193rd Special Operations Wing (193 SOW), a unit of the Pennsylvania Air National Guard operationally allocated to the Air Force Special Operations Command (AFSOC) and in Operation Odyssey Dawn operating out of Naval Air Station Sigonella, Italy. The aircraft was equipped with vertical trailing wire antenna under the fin, IR-countermeasures on either side of the rear fuselage, an underwing pylon (23x6ft) for equipment, and X-antennae on either side of the fin. The antennae under the fuselage had been upgraded as compared to previous versions of the aircraft. In politically sensitive or hostile territories, the Commando Solo often flew missions at night to reduce the risk of detection. (Artwork by Tom Cooper)

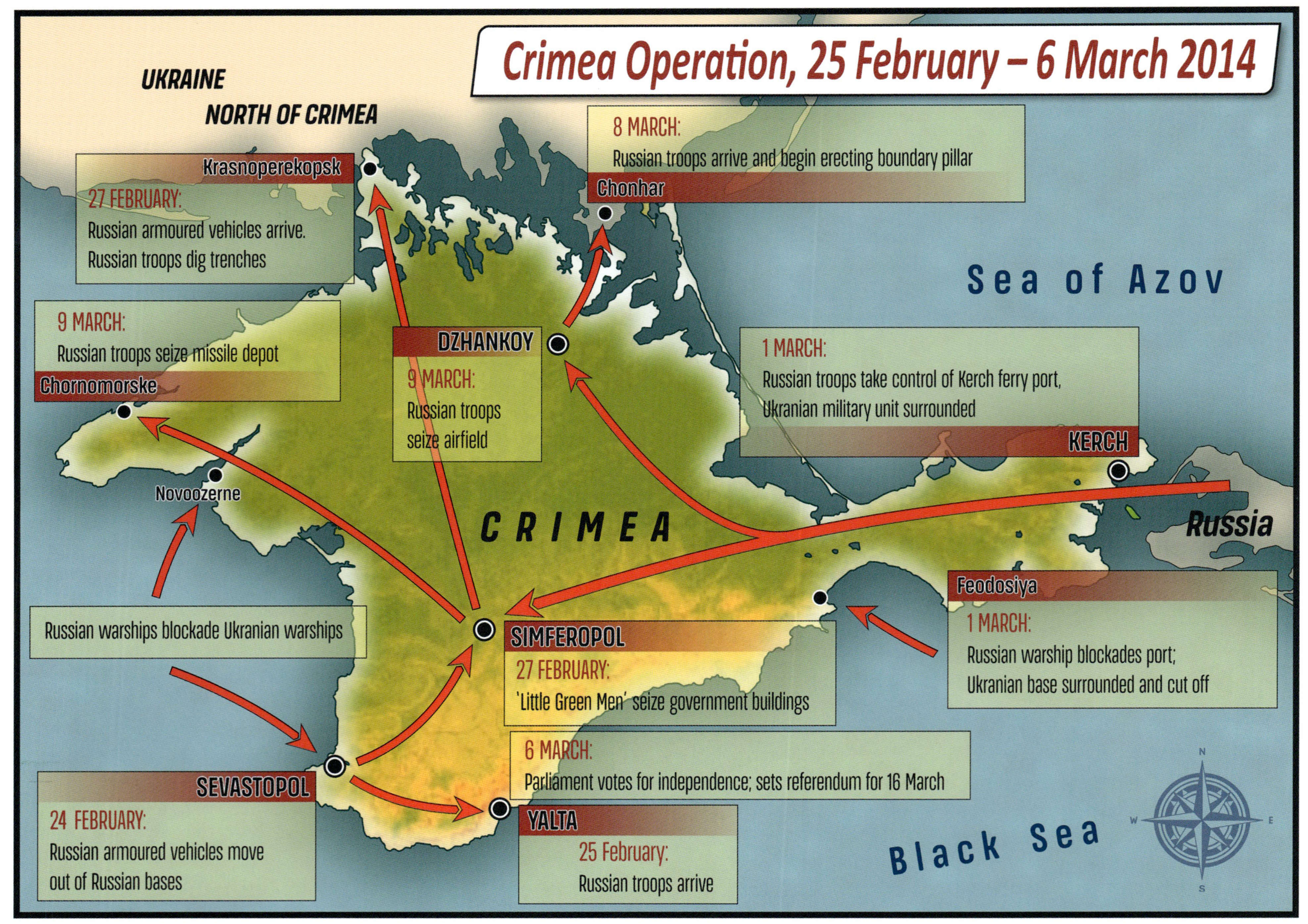

Russia's Crimea operation, 2014. (Map by Anderson Subtil)

affairs activities have helped enable Nord Stream maintain open dialogue with regulatory decision-makers and enhance information flow at an international level.'[49] In other words, Hill and Knowlton assisted Nord Stream AG with the EIA application process. The Hill and Knowlton agency was quite successful, and indeed won several awards in 2009 for its public relations activities on behalf of Nord Stream AG.[50]

The first line of the pipeline was eventually constructed according to plan, as adjusted for the delays in the EIA process, with work beginning in 2010 and the pipeline coming on line in November 2011. Several heads of government from EU member states attended the opening ceremony. The second line came on line in October 2012, with less pageantry and official representation.[51] Russia had succeeded in building a natural gas export pipeline with direct access to Germany, thus bypassing those transit states with which Russia had frequently encountered political problems. However, it had been a costly venture. The Nord Stream consortium claimed that Sweden's obstruction alone cost more than EUR 100 million in expenses related to the EIA process and associated lobbying activities, not counting almost two years of added time spent on the EIA process.[52] Both sides had carried out hybrid threats campaigns, and both had achieved some of their goals.[53]

In June 2015, Gazprom and several European energy companies agreed to initiate the Nord Stream 2 project, which aimed to add two new pipelines alongside the existing two Nord Stream pipelines, henceforth known as Nord Stream 1, and thereby to double the project's capacity for Russian natural gas supplies to Germany. The project was completed in September 2021, despite a wave of U.S. sanctions against it.

However, already in February 2022 Germany halted the project, as a means to respond to Russia's formal recognition of the Donetsk and Lugansk People's Republics in eastern Ukraine. On 26 September 2022, a series of underwater explosions and consequent gas leaks occurred on three of the four pipelines, which thereby were rendered inoperable.

Following a thorough investigation, the German authorities in June 2024 issued a European arrest warrant for a Ukrainian national living near Warsaw suspected of having used the yacht *Andromeda* together with two others to sabotage the Nord Stream pipeline in an operation under the control of the Ukrainian government.

Comparable Cases

Major pipeline projects seem particularly vulnerable to hybrid threats activities, since when a pipeline has been built, it cannot be moved. To invest in a pipeline leading to a single end customer makes the supplier vulnerable to demands from the customer to re-negotiate the price of energy or cancel imports, after the investments have already been made and the project is committed. Besides, geopolitical factors tend to complicate issues, while anybody can raise environmental concerns to oppose a planned project. The negotiations concerning the Turkmenistan-Afghanistan-Pakistan-India (TAPI) pipeline project shares many characteristics with those of the Nord Stream project. However, the original purpose of the TAPI project, first advertised by Argentina's Bridas Corporation in 1993–1994 but subsequently taken over by the U.S. firm Unocal, was to enable Turkmenistan to export natural gas through a new pipeline that would bypass Russia, which by then functioned as a transit country for Central Asian gas exports. In similarity to the

Pipes for North Stream 2 at Mukran Port in Sassnitz, Germany, September 2020. (Photo: Pedant01)

Nord Stream project, the TAPI project was characterized by frequent problems on the issue of investment costs and the pricing of gas exports. There was also the issue of how to deal with the Afghan Taliban which then controlled major parts of the transit territory.[54]

But real economic power is also deployed in the form of the interruption of supply of raw materials as a means to raise prices or force compliance with other demands. On 7 September 2010, a Chinese trawler, the *Minjinyu 5179*, collided with the Japanese Coast Guard vessels *Yonakuni* and *Mizuki* in the East China Sea. The Coast Guard arrested the trawler captain, Zhan Qixiong. Among the Chinese government's responses to the incident was a threat to interrupt the export of REEs to Japan. At that time Japan was dependent on China for nearly 90 per cent of imports of such materials. The threat accordingly shook the Japanese industry, especially the automobile sector for which REEs for the production of magnets were indispensable.[55] While the threat was serious, there is no evidence that a Chinese embargo, formal or informal, ever was introduced.[56] Nonetheless, the sales price of REEs soared, and journalists still regularly report the case as a case study of Chinese hybrid threats power. China applied other pressures as well. The crisis was eventually resolved by the release of the trawler captain.

Less noted is how Japan responded to the risk that supplies might be interrupted. The threat prompted the Japanese government rapidly to put together a package of comprehensive measures to diversify supplies and reinforce its supply chain against such interference. These included a supplemental budget of JPY 100 billion to develop technologies and support investment in equipment to reduce the overall use of REEs, develop technologies to use alternative materials, promote recycling of REEs through investment in recycling facilities and the development of more efficient recycling technologies, invest in REE mines in Australia and elsewhere, and the immediate stockpiling of REEs. As a result, Japanese dependence on Chinese rare earths dropped from 90 per cent to 60 percent, and the Japanese consumption of REEs fell to 50 per cent of what it had been.[57] The weapon that China thought it had was no more.

There should be a lesson learned in this. The sanctions policy that seemingly provides the foundation stone of current Western policy against rival powers is based on the same principle as the one China thought it might benefit from in 2010. Apart from rhetoric and feel-good politics (statements that make the political actor and his or her audience feel good about themselves as opposed to having a real impact), does it make sense to use sanctions as a means of political leverage against other countries? The 2010 case was only one of many which may throw some light upon the various issues of sanctions and dependence on others—and on how fear of dependence and indeed exaggerated views of dependence may influence policy in a detrimental way.

The introduction of sanctions is a double-edged sword since history shows that sanctions and embargoes, if serious enough, may engender unexpected responses. In August 1941, the United States embargoed its oil exports to Japan, which was 76.7 percent dependent on American oil.[58] The purpose was to coerce Japan into abandoning its war in China. The embargo caused the fall of the Japanese government and thereby became a decisive reason why Japan suddenly attacked the United States later in the same year.

In 1973, OPEC embargoed its oil exports to the Western countries to force them to abandon their support for Israel. The oil crisis hit hard but the effect became the opposite; methods were introduced to increase energy efficiency, so OPEC lost the leverage it thought it had. Western support to Israel increased.[59] Again political leverage was illusionary and quickly lost. Besides, it would seem that no serious raw materials exporter knowing of this case and the one in 2010 would willingly want to create a situation that ultimately causes its exports to decrease (although elected governments may choose to ignore the long-term national loss in exchange for fleeting short-term political gains). The dependence between exporter and importer is mutual.

Financial Power

In similarity to real economic power, financial power is mostly deployed by states. However, again some multinational firms and conglomerates have similar resources at their disposal as small states, so non-state actors are active within this domain, too. Financial power projection displays itself in a variety of activities, some of which overlap with real economic power projection. Most common seems to be the imposition of trade barriers, financial sanctions (in particular punitive tariffs and embargoes, which often are employed in conjunction with diplomatic sanctions), Foreign Direct Investment (FDI) including the strategic application of sovereign wealth funds to gain specific objectives, and the manipulation of exchange rates for reasons of speculation or for inducing targeted indebtedness in states regarded as adversarial. However, financial power projection can also be applied as a means to take advantage of manipulated stock market fluctuations. If so, the manipulation was typically carried out by other, non-financial means, which makes the activity a hybrid threat. However, FinTech (short for financial technology, which means the application of innovative technologies to products and services in the financial industry) and similar new technologies signify fresh vulnerabilities in this field.

Case Study: SWIFT, Unwilling Belgian Society for the Imposition of Sanctions, 2018

In 2018, the Trump administration of the United States imposed unilateral sanctions on Iran in an ongoing campaign that included the U.S. withdrawal from the Iran nuclear deal negotiated in 2012. The campaign, which was overt, included hybrid threats in primarily the domains of financial, diplomatic, and media power. Most were aimed at Iran, but some were aimed at entities and states which opposed the change in U.S. policy.

In 2012, both the United States and the EU had imposed sanctions on Iran in order to compel negotiations. However, in 2018 the EU had no intention of following the American lead. Realizing that U.S. sanctions alone would not carry the intended weight, the Trump administration decided to employ a non-state actor, the Belgium-based Society for Worldwide Interbank Financial Telecommunications (SWIFT) financial messaging service, as its proxy for additional impact. Specifically, the United States wanted SWIFT to suspend access to its service for Iranian banks and financial institutions. Since virtually all international financial transactions go through the SWIFT system, the suspension of access would mean that Iran no longer would be able to pay for imports and could not receive payment for oil exports. The suspension of access to SWIFT may be the most devastating application of financial power available to any current government.

SWIFT was a cooperative company under Belgian law, owned and controlled by its shareholders, which consisted of financial institutions from across the world. The shareholders elect a Board of independent Directors, representing banks across the world. Overseen by the G-10 central banks (Belgium, Canada, France, Germany, Italy, Japan, Switzerland, Sweden, The Netherlands, United Kingdom, and United States), as well as the European Central Bank, the lead overseer of SWIFT was the National Bank of Belgium.

In 2012, following an EU Council decision, SWIFT had discontinued its communications services to Iranian financial institutions as a result of European sanctions (specifically, EU Regulation 267/2012).[60] As a result, Iran's oil exports plunged and the sanctions imposed through the discontinuation of SWIFT services were widely seen as instrumental in bringing Iran to the negotiating table which led to the 2015 Iran nuclear deal. However, in 2018 no European sanctions had been imposed on Iran, since the EU disagreed with the U.S. policy.

To compel SWIFT into adhering to the U.S. sanctions despite the lack of EU support, the Trump administration noted that it would specifically include those who provided 'specialized financial messaging services to the Central Bank of Iran and Iranian financial institutions' among those against whom U.S. sanctions would be enforced.[61] The Trump administration had no intention to close down all SWIFT operations, however, since U.S. banks, too, depended on its services. Instead, the Trump administration noted that the relevant U.S. legislation (Section 220 of the Iran Threat Reduction and Syria Human Rights Act) allowed the Treasury Department, at its choosing, to impose financial sanctions on the banks represented on the SWIFT board or on individual SWIFT officials, rather than targeting the cooperative itself. Thus, SWIFT operations would not be interrupted by the sanctions, even though its shareholders and officials might be wiped out financially.[62]

On 5 November 2018, SWIFT announced that it would comply with the restored U.S. sanctions on Iran, despite the EU's efforts to defy the U.S. action with new EU rules that forbid companies from complying with the U.S. Iran sanctions.[63] SWIFT subsequently explained its action as follows:

> In exceptional circumstances, and where the interest of the stability and integrity of the wider global financial system are at risk, SWIFT may also need to restrict customers' access to the network. In an isolated event in November 2018 SWIFT thus suspended certain Iranian banks' access to the messaging system. This step, while regrettable, was taken in the interest of the stability and integrity of the wider global financial system, and based on an assessment of the economic situation.[64]

The SWIFT board had to choose between two legal threats, and it determined that the risk of U.S. sanctions against the personal estates of the board members, or the banks they represented, was the greater danger. (This threat was, of course, an application of judicial state power; it was only the subsequent use of SWIFT against Iran which was an example of non-state actor financial power deployment.)

The SWIFT case is significant, because SWIFT was an unwilling non-state actor proxy. The company did not share the U.S. strategic goals and received nothing in return for compliance. Yet, the threat of personal sanctions against the individuals who headed SWIFT compelled the introduction of institutional sanctions. Moreover, demands for the use of SWIFT as a means to impose sanctions occur regularly among a variety of actors, including those within the European Parliament.[65]

Besides, the case again shows how sanctions, not hard power and certainly not other types of soft power, have become the central element of Western countries' security policy and deterrence toolkit.

Comparable Cases

The SWIFT case was an overt application of the hybrid threats potential of financial power, which explains why the case is fully documented. Rumours about the covert application of financial power as hybrid threats appear from time to time, but they tend to be impossible to verify through open sources. One of these cases was the 23 April 2013 hack of the Twitter account of the U.S. news agency Associated Press (AP), for which the Syrian Electronic Army (SEA), a group of hackers who operated in support of the Syrian government, claimed responsibility. Three years later, the FBI charged three members of the SEA for this and other hacks. Having gained control of the AP Twitter account, the hackers asserted that President Barack Obama had been wounded in an explosion at the White House. Reportedly more than 1.9 million people followed the AP reports on Twitter. As a result, the amount of USD 136.5 billion was erased from the US S&P 500 stock index value and the Dow Jones Industrial Average index dropped 0.98 percent within seconds. Although the market quickly recovered, the SEA hack showed the vulnerability of the financial sector.[66] If such a group of hackers indeed aimed to cause a negative impact on the financial markets on behalf of a state actor, and if the state actor was in position to take advantage of the market impact, neither of which seems to have been the case at this particular time, then it would have been a covert application of financial power as a hybrid threat, since the operation would affect the financial, media, and cyber domains. Mere cyberattacks against the capability of individual banks to employ SWIFT services might produce a short-term effect but would not reach the strategic threshold for a hybrid threat.

Symbol of Syrian Electronic Army. (Image: SEA)

Diplomatic Power

Diplomatic power is typically deployed by states, and organizations that with more or less justification claim to be states, such as the Afghan Taliban movement. They customarily involve threats, sanctions, and the crafting and introduction of resolutions by international organizations over which the state has some lever of influence or in which it is able to find support from like-minded states. Intimidation, often by statements referring to military means including the use of nuclear weapons, is a form of diplomatic power. The purpose is often to isolate the target state from the international community in order to reduce its freedom of manoeuvre which translates into the reduction of its potential as a threat. A dominant state might be able to utilize an international organization as a proxy, in which case the international organization functions as a non-state actor in relation to the state actor and the activity, if carried out in conjunction with the application of other powers, may qualify as a hybrid threats campaign. However, international organizations may have agendas of their own and employ hybrid threats means of their own making. The same goes for some other types of non-state actors, notably insurgent organizations and governments-in-exile, which frequently employ their diplomatic power, such as it may be, in hybrid threats activities.

Case Study: Afghan Taliban, Pashtun Proxy with Own Agenda, 1994–2020

When Pakistan in 1994 provided the necessary support and logistics to set up the Afghan Taliban movement, a predominantly Pashtun group, it had multiple reasons for doing so.[67] The idea to use the nascent Taliban movement as a proxy for diplomatic power was presumably not the primary motive. However, it was part of the plan. Afghanistan's seat in the United Nations was then held by a party which, although previously a Pakistani proxy, no longer complied with Pakistani demands. Hence, if Pakistan could make the Afghan Taliban movement recognized as the new government of Afghanistan, it might find the latter a friendly proxy for Pakistani interests. For this reason, efforts were made to persuade important states to grant the Afghan Taliban diplomatic recognition. By 1996, the United States had initiated diplomatic links with the Taliban government, and the issue of the United Nations seat came up in the discussions.[68] Meanwhile, Pakistan found allies to recognize the Taliban government as Afghanistan's legitimate government. In May 1997, Pakistan, Saudi Arabia, and the United Arab Emirates, in this order, recognized the Taliban Emirate of Afghanistan.[69] However, other events ultimately blocked the development, and the Afghan Taliban, once established, proved little more cooperative than Pakistan's previous proxies in Afghanistan. The use of the Afghan Taliban as a non-state actor proxy in diplomatic power had failed (if it had succeeded, the non-state actor would then of course have been transformed into a state actor).

Besides, after the 2001 invasion of Afghanistan the Taliban developed their own hybrid threats capacity, including in diplomatic power projection. It focused on two distinct targets: the International Security Assistance Force (ISAF) member states and the worldwide Muslim community.[70] Against the ISAF member states, a major aim was to negotiate the withdrawal of the international coalition, with threats if necessary, so that the Taliban could return to power. For this task, the Taliban relied on diplomatic power, with negotiations conducted through friendly Muslim countries such as Pakistan, Saudi Arabia, the United Arab Emirates, and Qatar. These countries were not chosen by random; as we have seen, it was only Pakistan, Saudi Arabia, and the United Arab Emirates which had recognized the Taliban Emirate of Afghanistan. The diplomatic process against ISAF member states can be said to have begun in 2009 in Dubai, United Arab Emirates. At the request of the Taliban, German intelligence then held the first of a series of meetings with Taliban delegations. Through these meetings, the Taliban aimed to persuade the United States to lift sanctions, release high-level Taliban prisoners, and allow the opening of a Taliban representative office in a Muslim country.[71] These meetings all took place in secret, and at the time there was little chance for the Taliban to gain a negotiated American withdrawal. However, the Taliban diplomatic campaign eventually paid off in the form of a more public, international diplomatic presence, aimed less at the West than the worldwide Muslim community, against whom the Taliban leadership wished to appear as a responsible and religiously legitimate party.

In 2018, Taliban representatives took part in an international meeting in Moscow with Russia, China, Pakistan, Iran, India, the five Central Asian republics, and the United States, which formally attended with observer status. The Afghan government was not formally represented, but the Minister of the Interior, Wais Ahmad Barmak, was in Moscow during the negotiations, and he regarded the meeting favourably. The Taliban included Sher Mohammad Abbas Stanikzai, head of the Taliban's political council in Qatar, who in his then role as Taliban acting foreign minister already in 1996 had visited Washington, D.C., to ask the Clinton administration to extend diplomatic recognition to the Taliban.[72] Then, in early 2020, the Taliban announced that a peace agreement had been reached with the United States.[73] On 29 February, as planned, the United States and the Taliban signed the agreement at a meeting in Qatar. The Taliban referred to the agreement as 'Termination of Occupation Agreement' and a 'collective victory of the entire Muslim and Mujahid nation', while the Trump administration called it an 'agreement for bringing peace' to Afghanistan.[74] Since the Afghan Taliban deployed their diplomatic power in conjunction with several types of hard power, notably privatized and terrorist power, the Taliban activities qualified as a hybrid threats campaign.[75]

Comparable Cases

Whenever a non-state actor has the ambition to remake itself into a state, it will sooner or later have to create a capacity in diplomatic power. As long as the non-state actor in question enjoys state support, it may well be treated as a diplomatic proxy. For this reason, the development of the Afghan Taliban movement is far from unique. Most successful insurgent movements throughout history at one time or another went through a parallel development.

Civil Power

Civil power can be described as the soft-power version of people's power. It is customarily deployed by NGOs, charities, law firms and PR agencies which operate on behalf of interested parties, and some international organizations. Civil power is commonly deployed as protests, demonstrations, consumer boycotts, fundraisers, and the like.

As with people's power actors, civil power representatives may function as proxies in hybrid threat operations for hostile powers, or for foreign organizations. Global links and events influence population segments in many countries, especially in diaspora groups, so it is often difficult to distinguish between genuine popular discontent and hostile activities directed from abroad. Not every hostile action is a hybrid threats operation.

Case Study: International University Exchange Fund, Well-endowed Nordic Proxy, 1969–1980

The International University Exchange Fund (IUEF) was established in 1961 to fund students from southern Africa, primarily South Africa, who had fled to Europe because of racial discrimination. Following an internal scandal over funding which ultimately derived from CIA, the organization was in 1969 moved to Switzerland and reorganized under a board of NGO representatives from the Nordic countries, primarily Sweden and Norway. Sweden was the major source of the IUEF's budget, and the bulk of this contribution derived from Swedish government funds. Swedish NGOs provided some additional funds, which were raised during humanitarian fundraising campaigns. It was no coincidence that Sweden funded most IUEF activities, and also supplied the organization's chair; by then, the Swedish government had embarked upon a policy to provide secret funding to the African National Congress (ANC) in order to topple the South African government as part of the struggle against the Apartheid regime. Sweden gave full support to the clandestine segments of the ANC, including the provision of safe houses within South Africa, facilitation for clandestine border crossings, and the use of Swiss bank accounts for the transmission of

American diplomat Zalmay Khalilzad (left) and Taliban diplomat Abdul Ghani Baradar (right) signing the peace agreement in Doha, Qatar, 29 February 2020. (Photo: U.S. Department of State)

covert funds. It was a covert hybrid threats campaign which involved people's power, financial power, diplomatic power, civil power, and media power. The campaign was led by the Swedish Humanitarian Working Committee (better known under its Swedish abbreviation, *Humanberedningen*), a group of Swedish civil society notables who, as government employees, coordinated government-sponsored clandestine activities outside regular channels, apparently reported to the Swedish Minister of Foreign Affairs, and whose activities were highly classified. Because of the gravity of the clandestine activities (the ANC had carried out several bombings of civilian targets, and a former Swedish Prime Minister later admitted that Swedish funds may have supported these activities), plausible deniability was required. For this reason, the IUEF was chosen as one of several suitable non-state actors through which to carry out activities. The use of the IUEF was at first successful. However, in 1977 South African intelligence infiltrated the IUEF, embezzled a major share of its operating budget, and essentially crippled the organization.[76]

Comparable Cases

Although the use of civil society for hybrid threats activities has a long history (in early times, religious movements were frequently utilized in this role), the method became increasingly widespread during the Cold War. Perhaps the best comparable case is that of how Soviet intelligence during the Cold War infiltrated and gained control over parts of the extensive anti-war and anti-nuclear protest movement in North America and Western Europe, thus turning them into hybrid threats actors against the Western alliance and its ongoing reliance on nuclear weapons for deterrence. Although the degree of impact was different in each country, the Soviet influence in Cold-War Sweden has been recognized by both security service officials and scholars.[77]

Scientific & Technological Power

Scientific and technological power, that is, the result of research into new technologies, can be utilized, in part or in whole, to further a political or economic agenda. This type of power is frequently deployed by state actors, but non-state actors in the form of certain multinational firms and conglomerates have the capacity, too. The new technologies can be used either as enablers or influencers. When used as enablers, they can, for instance, be used as means for intelligence collection, which is illustrated by the case study presented below. However, new technologies can also be used as influencers. A hypothetical case of the latter type would be the influence exerted by major pharmaceuticals manufacturers on the public health service. This has the potential to go beyond the influence exerted in traditional commercial marketing campaigns. Under the conditions of a medical emergency, such as an epidemic or pandemic, it would be possible to employ deliveries of medicines as levers of influence in small states, since they tend to be dependent on the pharmaceuticals manufacturers of other states. Assuming the intention is there, either the manufacturers themselves, or the states under which jurisdiction they operate, could use the supply, or denial, of medical products to induce a state of panic in a population which has an urgent need for them. Such panic might under certain circumstances provide fertile ground for social destabilization which easily could be translated into acquiescence in the face of political or economic demands. If so, scientific and technological power would be applied in conjunction with other powers, thus producing a hybrid threats operation.

Anti-nuclear weapons protest march in Oxford, 1980. The protestors, seen here marching past Oxford's Town Hall, objected to the proposed stationing of cruise missiles at the U.S. Air Force base at Upper Heyford. (Photo: Kim Traynor)

Case Study: MINERVA, Swiss Manufacturer of Backdoors, 1970–1995

In 2020, the Swiss government issued a report which described how U.S. and German intelligence had utilized a commercial Swiss manufacturing company as a means for intelligence collection. From some point in the 1950s until at least 1995 the intelligence services had used the Swiss company, then known by its cover name MINERVA, in a secret operation to provide the governments of certain countries with encryption machines with built-in backdoors and weaknesses, so that the two intelligence services could intercept and read their encrypted communications. After some years, the two intelligence services had acquired joint ownership of the company so as to ensure smooth operations. Swiss intelligence, too, had been party to the cooperation.[78]

While the utilization of a non-state actor such as MINERVA certainly included the application of scientific and technological power, and presumably was significant for intelligence collection, there is no information to suggest that the operation formed part of a hybrid threats campaign. To the contrary, it can be assumed that the intelligence services involved treated the results of their utilization of MINERVA as top secret, simply to protect the operation so that it might continue over time. Moreover, for states the carrying-out of intelligence collection aimed at other states is generally regarded as a legitimate (although not necessarily legal) activity, which customarily is not regarded as a breach of international protocol. Having said this, the information exposed by the operation could have been employed for other purposes in a hybrid threats campaign, had the intelligence services been so inclined.

Comparable Cases

In February 2020, U.S. officials announced that China had the capacity covertly to access Huawei Technologies Co.'s mobile networks through backdoors.[79] This would put Huawei in a similar position to that of MINERVA, but on a larger yet less exclusive scale. Most people rely on mobile networks, while only certain security-conscious state institutions purchased the technology provided by MINERVA. Perhaps the temptation to use manufacturers of encryption technology as vehicles for intelligence collection is too high to be disregarded.

Yet, there are less well-known but more comprehensive methods of intercepting – and manipulating – telephone and data traffic. Presently, underwater cables carry almost all intercontinental data traffic. Automated protocols based on software-defined networking (SDN) control how data travels through the underwater cables. SDN is an approach to network management that aims to improve network performance and monitoring in a manner more similar to cloud computing than to traditional network management. The protocols determine the pathways the data takes, which in turn affects transmission speed and costs, but also exposure to interception. SDN allows data traffic to be managed and optimized

Huawei expo at IFA 2018 in Berlin. Huawei has firmly denied allegations that the corporation would install backdoors on behalf of the Chinese government. (Photo: Matti Blume)

in real time in order to improve efficiency further. However, this also enables the firms that develop and control the SDN protocols to manipulate data flows. Data traffic from Europe to Africa can, for instance, be surreptitiously rerouted through landing stations at Shanghai or Guangzhou, which would expose the entire data stream to interception in China.

Chinese tech companies like HMN Tech (formerly Huawei Marine Networks), ZTE, and China Unicom are currently market and innovation leaders in SDN development. There is no suggestion that either of these companies aims to manipulate SDN protocols in the manner described here. Yet, present technology allows any company which develops and controls the SDN protocols, regardless of nationality, to manipulate them, if the company for whatever reason finds this action desirable. Hypothetically, this power would enable a state actor not only to intercept and manipulate data but also to degrade or even sever internet connectivity for rival nations. This would isolate the target country from global markets and disrupt its financial transactions and foreign trade, including supply chains.[80]

Moreover, even the minuscule delays that can be induced by rerouting data for financial trading have the potential to induce major losses in automated stock market trading systems. Automated or algorithmic trading enable traders to establish specific rules for both trade entries and exits that, once programmed, can be automatically executed via a computer. This is significant, since an estimated 70 to 80 per cent of shares traded on U.S., European, and major Asian stock exchanges presently derive from automated trading systems.

In short, scientific and technological power should not be underestimated in scenarios for the disruption of trade and financial systems and, because of the mostly unforeseeable consequences, destabilization of a country so targeted.

Media Power

Media power is deployed by almost all actors engaged in hybrid threats activities, including both state actors and non-state actors. The deployment of media power is probably the most pervasive means of influence. Its impact has been unparalleled since the fifteenth-century introduction of the movable-type printing press which enabled the mass production of printed leaflets and newsletters. The use of such media for purposes of propaganda and disinformation began almost at once, and even though the media currently employed is different, the nature of media power remains unchanged. Media power is deployed to direct and influence public opinion, whether in the cyber domain, in social media networks, or by means of traditional mass-media coverage. Non-state actors involved in media power projection commonly include NGOs, media firms, and PR agencies, but also other non-state actors such as insurgent and terrorist groups as well as commercial entities.

Beyond the lofty ideal of enabling the free exchange of ideas in liberal democracies, media power is customarily employed to attain two linked but quite different objectives: (1) as a means to exert influence on states and societies through information, disinformation, propaganda, and manipulation of information, based on the principle that what is perceived becomes the truth; and (2) as a means to interrupt an adversary's main channels of communicating with the public and the denial of access, for the adversary, to alternative sources for media dissemination. Denial of access may consist of denial of service by physical means or the successful mobilization of available media sources. Either method translates into supremacy within the information domain. If the media power deployment takes place in conjunction with other means, the activities qualify as a hybrid threats campaign.

After the Cold War, it became increasingly common for states to hire PR agencies as means to manage and win conflicts. The global public relations agency Hill and Knowlton, which we last met facilitating the Nord Stream pipeline, already in 1990 was hired by a proxy NGO established by the Kuwaiti government to pave the ground for a U.S. war against Iraq in retaliation for the Iraqi invasion of Kuwait. The firm's most spectacular triumph was the false testimony to the U.S. Congress given by Nayirah al-Sabah, the daughter of Kuwaiti ambassador Saud Nasser al-Saud al-Sabah. The 15-year-old girl, who hid her real identity, falsely claimed that she had been a volunteer nurse in Kuwait, where she said that she had witnessed Iraqi soldiers removing babies out of hospital incubators to steal them, leaving the babies to die on the floor. Young Nayirah performed brilliantly, choking with tears at the opportune moment, her voice breaking as she seemingly struggled to relate her tale. Her claims were widely publicized and cited numerous times in the U.S. Senate and by U.S. President George H. W. Bush as reasons for pursuing military action against Iraq. Her portrayal of Iraqi war crimes was a major reason for the U.S. decision to go to war against Iraq, and for other countries to join the U.S.-led coalition.

But the false testimony to the U.S. Congress was not the end of the media campaign. A few weeks later, Hill and Knowlton produced what the firm claimed to be eyewitnesses to give testimony to the United Nations about Iraqi atrocities. It was later found that the seven witnesses used false names and, in at least one case, a false identity. Moreover, the United States presented a video expertly produced by Hill and Knowlton to the Security Council. As a result, the United Nations authorized use of 'all means necessary' to eject Iraq from Kuwait. Soon afterwards, the U.S. Congress authorized the use of military force.[81]

Other PR agencies soon signed on to demonize other adversaries. The list is too long to mention here, but the work by the agency Ruder Finn to undermine Serbia's standing during the Balkan wars deserves a special mention, since its narrative continued to resonate for years afterwards.

The PR agency successes were facilitated by two trends in journalism that may not be consistent with the ideal of a free press but nonetheless are present in the media industry. First, the press is generally less interested in objective facts than stories about victims and villains. When a PR agency presented such a tale, its publication would assuredly entice readers and viewers. Second, in time of conflict, media representatives tend to rally around the flag and support their government's line.

Almost no international journalists were present in the battle for Aleppo 2012–2016 during the Syrian insurgency. Instead, the international media outsourced reporting to locals representing the insurgents, particularly the jihadis of Jabhat al-Nusra (Al-Nusra Front), at the time the Al-Qaida subsidiary in Syria, who held the eastern parts of the city. The jihadis used graphic images of injured and dying children to win the sympathies of world viewers. The jihadis also used social media to great effect to promote fake and distorted news, with an emphasis on the suffering of civilians. Satisfied with the theme of the stories and images of victimhood, the international media did not question the reports from Aleppo. The coverage of the siege of Aleppo in the international media accordingly amplified the jihadi narrative, which greatly influenced the Western response to the conflict in Syria.[82] And when Western governments bought the stories and made them the foundation-stone for Western policy, their media predictably rallied around the flag, producing yet more stories along the same lines.

With Western policy set, American and British contractors were tasked to develop additional infrastructure for the production of propaganda to stimulate support in the West, as well as support within Syria, for the insurgents. The contractors developed a network of opposition media activists inside Syria, flooded Syria with opposition propaganda including tens of thousands of posters, flyers, newspapers, and booklets, and yet more importantly, made sure that numerous articles and videos that sowed hatred toward the Assad government were planted in Western and Arab mass media, which then went on to amplify these materials. The contractors supported groups such as the Free Syrian Army (FSA) but also Jabhat al-Nusra which they, apparently successfully, worked to re-brand as a political activist organization known first as Jabhat Fatah al-Sham and subsequently as Hay'at Tahrir al-Sham.[83] Meanwhile, the successful mobilization of available media sources meant that the Syrian government effectively was denied access to most international media. With headlines fully focused on the insurgent narrative, there was simply no space left for alternative narratives.

As a result, protests intended to show solidarity with Aleppo's besieged insurgents, as well as demonstrations against the Syrian government and its Iranian and Russian allies, were soon held in many cities across the world. In Paris, the lights on the Eiffel Tower were turned off on 14 December 2016 as a symbol of solidarity, and thousands protested against Russia's role in the destruction of Aleppo. Protests were also held in London, Sarajevo, Istanbul, Jerusalem, Gaza City, and Amman. Some protesters burned photos of Vladimir Putin because of Russia's support to the Syrian government.[84] The application of media power had then gone full circle, beginning with the international media's desire for stories and images of victimhood, the impact of which heavily influenced government policy. The immediate result became the provision of active media support to the insurgents, which caused yet further demonization of the Syrian government and its allies. This, in turn, enabled the media to produce stories of appropriate villains in addition to victims, which naturally enflamed passions, and thereby policy, further. The symmetry was beautiful, while the state of symbiosis between free media and government stands out for its unity of vision and fruitful cooperation.

There were elements of hybrid threats operations in this symbiosis, although it is difficult to say who led whom: the media, Western governments, or the Aleppo insurgents. For more definitive hybrid threats operations involving media power, we will have to look elsewhere. Since the deployment of media power probably is the most pervasive means of influence, and since there are real differences between traditional and social media operations, the subject of media power merits no less than three case studies.

Case Study: Patriot and Blitz, Indian Purveyors of Active Measures, 1980–1982

For a case study of hybrid threats operations in traditional media power, it is best to turn to the Cold War. The Soviet Union attempted to split the unity of the Free World with what it referred to as 'active measures'. The primary target was the concord between the United States and Western Europe but active measures were also used to split national unity within these countries. Active measures encompassed various means including clandestine support to local communist parties and activist organizations such as those within the peace movement.[85] The goal of active measures was regarded as distinct from both espionage and counterintelligence, on the one hand, and from traditional diplomatic and informational activities, on the other. Relying on deception, the goal of active measures was to influence the opinions and/or actions of individuals, governments, and/or the public.[86] The Soviet foreign intelligence service, the KGB, in an internal dictionary defined active measures as 'Agent-operational measures aimed at exerting useful influence on aspects of the political life of a target country which are of interest, its foreign policy, the solution of international problems, misleading the adversary, undermining and weakening his positions, the disruption of his hostile plans, and the achievement of other aims'. With particular regard to the KGB, active measures were explained as:

> Agent-operational measures directed at exerting influence on the foreign policy and the internal political situation of target countries in the interests of the Soviet Union and of other countries of the socialist community, the World Communist and National Liberation Movement, weakening the political, military economic and ideological positions of capitalism, undermining its aggressive plans, in order to create conditions favourable to the successful implementation of the Soviet Union's foreign policy, and ensuring peace and social progress.[87]

In February 1980, KGB Chairman Yuriy Andropov approved a KGB action plan for active measures abroad which focused on Pakistan. The plan's objective was to shape foreign policy and public opinion with regard to the Soviet intervention in Afghanistan which had taken place in December 1979. It entailed the planting of information through a wide variety of means and in a wide variety of sources, including in the local press in Pakistan and other target countries, publications issued by real and fictitious civil organizations (among them cultural association, student organizations, religious groups, and diaspora-based organizations), and statements from public and political personalities and leaders of the main opposition parties in the target countries (who might not necessarily be Soviet proxies but had personal reasons to ask provoking questions to their political rivals, if provided with relevant materials). One part of the plan involved two Indian publications: the daily newspaper *Patriot* and the weekly *Blitz*. The KGB managed to plant partially false information in both publications. Then, the Soviet press agency TASS picked up the stories and distributed them throughout the world, thus amplifying the effect.[88] In particular *Blitz* was a well-known propaganda outlet for the KGB and had been used for this purpose for decades.[89] So was *Patriot*, which the KGB used again and again for placing articles.[90] In fact, the Soviet embassy in New Delhi controlled as many as 53 front organizations (friendship societies, youth and student organizations, workers' and farmers' associations, and so on). The front organizations ran 47 newspapers and periodicals and also published books and leaflets. Among them were publications that for years had been ready to accept items for publications, including the aforementioned daily *Patriot* and *Blitz* but also several others.[91] Ultimately, the KGB active measures campaign was successful on some issues, but not all. Taken as a whole, the campaign certainly involved hybrid threats, since it involved numerous domains beyond the obvious one of media power.

The essence of active measures was deception, and the desired result was typically the imposition of disunity among the adversaries. Since active measures was a well-known feature of Soviet policy, we will see that present-day Russian intelligence is aware of the method and at times has aimed for a similar divide and rule policy. Even so, one lesson from the Cold War to keep in mind is that active measures were not aimed at the Soviet population. There was certainly domestic propaganda, but this was a separate phenomenon.

Moreover, in those days the United States at times reported active measures that seem not to have been devised by the Soviets.[92] In most cases, it seems that it was Soviet propaganda aimed at a purely domestic audience that was mistaken for active measures against the Western countries. This might have been a misunderstanding among Western analysts; however, it seems to have been common in the West to assume that every Soviet exaggeration or outright lie was a deliberate attempt to influence the West. There was, no doubt, a shared interest among Western intelligence analysts and the Western press to report Soviet active measures as particularly prevalent and efficient, even when evidence was slim or non-existent. In short, the analysis credited Soviet active measures with being more prevalent and more damaging than even the KGB could have hoped for.

The motives behind active measures campaigns were, and remain:

- To create disunity and dissent among adversaries
- To cause and spread confusion
- To tie-up adversaries' attention and resources
- To discredit rival political figures and movements
- To give an impression of power; suggest a subtle threat
- To change others' policies or behaviours.

To cause the actual change of an adversary's policies or behaviours would, no doubt, be the Holy Grail of any disinformation campaign. However, while this simultaneously would represent the ultimate success for a disinformation professional, it is unlikely that any professional really expects to reach this objective. To stir up trouble between allies is a more realistic aim, and is considered a success in itself. However, success and failure are unpredictable. The same goes for the effect on non-adversarial states. A disinformation campaign may easily create a reaction contradictory to the one hoped for.

One reason for this is that disinformation campaigns rely on the power of fear. Successful campaigns typically exploit the fear of traditional enemies, or other ethnic groups, or the rise to power of a rival ideology or nation. The seed of apparent truth, accuracy, or plausibility that underlies the disinformation is what makes a campaign all the more credible and persuasive. More often than not, disinformation campaigns involve the straightforward stoking-up of tension that already exists between rival parties. They fan existing conflicts, disputes, suspicions; they do not invent new ones. Yet, the two distinguishing characteristics of disinformation are that they involve deception and secrecy. An active measure or disinformation campaign is never an honest activity designed to impart accurate information for altruistic purposes; it is a dishonest activity designed to impart information, which commonly is adulterated, to create a desired outcome. If exposed, the dishonesty is likely to produce fear of another kind, which may result in the additional buttressing of the very unity which the campaign intended to destroy.

Finally, the disinformation activities of allies and 'friendly' organisations with their own agendas should never be overlooked or underestimated. Deception is, like fear, a natural survival instinct which is deeply rooted in the human psyche. There is probably no country or organization which does not employ methods of deception for at least some purposes.

The party to be influenced by a disinformation campaign is often, purportedly, a friend or ally. The disinformation takes the form of helpful advice or an important strategic tip-off, given in good faith. Yet, in the next moment, this friend or ally might become a party who is being used or accused in disinformation aimed at other recipients. This suggests that disinformation campaigns may entail deceiving one's supposed allies just as much as one's enemies. The deceptive activities of 'friendly' powers can be especially problematic for major powers such as the United States, which needs its allies to maintain a global presence.

Case Study: Ghostwriter, Composer of Fabricated Content, 2017–2022

The KGB 'active measures' campaigns of the Cold War employed essentially the same methods as those used in pro-Russian disinformation campaigns today, except that modern cyber technology has facilitated and speeded up the production and dissemination of disinformation. The present author's aforementioned analysis of the Cold War campaigns, in particular those that related to Afghanistan, enables us to identify their structure as well as the motives and ambitions that lay behind them.[93] A comparison with what is known of modern-day disinformation campaigns shows that there are significant structural similarities between the active measures campaigns of the Cold War and disinformation campaigns employed today. Moreover, the analysis shows that many campaigns, then and now, involve three parties: those to be deceived, those cited or used in the disinformation, and those to be maligned – that is, cast as the main 'villain' – by the disinformation. Others have a bipartite structure, consisting of direct threats or criticisms toward the opponents, although still made via covert activity such as the secret planting of newspaper articles or via third parties. The analysis also shows that the disinformation activities of allies and 'friendly' organisations with their own agendas should not be overlooked or underestimated, and friendly nations are just as likely to be deceived as much as adversaries are. It is relatively rare for disinformation to be pure fabrication. Campaigns commonly involve exaggerated or adulterated versions of information that is true, or has some truth in it. Often, the exaggeration takes the form of alarmism; suggesting that a worst-case scenario is bound to arise from a situation that is known already to be problematic or threatening. Campaigns typically exploit the fear of traditional enemies, other ethnic groups, or the rise to power of a rival ideology or nation. Finally, the analysis shows that there is only a fine line between disinformation campaigns, news reporting, and diplomatic 'influencing'. A dizzying array of actors and topics may be used in disinformation.[94]

While the historian has the luxury of scrutinizing evidence from active measures campaigns in long-forgotten archival documents, it is notably more difficult to assess contemporary disinformation campaigns. However, the fundamental conclusions drawn from the aforementioned investigation into the 1980s KGB campaigns seem to hold true also for the present. This is evident from a perusal of the data provided by FireEye, a well-known cyber security company presently known as Mandiant and owned by Google, with regard to what has become known as the Ghostwriter influence campaign.[95] In an ongoing project, FireEye managed to find links between several information operations that the security company assessed to form part of a broader influence campaign aligned with Russian security interests.

The name Ghostwriter derived from the group's first operations, in which Ghostwriter actors would steal credentials of journalists or publishers and publish fake articles using those credentials. The Ghostwriter campaign has been in operation since at least March 2017 and at first primarily targeted audiences in Lithuania, Latvia, and Poland with anti-NATO narratives. The campaign included fabricated content, among which was falsified correspondence from military officials (who for this purpose were 'used' in the campaign). FireEye reported that several disseminated narratives had been identified. Although the details obviously differ, these nonetheless correspond to the tripartite structure employed in the 1980s by the KGB. Then, many active measures involved three parties: those to be deceived, those cited or used in the disinformation, and those to be maligned – that is, cast as the main 'villain' – by the disinformation. The same framework was used in the Ghostwriter campaign. Some of the narratives, too, were similar to those employed earlier by the KGB. A selection of the Ghostwriter narratives is presented in Table 4.[96]

The Ghostwriter campaign was later extended to other European Union/NATO countries. In March 2021, the German news magazine *Der Spiegel* reported that seven members of the federal parliament and 31 members of regional parliaments were targeted by a phishing campaign with fake emails suspected to be conducted by Ghostwriter and in extension, the Russian military intelligence service, the GRU.[97] In September, Germany's foreign ministry formally blamed Russia for being behind the phishing campaign, noting that the campaign included apparent attempts to hack into confidential information that could be used to influence the forthcoming election.[98] In an obviously linked development less than three weeks later, the High Representative of the European Union for Foreign Affairs and Security Policy, Josep Borrell, published an EU Declaration that some member states had observed ongoing malicious cyber activities linked to Ghostwriter, and associated these with the Russian state.[99]

Interestingly, cyber security specialists at Mandiant (ex-FireEye) may not agree with the attribution to the GRU. Without making their data public, they have instead pointed the finger at Belarusian military intelligence.[100] Be that as it may, Microsoft, Google, Facebook, and the Ukrainian government in early 2022 accused Ghostwriter of also launching phishing campaigns followed by subsequent successful hacks against Ukrainian email addresses and military accounts.[101]

Case Study: CENTCOM and Operation Earnest Voice, Bot Operator and Fabricator of Fake Online Personas

Although Ghostwriter employed modern cyber technology, the campaign fundamentally relied on disinformation messages crafted in the traditional manner, that is, by humans. This is no longer required. Artificial intelligence (AI) can be employed to generate disinformation content that barely can be distinguished from content created by humans. With the emergence of social media networks, content can also be disseminated by bots. An Internet bot, web robot, or simply bot is a software application that runs automated tasks (scripts) on the Internet. The bot is designed to imitate human activity on a large scale. Early on, bots were deployed in networks which could be used to carry out a distributed denial-of-service (DDoS) attack, in which the attacker floods a server with internet traffic originating from many different sources to prevent legitimate users from accessing connected online services and sites. However, in social media networks individual bots can be used for large-scale messaging.

Besides, anybody wishing to promote content on social media can easily amplify the dissemination by manipulating the key social media metrics – followers, views, likes, comments, and shares. Users can purchase a range of legally available, paid advertising tools and services for social media manipulation to promote their posts beyond their existing set of followers. These tools include the use of fake online personas. Such deceptive practices are presently commonplace in marketing, but also in propaganda activities.

As a result, it is possible simultaneously to conceal an agenda and amplify its effect on the public through social media networks. This opens up vast new opportunities for exerting influence on a given population, its media, and thereby its government. Present hybrid threats operations take full advantage of these technical solutions.

One state actor which early took advantage of the new possibilities was U.S. Central Command (CENTCOM), responsible for military operations in the Middle East and Central Asia. The operation apparently originated in the psychological warfare programme called Operation Earnest Voice (OEV), which was first developed in Iraq as a weapon against the online presence of jihadis and insurgents who opposed the U.S.-led coalition forces there. CENTCOM personnel used fake online personas secretly to manipulate social media sites by influencing online conversations and spread pro-American propaganda among those susceptible to jihadi or insurgent agitation.[102]

CENTCOM soon also deployed an interconnected web of accounts on Twitter, Facebook, Instagram, and five other social

Table 4: Ghostwriter narratives concerning Lithuania, Latvia, and Poland

Measure	Influenced	Used	Accused
Place articles online claiming that…			
Commanding General of U.S. Army in Europe criticizes Polish, Baltic militaries	Polish, Baltic militaries	General of U.S. Army	U.S. Army
Canadian forces brought COVID-19 to Latvia	Latvian population	NATO Commander	Canadian military
NATO withdraws from Lithuania over COVID-19 concerns	Lithuanian population	Secretary General NATO	NATO leadership
U.S. soldiers involved in carjacking in Lithuania	Lithuanian population	Vilnius Chief of Police	U.S. Army
German soldiers desecrated Jewish Cemetery in Lithuania	Jewish population	Local Jewish organization	German military
Lithuanian Minister of Defence committed sexual assault	Lithuanian population	Alleged Victims	Minister of Defence
NATO places Baltic populations at risk of pre-emptive military strike	Baltic populations	News web site	NATO
Poland is at the epicentre of the coming war between NATO and Russia	Polish population	News media	NATO
Polish Members of Parliament call pro-choice activists 'drug addicts-prostitutes and child killers'	Polish population	Pro-choice activists	Polish MPs
Radioactive waste leaked from Lithuanian nuclear plant poses danger to Poles living near border	Polish population	Social media	Lithuanian government

media platforms which used deceptive tactics aimed at the Middle East and Central Asia to promote the interests of the United States and its allies while opposing geopolitical rivals, primarily Russia, China, and Iran. Anti-Russian propaganda became particularly virulent and pervasive after Russia's invasion of Ukraine in 2022. Notably, Russia was not within CENTCOM's geographical area of responsibility, but support for Russia in the Middle East and Central Asia was. Meanwhile, a small portion of the social media activity still aimed to influence those susceptible to jihadi agitation – the original purpose of Operation Earnest Voice. The social media accounts were created with fake personas with AI-generated faces. They posed as independent media outlets, launched hashtag campaigns and online petitions, and leveraged memes and short-form videos, that is, video content from five to about 60 seconds in duration, which marketers believe has maximum impact on a young audience since it gives instant gratification. The accounts also shared news articles from U.S. government-funded media outlets, such as Voice of America and Radio Free Europe/Radio Liberty, and links to websites sponsored by the U.S. military.[103]

Not to be outdone, another U.S. military unit, reportedly linked to the Pentagon but possibly the U.S. Indo-Pacific Command (USINDOPACOM), initiated a covert anti-China campaign targeting the Philippines. The clandestine operation aimed to sow doubt about the safety and efficacy of vaccines and other life-saving aid that China provided to the Philippines during the COVID-19 pandemic.

Relying on at least 300 fake personas with accounts on Twitter designed to impersonate Filipinos, almost all of which created in the summer of 2020, the operation launched the hashtag campaign #Chinaangvirus, meaning 'China is the virus' in Tagalog. In its eagerness to persuade Filipinos not to accept the first vaccine that would become available in their country – China's Sinovac – the operation soon transformed into an open anti-vax campaign. The generated social media posts advised the public not to use face masks or COVID test kits because of their alleged low quality. One could easily argue that the U.S. military operation likely killed civilians by persuading them not to accept the only vaccination that was available at the time.[104]

Comparable Cases

The *Patriot* and *Blitz* case was unambiguous because it involved the commercial press, that is, non-state actors, which were manipulated into functioning as part of a hybrid threats campaign under the control of a foreign intelligence service. More ambiguous are those cases which involve news organizations that depend on government funding. In these cases, management and editors may feel that they have to adhere to certain agreed or unspoken policy guidelines in their choice of what is newsworthy and in the presentation thereof, which may result in biased reporting. While biased news reports may be easy to recognize and refute, the bias itself is often notoriously difficult to prove. During the Cold War, the government-funded Radio Free Europe (RFE) and Radio Liberty (RL) were established to broadcast pro-Western news and propaganda to the Soviet Union and its allies. Working with diaspora entities and defectors, the CIA and RFE/RL carried out a number of operations which today would be termed hybrid threats activities, including the sending of printed propaganda to Eastern Europe through the use of weather balloons.[105] While the RFE/RL-CIA link remains the best documented case of the use of media power in hybrid threats campaigns – because of the U.S. declassification of formerly secret documents – the Soviet Union, People's Republic of China, and Warsaw Pact countries maintained comparable news organizations which were used for similar purposes. In present times, RFE/RL remains government-funded and continues to broadcast news with a focus primarily on countries outside the Western alliance but also those deemed at risk of abandoning pro-Western policies (Bulgaria, Romania, and Hungary). Another contemporary case is the Russian government-funded RT television network, which like the RFE/RL describes itself as an autonomous nonprofit organization. Some might feel that the comparison of these two news organizations is inappropriate due to the differences in the content which they broadcast; however, from a strict hybrid threats perspective they operate in essentially the same manner within the domain of media power.

Meanwhile, hybrid threats operations employing social media networks and bots were easily identified in numerous Russian and Chinese propaganda operations. These were undistinguishable from those carried out by Western military units.[106]

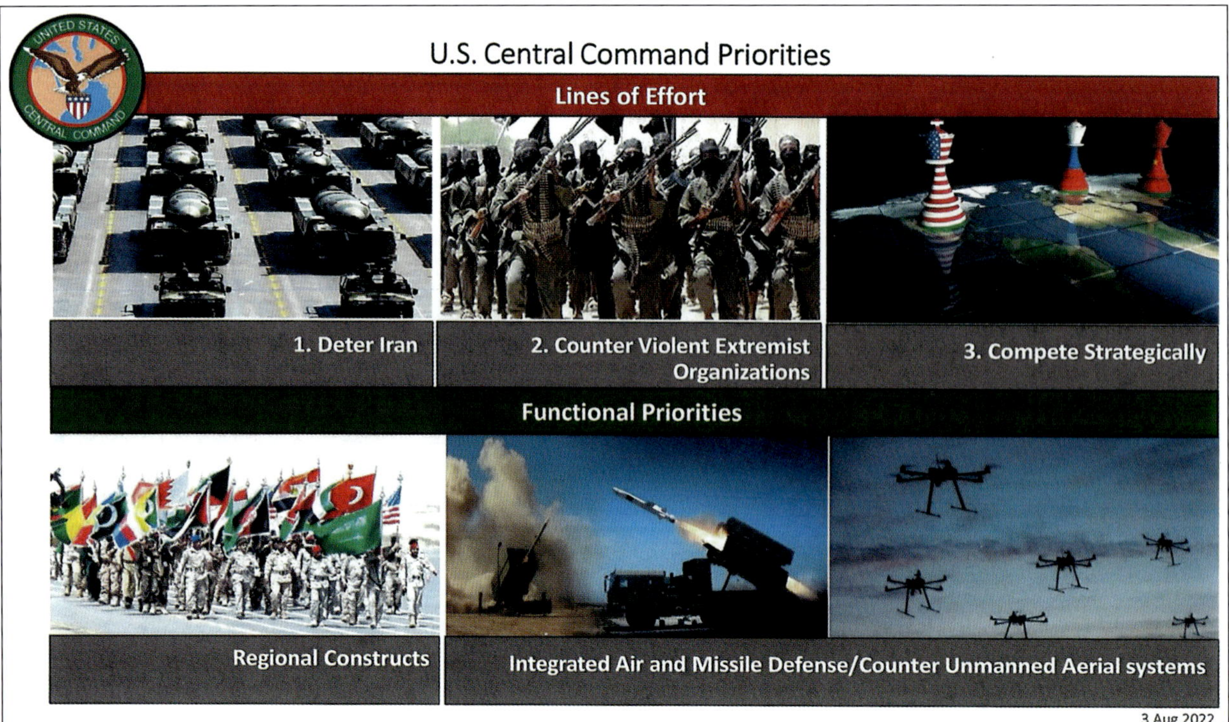

CENTCOM's priorities included the strategic contest with Russia and China. (Image: CENTCOM)

3

NON-STATE ACTORS

Acting as States

Under certain conditions, some non-state actors do exceed the threshold which turns them into genuine hybrid threats. In short, they assume state-like powers and begin to act as states, including claiming the right to declare war and peace.

Already Frank G. Hoffman mentioned the hybrid threats capacity of Hezbollah and Hamas. Of these two organizations, Hezbollah at times certainly exceeded the threshold which turned it into a hybrid threats actor. A Lebanese Shia Islamist political party with a paramilitary wing, Hezbollah was formally established in 1985 by Lebanese Shia groups that in 1982 began to operate against Israeli targets in response to the Israeli invasion of Lebanon in the same year. Inspired by the Iranian Revolution of 1979, Hezbollah established strong ties with Iran and from time to time operated in support of Iranian objectives. Although on these occasions an Iranian proxy, Hezbollah primarily followed an independent agenda and had objectives of its own.

Hamas, a Palestinian Sunni Islamist political party and paramilitary group, was founded in 1987 by Palestinian Islamic scholar Ahmed Yassin after the outbreak of the First Intifada against the Israeli occupation in this year. Although the party from time to time used hybrid threats, Hamas generally followed an independent agenda and the party's own objectives.

Organized Crime

However, organized crime groups too may exceed the threshold which turns them into genuine hybrid threats. In Colombia, Medellín Cartel leaders such as Pablo Escobar and Carlos Lehder by 1984 initiated a terror campaign of indiscriminate violence against shopping malls, theatres, newspaper, and banks with the aim to coerce the government into refusing their extradition to the United States. The campaign went far beyond that of privatized power, since it included terrorist and media powers as well, for which reason it should be labelled an attempt to use hybrid threats against the state.

Calling themselves *Los Extraditables*, they even issued communiqués that explained their cause:

> We declare total and absolute war on the government, the industrial and political oligarchy, the journalists who have attacked and outraged us, the judges who have sold themselves to the government, high court extraditing judges and presidential and sectorial (social, business and labor) associations, and all who have persecuted and attacked us... . We will not lower our flag, and we will continue our struggle and our total war against the anti-nationalists and the sellers of the motherland... . We prefer a tomb in Colombia to a jail in the United States.[1]

The terror campaign reportedly included the assassination of the Minister of Justice, Rodrigo Lara Bonilla, the deadly 1985 attack on the Palace of Justice by the 19th of April Movement (in Spanish: *Movimiento 19 de abril*, M-19), a guerrilla group employing terrorist tactics, and the 1989 bombing of an Avianco airliner, which was lost with no survivors.[2]

The Medellín Cartel was essentially a rival to the state, with its implied monopolies of violence and theft. Besides, before Pablo Escobar and Carlos Lehder declared 'war' on the state for political power, they both aimed to build political support bases within the system. Escobar gathered supporters to be elected to Congress, while Lehder founded a nationalist political movement.[3]

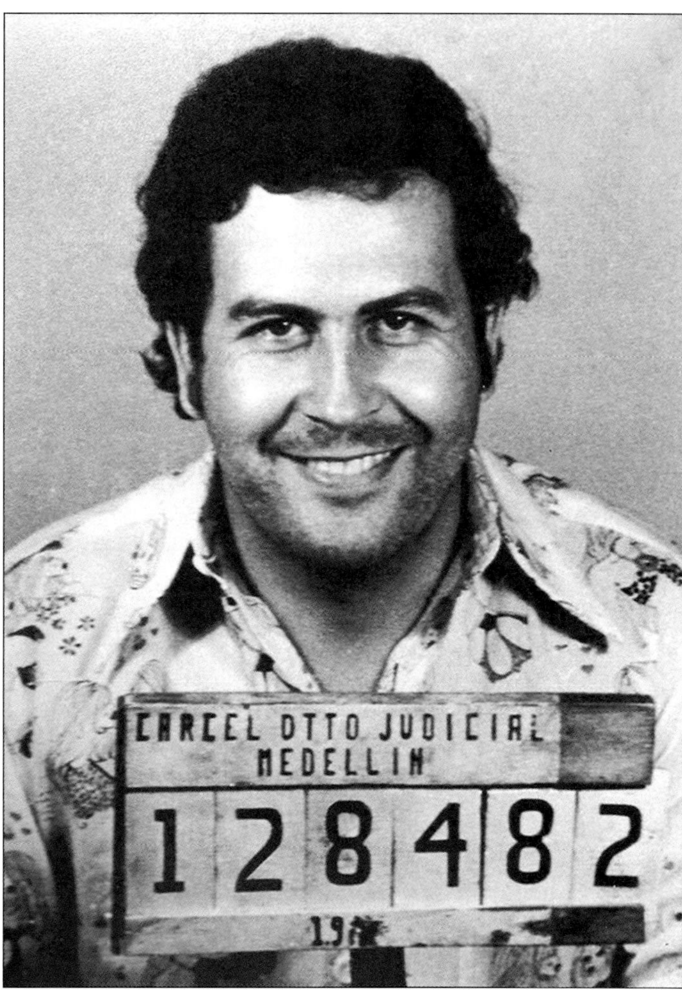

Pablo Escobar, 1976. (Photo: National Police of Colombia)

A similar terror campaign took place a few years later in Italy. In 1992, the Sicilian Mafia assassinated antimafia judges Giovanni Falcone and Paolo Borsellino in a series of car bomb attacks, which also killed Falcone's wife and eight bodyguards. As a result, new legislation was introduced to combat Mafia activities. In response, the Sicilian Mafia in May 1993 carried out a series of car bomb attacks in Rome and Florence. The Rome attack targeted TV talk show host and antimafia campaigner Maurizio Costanzo, while the attack in Florence aimed to devastate the world-renowned Uffizi Galleries. In July 1993, another series of bombings took place. In Rome, the attacks targeted the famous churches of St. John Lateran and San Giorgio in Velabro, while in Milan the target was the Pavilion of Contemporary Art. The targets were chosen so as to terrorize the public and government into abolishing the antimafia legislation.[4]

A Colombian Police Bell 212 helicopter deploying troops on the roof of the Palace of Justice, Bogotá after its takeover by the M-19 guerrilla group, 6–7 November 1985. (Photo: National Police of Colombia)

Why did the Mafia engage in terrorism? According to the testimony of one member, Sicilian Mafia chief Salvatore 'Totò' Riina had explained: 'If you don't make war, how can you negotiate peace?'[5] With the activities spanning privatized power, terrorist power, and – through attacks on the media – media power, there is no doubt that the 1993 events can be labelled a hybrid threats campaign.

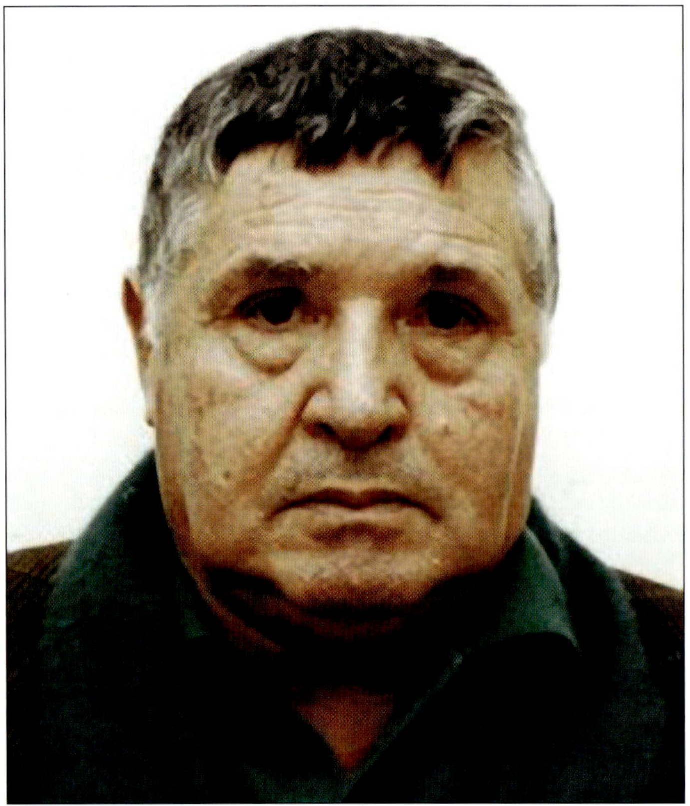

Salvatore 'Totò' Riina after his arrest on 15 January 1993.

Meanwhile, the Kurdistan Workers' Party (PKK) attempted to use hybrid threats including terrorist power to maintain control over the Kurdish population of Sweden, and for that matter, other European countries in which large Kurdish populations had received asylum. As part of the campaign, the PKK murdered two defectors (Enver Ata in Uppsala in 1984 and Çetin Güngör in Stockholm in 1985). However, the method backfired. As a result of widespread media reporting, some of which derived from the PKK itself, the organization for some time found itself in the unenviable position of being treated as the prime suspect of the 1986 murder of Swedish Prime Minister Olof Palme. The powers employed by the PKK included privatized, terrorist, civil, and media powers, so the campaign certainly exceeded the threshold which turned them into genuine hybrid threats.[6]

Similar developments took place in Mexico. From 2009 onwards, the Mexican criminal group *Los Zetas* carried out several massacres of civilians and also, among other murders, killed a female police officer in front of a group of colleagues so as to intimidate them into obeying. In Mexico, this strategy of intimidation – toward law enforcement, the public, and rival groups – worked to the group's advantage. This was another case of an organized crime group employing privatized power as well as terrorist power, thus reaching the threshold which turned them into genuine hybrid threats (although admittedly to a lesser extent than the similar Cartel, Mafia, and PKK cases). *Los Zetas* also operated in the United States, but there they did not attempt to use indiscriminate violence, presumably because they realized that this would result in a far harsher government response, which would cut into the profits from drug sales north of the Mexican-U.S. border.[7]

Murder of judge Paolo Borsellino and his escort, 19 July 1992. (Photo: PD-Italia)

Bombing of the Pavilion of Contemporary Art in Milan, 28 July 1993. (Photo: Unknown)

The Afghan Taliban

However, the non-state actor that reached highest on the scale with regard to hybrid threats power and the desire to act as a sovereign state was arguably the Afghan Taliban movement after it had been forced out of Afghanistan. Hamas and Hezbollah certainly acted as sovereign states, but they never actually claimed state power, which the Afghan Taliban did already in 1994. Despite, or perhaps because, being a dispossessed non-state actor, the Taliban movement managed to deploy a full spectrum of powers.[8] This is particularly interesting since we will see that the Afghan Taliban was not a spontaneous movement but a proxy organization deliberately formed as such by the Pakistani government.

Moreover, the hybrid threats capability and operations of the Afghan Taliban makes an excellent case study. Unlike the situation with many well-established states, we have a relatively complete knowledge of the hybrid threats capabilities and plans which the Afghan Taliban employed during its period in exile. An examination of the hybrid threats of the Afghan Taliban accordingly enables a full-spectrum glimpse into how major hybrid threats actors operate in both long- and short-term perspectives. For this reason, it also makes a fitting end to this recognition guide.

When the Afghan Taliban leaders in late 2001 withdrew into Pakistan, they had no intention to surrender the struggle against the U.S.-led international coalition which had forced them out of Afghanistan. Yet, with a substantial international military presence firmly entrenched in Afghanistan, there was no way that the Taliban could regain power by conventional military means. Even with Pakistani military support, the Afghan Taliban movement could not have repeated the 1994 invasion of Afghanistan in the face of such military opposition.

For this reason, the Afghan Taliban soon after its forced withdrawal into Pakistan began to employ the means and methods of hybrid warfare and hybrid threats. This was a result of strategy debates within the Taliban top leadership, likely with the support of political agents and military advisors from the Pakistani Inter-services Intelligence agency (ISI). Pakistan had long considered influence in Afghanistan a vital component of national security policy and was reluctant to surrender its influence. The policy is generally regarded as having originated from two perceived strategic needs: (1) to allow Pakistan the use of Afghanistan's territory for strategic depth in a conventional war against India; and (2) to ensure friendly Pashtun hegemony in Afghanistan so that ethnic Pashtuns on either side of the Pakistan-Afghanistan border would drop any plans to unite in a single Pashtun nation, and thereby compromise Pakistani territorial integrity.[9] During the 1990s, Pakistani specialists were certainly dispatched into Afghanistan when the Taliban movement aimed to establish a new front, or when combat conditions were particularly difficult. It is likely but not conclusively proven that Pakistan modelled its support to the Taliban on that provided to favoured Afghan insurgent leaders within the U.S.-sponsored mujahidin front in the 1979–1989 Soviet

Mullah Abdul Salam Zaeef (centre), the Taliban ambassador to Pakistan, his translator Ahmed Ratib, and Deputy Ambassador Sohail Shaheen take journalists' questions during a press conference in Pakistan's capital Islamabad, 29 October 2001. Pakistan provided the Afghan Taliban leadership with sanctuary after the U.S. invasion of Afghanistan and essentially let them continue the struggle from Pakistani territory. (Photo: Jacob Freeze)

war in Afghanistan.[10] Even so, there is little doubt that it was the Afghan Taliban leaders, not their Pakistani advisors, who formulated policy, including with regard to hybrid warfare and hybrid threats.

The hybrid threats capability developed by the Afghan Taliban (here defined as the Afghan Taliban movement with affiliates, excluding allied but independent international terrorist groups such as Al-Qaida or foreign terrorist groups such as the Pakistani Taliban) included different tactics and strategies to be employed at home and abroad. From 2002 onwards, the Afghan Taliban movement developed a considerable capability for hybrid threats power projection. Being at war, in Afghanistan the Taliban movement, unsurprisingly, engaged in hybrid warfare. Abroad, the movement utilized its capacity for hybrid threats. For this reason, the domestic threat in Afghanistan deriving from the Taliban and the international threat of the movement were quite different in character.

While the Afghan Taliban movement had no expressed policy on the concept of hybrid warfare or hybrid threats as such, the movement was obviously aware of the means and potential of the concept. So were, for instance, the entire first two sections of the Taliban *Code of Conduct for the Mujahidin of the Islamic Emirate of Afghanistan* primarily focused on the effect that the means of intimidation would have to compel the population into joining the Taliban, and how ordinary people and collaborators should then be treated.[11] In addition, the *Code of Conduct* emphasized that all who worked for the Taliban Islamic Emirate must strive to force those who supported the infidels to acknowledge and surrender to the Taliban.[12] It was clear from the *Code* that this encompassed threats and propaganda as well as fighting. The *Code* stressed the need to win the hearts and minds of the population. Article 78 translates as 'The mujahidin are duty-bound to show good character and Islamic behaviour to the nation. They should win the hearts of Muslims at large.'[13] The Taliban *Code* in these respects mirrored the counterinsurgency strategies adopted by Western countries, in their emphasis on winning the hearts and minds of the contested population.[14] In this respect, there was no great difference between Western and Taliban views on warfare. Nor was there such a difference in the view on new tactics and technologies. The Taliban movement, in similarity to other military organizations, displayed a learning curve, in which new methods, tactics, and technologies were adopted to stay abreast of developments.[15]

In fact, the hybrid threats capability of the Afghan Taliban movement soon grew to encompass several distinct types of powers, in both domestic and international dimensions. Many of these powers were exercised from Afghanistan, but in particular those with an international dimension more often geographically originated in Pakistan, where the Taliban leadership enjoyed safe havens. The full hybrid warfare and hybrid threats capability of the Taliban is summarized in Table 5, and will be further explained below.

Table 5: Afghan Taliban Movement hybrid threats capability

Domestic Threat						
Type of Threat	**Target**	**Means and Method**	**Purpose**	**Geographic Origin**	**Effect**	**Defensive Actors**
Military (State) Power	ISAF/ANSF	Guerrilla attacks, IEDs	Defeat or intimidate enemy	Afghanistan/ Pakistan	High	Armed forces, police, intelligence
Terrorist Power	ISAF/ANSF	E.g. suicide bombers	Intimidate enemy	Afghanistan/ Pakistan	High	Armed forces, police, intelligence
Terrorist Power	Population	E.g. killings, mutilations	Intimidate population	Afghanistan/ Pakistan	High	Armed forces, police, intelligence
Media Power	Population	E.g. night letters, proclamations, videos	Propaganda	Afghanistan/ Pakistan	High	Armed forces, police, intelligence
Organized Crime (Privatized) Power	ISAF/ANSF	Support to bandit gangs	Cause disruption	Afghanistan/ Pakistan	Medium	Armed forces, police, intelligence
International Threat						
Diplomatic Power	ISAF member states	Negotiations	Negotiate withdrawal	Pakistan	Medium	Foreign Ministry, international organizations
Diplomatic Power	Worldwide Muslim community	Negotiations	Appear as responsible party	Pakistan	Medium	Foreign Ministry, international organizations
Media Power	ISAF member states, worldwide Muslim community	*Afghanistan In Fight*, Internet, Twitter	Propaganda	Pakistan	Low/medium	Media houses, government institutions, think tanks, NGOs
Terrorist Power	ISAF soldiers' family members	Threats by telephone or SMS	Intimidate individual to resign	Afghanistan, ISAF member state	Low/medium	Security service, intelligence service, police
Terrorist Power	Attacks	Not used	Intimidate enemy to withdraw	Pakistan	None	Security service, intelligence service, police

Background

The Taliban Movement in the 1990s

To assess the Afghan Taliban movement's capability for hybrid warfare and hybrid threats, it helps first to explain the origins of the movement. The Afghan Taliban movement arose as a military force in 1994, when it was created, in all essentials, by and for Pakistani interests.[16]

The emergence of the Taliban movement as a fighting and political proxy for Pakistani interests was the result of a policy shift in Islamabad. As noted by General Pervez Musharraf, President of Pakistan in 2001–2008, it was 'true that we had assisted in the rise of the Taliban' which was created by and for Pakistani interests.[17] The fact that few, if any, Taliban leaders subsequently were much concerned about following Pakistani orders does not change the fact that without Pakistani support, the movement would have become nothing more than one among many armed bands then operating in Afghanistan.[18] In Musharraf's words: 'After the Taliban came to power, we lost much of the leverage we had had with them.'[19]

The Taliban movement's leaders at the time regarded themselves as the world's perhaps only true Islamic government, on the lines of the righteous caliphate of the early years of Islam.[20] The Taliban government accordingly styled itself the Islamic Emirate of Afghanistan.[21]

The Taliban were reinforced by large numbers of Pakistanis, religious volunteers as well as regular Pakistani military units. Indeed, the very first Taliban incursion into Afghanistan in 1994 was reportedly supported by Pakistani Army artillery fire and motor transportation from the Pakistani side of the border.[22] The volunteers, who first were reported by the Pakistani press in mid-June 1997,[23] were initially mostly Pashtuns of Afghan or Pakistani origin but from 1999, Pakistani Punjabis arrived in increasing numbers and eventually formed the majority of the Pakistani volunteers.[24]

The Pakistani military played a considerable role in the military success of the Taliban. Senior Pakistani intelligence and army officers were involved in strategic planning. Regular Pakistani soldiers served as units in combat roles, or were detached from their units for the provision of special skills such as those of tank drivers and aircraft pilots, in technical and rear support, maintenance, and administrative functions. Pakistani aircraft assisted with troop rotations for Taliban forces during combat operations at least in late 2000. Pakistani military officers from the ISI as well as commandos from Pakistan's Special Services Group (SSG, a special forces regiment based near Peshawar) also appeared to take considerable responsibility for the planning and execution of major operations. This was shown by the impressive use of mobility, speed, logistics support, as well as efficient contemporary command, control, communications, and intelligence procedures displayed by the Taliban. This was on a level hitherto never seen among Afghan troops and certainly not to be expected from such a comparatively new military formation, even considering the fact that the Taliban also recruited numerous officers and men of the pre-1992 Afghan army, many from the hardline, Pashtun nationalist Khalq ('Masses' or 'People') wing of the Communist Party.[25]

Pakistan-based Western diplomats knew that the ISI was instrumental in forming and supporting the Afghan Taliban movement. While there was some understandable initial confusion about the identity and purpose of the new movement, U.S. diplomatic observers immediately noted that the origin of the movement was linked in time with a Pakistani vehicle convoy that formed part of 'Pakistani Interior Minister Babar's vision of opening up trade between Pakistan and the Central Asian states' and, since the Taliban had been armed 'with brand new weapons', it was immediately suspected that the new movement had been formed with the 'active support' of the government of Pakistan.[26] A few weeks later, U.S. diplomatic observers remained undecided about the nature of the Taliban movement. However, they remained suspicious about Pakistan's involvement. For instance, the 'appearance of a new force, with new weapons, at the precise moment that Pakistan claimed that opening the road from Chaman to Kandahar, Herat, and on to the CAR [the formerly Soviet Central Asian republics] was one of its priorities was too much of a coincidence.' Yet, although there were suspicions that Interior Minister Babar was 'one of the initial sponsors', these observers – whether out of political caution or perspicacity – concluded that Pakistan no longer controlled the movement.[27]

That Interior Minister Babar assisted in launching the Taliban movement has since been recognized in Pakistan.[28] U.S. diplomats had heard about it at the time. A memorandum to the State Department's Afghanistan Desk dated 5 December 1994 noted that the Pakistani intelligence service, ISI, was 'deeply involved' in the Taliban movement. The memorandum also reported Pakistani Air Force and Pakistani military support to the Taliban, together with the recruitment of former Khalq members with a military background. However, Babar's involvement was known too. At the bottom of the memorandum, a handwritten note states, 'This AM I've heard that General Babar is running this Taliban op'.[29] On the following day, yet another report – this time classified as secret – noted that the Taliban was 'directly supported by Pakistan' and that General Babar was involved. The Pakistani support included fire from artillery units and 'coordination provided by Pakistani officers on the scene.' Taliban use of tanks and helicopters too supported the claims of Pakistani direct military support.[30] In another secret report, dated 26 January 1995, the Taliban use of helicopters, unexpected military discipline, and large volumes of fuel supplies from Pakistan again indicated Pakistani involvement.[31] Subsequent reporting from U.S. diplomats, to the extent that these have been declassified, generally confirms the picture of unexpected military efficiency, again quite likely because of Pakistani military support. Indeed, an American observer noted that, among the Taliban who conquered Herat in September 1995, 'there were quite a few Taliban who only spoke Urdu', which clearly signifies that these Taliban members were Pakistanis. Further, since Pakistani Pashtuns speak Pashto, this observation indicates that these Taliban were from Pakistan's relatively distant Punjab province.[32]

Lest it should be claimed that the diplomatic cables misinterpreted the situation, or that the Pakistani support ended after the Taliban conquest of Kabul, a Taliban representative in December 1996 acknowledged to Robin L. Raphel, U.S. Assistant Secretary of State for South Asian Affairs, that Pakistani support was 'extensive and largely provided by the ISI.' According to the Taliban representative, 'Pakistani support ranged from cash to supplies to logistical support to on the ground military/intel advisers.' The Pakistani Ministry of Foreign Affairs 'actually drafted letters for the Taliban'. Among the Taliban soldiers, there were both 'educated army officers with the ISI and uneducated recruits from rural areas'. The report ends with the comment that the U.S. representatives had recently received credible information about the extent and origin of Pakistani assistance and support to the Taliban from other sources, and that the Taliban representative's account was consistent with other information.[33] This cable was written, it should be remembered, at the time when the United States was initiating diplomatic links with the Taliban government and when Pakistan remained being seen as a close ally of the United States. If reports of Pakistani military support to the Taliban had not been so pervasive at the time, it is unlikely that the issue would have been discussed at all. Washington then had other priorities. Incidentally, the Taliban envoy who met Raphel was the Taliban-designated United Nations representative, Hamid Karzai, whom the United States a few years later made president of Afghanistan.[34] This was not surprising; by the mid-1990s Karzai had good relations with the Taliban, was 'enthusiastic' about the movement, and knew many of their leaders on a personal basis.[35]

However, following the 11 September 2001 terrorist attacks, the creation of the Afghan Taliban movement as a Pakistani non-state proxy was seldom mentioned so as not to embarrass Pakistan and cause further tensions in an already dangerous domestic political environment.

Weapons being abundant in Afghanistan, the Taliban did not really have a supply problem with regard to personal weapons. Fuel, heavy weapons, and ammunition were another matter. The Taliban depended on Pakistan for delivery of ammunition, particularly for tanks and artillery, some small arms, pick-up trucks, and petroleum (both motor and aviation fuel), oil, and lubricants. They also received financial payments. A significant share of the Taliban procurement of arms, munitions, and spare parts was handled by Pakistani private companies, often run by retired military officers. They bought considerable quantities from Chinese manufacturers through dealers in Hong Kong and Dubai (United Arab Emirates). The supplies were usually shipped in sealed containers to the Pakistani port of Karachi, whence they were trucked to Afghanistan without normal customs inspection, since this was not required by the two countries' trade agreement, the Afghan Transit Trade Agreement (ATTA).[36] Some were probably paid for through financial assistance to the Taliban from private or state supporters in the Arabian peninsula through the use of Islamic charities such as the Al-Rashid Trust, since accused of smuggling weapons and supplies, disguised as humanitarian aid, to the Taliban.[37] The Taliban were funded partly from contributions from supporters abroad, typically on the Arabian peninsula, partly from taxes, in particular deriving from narcotics production in Afghanistan.[38] It was not unknown for Taliban leaders to maintain foreign bank accounts. So did, for instance, Taliban supreme leader Mullah Muhammad Omar have accounts in the Laskari Bank in Islamabad and the National Westminster Bank in Britain. Both were allegedly opened for him by the ISI.[39] Many Pakistanis too profited from business connections with the Taliban. Taliban leaders soon developed relations with a number of Pakistani businessmen close to Asif Ali Zardari, the husband of Pakistan's prime minister 1993–1996, Benazir Bhutto, who in turn were given highly lucrative permits for fuel deliveries from Pakistan to the Taliban. Pakistan also assisted in the development of necessary infrastructure in Taliban-controlled Afghanistan. So did, for instance, Pakistan Telecom set up a microwave telephone network in Kandahar. This became part of the Pakistani telephone grid. Kandahar received the same prefix (081) as that for Quetta, so Kandahar could be called from Pakistan as a local call.[40]

In the early years of the movement, the Taliban received considerable material and financial support also from Saudi Arabia. By then, every major Taliban offensive seemed to be preceded by a visit from Prince Turki ibn Faisal al-Saud, head of the Saudi General Intelligence Agency (*al-Istakhbarah al-Amah;* or simply *Istakhbarat*), and his staff. Earlier, Prince Turki also played a major role in organizing the mujahidin front against the Soviets during the 1979–1989 war.[41]

The Taliban military chain of command at the time was vague and ill-defined. The top decision-making body was the Rahbari Shura (Leadership Council, often referred to as the Supreme Shura) in Kandahar, headed by Mullah Omar. There were also other, lower shuras that reported to the Kandahar Leadership Council, such as the Kabul Shura and the Military Shura or Military Commission. The Kabul Shura was fundamentally a cabinet of acting ministers in Kabul. They primarily dealt with day-to-day problems and local military and political activities, since all important decisions were taken in Kandahar. The Military Commission, another loose body of senior Taliban officials, was technically in authority of military affairs. However, Mullah Omar remained head of the Taliban armed forces, and the Military Commission accordingly seemed to limit itself primarily to strategic planning. However, it had no strategic decision-making powers, and all decisions on military strategy, appointments of key commanders, and the allocation of funds were taken by Mullah Omar. Under Mullah Omar, there was a chief of the general staff and chiefs of staff for the army and air force, supposedly in command of ground operations and air operations, respectively.[42] Military operations were supposed to be directed by the minister of defence or the military chief of staff. However, it seems that ground operations remained in the hands of various local task force commanders, several of whom were also members of the Taliban government.[43] The Taliban ran an intelligence service, the *Istakhbarat* (named after, and no doubt at first assisted by, Saudi intelligence).[44]

The early Taliban movement because of its foreign support operated more as a conventional although semi-irregular military force than as an actor in hybrid warfare. For all its harsh policies, the Taliban movement never engaged in terrorist activities against neighbouring states.[45] However, the movement at times during its offensives indulged in what can only be called terrorist activities aimed at its Afghan enemies. Examples include the torture, castration, and killing of former President Sayyid Muhammad Najibullah in 1996, followed by the public display of his corpse, and the massacres of an estimated 6–8,000 civilians in Mazar-e Sharif, Maimana, and Shiberghan in 1998. These acts of terrorism were ordered by the Taliban leadership, and can be interpreted as an active strategy of intimidation directed against the Afghan population.[46]

The Taliban forces varied widely in training and experience. Some had considerable military experience, and many men had received military training in Pakistan, around Kabul, or in other quiet areas of Afghanistan. Others, however, especially some of the recent recruits from Pakistan, had received virtually no training and were frequently trucked straight to the front to take part in combat operations.[47] Most Taliban soldiers received regular salaries. Among those who did were the professional soldiers from the former communist armed forces, serving in the capacity of gunners, tank drivers, mechanics, and aircraft pilots. Although the majority of the professionals were Pashtuns, they were seldom as religiously motivated as other Taliban soldiers, in particular the volunteers from Pakistan.[48]

This description of the first years of the Afghan Taliban movement shows that far from being a tribal army, the early Taliban leaders and in particular their Pakistani supporters were often reasonably sophisticated fighting men, aware of the practicalities of both conventional and irregular warfare. While their military capabilities in the 1990s should not be exaggerated, the Taliban understanding of tactics and strategy was not much inferior to that of their neighbours, something which is easily forgotten in light of the speed in which their state collapsed in the face of the Afghan Northern Alliance campaign on the ground supported by American-led air support in late 2001, which drove the Taliban movement away from Kabul and into Pakistan.[49]

The Post-2001 Taliban Movement

With the invasion of U.S.-led forces in October 2001, the Taliban movement retreated into Pakistan. Following the withdrawal, it took some time before the Taliban movement fully reorganized and reconstituted itself as a military force. Due to the large and resilient support system the Taliban had acquired during its rule prior to 2001, the Taliban remained the largest threat to stability in Afghanistan.[50] This was facilitated by the fact that until 2005, the Taliban were not under serious military pressure.[51] In Pakistan, the Taliban movement continued to receive substantial support from Pakistani sources.[52]

From the viewpoint of the international coalition, the conflict in Afghanistan can be summarized as having consisted of four phases. In 2001–2005, the international forces followed the Light Footprint approach, which resulted in modest and insufficient foreign military and financial aid to the government of Afghanistan. The U.S.-led coalition was from 2003 onwards also distracted by the Iraq War. In 2005–2009, a Taliban resurgence took place, largely as a result of the Light Footprint of previous years and the existence of Taliban sanctuaries in Pakistan. By then, foreign aid was increasingly used as a tool for short-term stabilization in response to Taliban activity, instead of for much-needed long-term developments. The years 2009–2011 saw a U.S. military and civilian surge, accompanied by a substantial increase in aid. Unfortunately, the surge did not succeed in uprooting the Taliban insurgency. The years 2011–2014, finally, were characterized by the concept of transition intended to accomplish Afghan assumption of full sovereignty. Paradoxically, transition and full sovereignty were accompanied by almost complete foreign aid dependency, since insufficient long-term developments had taken place to ensure Afghanistan's economic future.

It follows from this that the Taliban movement was granted several quiet years in which to grow in strength, without being under serious military pressure anywhere. Yet the movement was an exile organization, without the benefits of being in control anywhere outside its Pakistani sanctuaries. The Taliban movement accordingly came to fragment into several semi-autonomous organizations, nominally united under Mullah Omar and what became known as his Quetta Shura, so named since it was for many years based in the Pakistani city of Quetta.

The Taliban was never a homogeneous movement, not even in the 1990s, and the divisions remained and to some extent deepened in exile. Mullah Omar and the Quetta Shura had one agenda, which the affiliated and allied groups only shared in part, since they had agendas of their own. In addition, even the Quetta Shura was a decentralized organization and in most cases consisted of loose units independent of each other, even though they all claimed allegiance to Mullah Omar. In fact, the Quetta Shura itself fragmented. In 2012, a power struggle emerged within the Shura, and internal rivalries sharpened in 2013.[53] By mid-2013, Mullah Omar remained the nominal head of the movement, although its members sometimes believed that he was held captive in Pakistan, or even was dead (he was not, as it turned out).[54] The Taliban movement was then widely regarded by its own members as having become divided into several largely autonomous alliances. These were the original Leadership Council in Quetta,[55] Abdul Qayyum Zakir's alliance within the Quetta Shura,[56] Akhtar Mansur's alliance within the Quetta Shura,[57] the Peshawar Shura,[58] and the Miram Shah Shura, also known as the Haqqani Network.[59] However, by April 2014 some of the tensions and divisions were resolved with the (temporary) removal of Abdul Qayyum Zakir from the Military Commission, ostensibly for reasons of illness.[60]

Nominally, the organization known among Western analysts as the Haqqani Network but in Afghanistan more often referred to as the Miram Shah Shura formed a part of the Peshawar Shura. However, being the most formidable of the various alliances within the Taliban movement, this was a fundamentally autonomous wing of the Afghan Taliban movement based in Miram Shah in Pakistan and named after its leader, Jalaluddin Haqqani.[61] The Haqqani Network was a distinct military and political organization created by Jalaluddin Haqqani during the 1980s which after the war against the Soviet Union remained a source of power in the borderlands shared by Afghanistan and Pakistan. The Haqqani leaders were experienced, having survived three decades of warfare, educated in theology, and had a sophisticated understanding of international trade and politics. Their patriarch, Jalaluddin Haqqani, had earned the name Haqqani as a honorific title as a result of his studies at the prestigious Dar ul-Ulum Haqqaniyyah *madrasah*. He spoke excellent Arabic, as did his son Sirajuddin, and both had first-rate connections in the Arab world. The Haqqanis could discuss the intricacies of Islamic theology in the language of the Prophet, and kept a low profile by avoiding Western journalists, thus for decades also avoiding the taint of international terrorism, despite close links to Al-Qaida.[62]

Affiliated to the Taliban movement but even older than the Haqqani Network was the Hezb-e Islami of Gulbuddin Hekmatyar (HIG), popularly named for its leader Gulbuddin Hekmatyar, a former Afghan warlord and prime minister and one time ally of the United States. Originally a political party in the 1980s involved in the war against the Soviet Union, HIG had political allies in the Afghan parliament, may have supported its own candidate in the 2014 presidential election (possibly Qutbuddin Hilal who once served under Hekmatyar),[63] and was maybe the politically most sophisticated and well-established Afghan insurgent group. Most Hezb-e Islami members were then detribalized Pashtuns from the state-educated state intelligentsia. The leaders were primarily intellectual Islamists from an urban background, so the party lacked a firm tribal base. This was in fact an advantage, as the party tended to recruit where tribal structures had broken down, which made it highly popular in Pakistani refugee camps. The party, radical Islamist in world view, was regarded as the best organized and most disciplined party within the anti-Soviet resistance. However, Hekmatyar's organization collapsed as Pakistani funds from 1994 were diverted from it to the newly created Taliban movement. Reportedly with thousands of sympathizers and fighters, HIG had strong relations with Al-Qaida and was closely linked with the Afghan Taliban. Hekmatyar and his followers were believed to have remained operating chiefly in Kunar Province, Afghanistan.[64]

Then there were several similarly autonomous groups of foreign fighters, including the remnants of the Al-Qaida core as well as groups such as the Uzbek-led Islamic Movement of Uzbekistan (IMU) and the Pakistani, ethnically Pashtun terrorist group, the Tehrik-e-Taliban Pakistan (TTP, 'Movement of Pakistani Taliban'). All these groups enjoyed bases and sanctuaries in Pakistan.

It was never known how many insurgents operated in Afghanistan. Besides, many were at any given moment based on the Pakistani side of the border. A common estimate was up to 25,000 Quetta Shura Taliban fighters, in addition to about 3,000 Haqqani fighters and 1,000 HIG fighters. As for Al-Qaida and other foreign fighters, their total number in Afghanistan was unlikely to exceed 1,000 and was likely far fewer, probably only numbering a few hundreds.[65] Since the foreign fighters played strictly a supporting role in Afghanistan, their means and motivations will not be further covered here.[66]

The post-2001 Taliban movement was, as a military force, less conventional in outlook than the old 1990s Taliban, but no less sophisticated and not lacking connections in a large number of countries. Besides, the existence of sanctuaries in Pakistan enabled the movement to develop strategies based on hybrid warfare and hybrid threats.

Hybrid Warfare and Hybrid Threats

As noted, the hybrid warfare and hybrid threats capability developed by the Afghan Taliban included different tactics and strategies to be employed at home and abroad. From both an analytical and practical perspective, these two theatres of war are best described as distinct from one another.

Being at war, in Afghanistan the Taliban movement engaged in hybrid warfare. Abroad, the movement instead utilized its capacity for hybrid threats. The domestic threat in Afghanistan deriving from the Taliban and the international threat of the movement were accordingly quite different in character.

The Domestic Theatre: Hybrid Warfare

Military Power Projection against ISAF and ANSF

In Afghanistan, the Taliban soon began to carry out a hybrid warfare campaign against the international coalition (Operation Enduring Freedom and the International Security Assistance Force, ISAF) and the fledgling Afghan National Security Forces (ANSF). The purpose of the campaign was to defeat or at least intimidate the coalition. Some Taliban leaders conceived that inflicting casualties on the foreign military forces would demoralize public opinion in their country of origin, causing panic among politicians, and thereby force a withdrawal.[67]

The hybrid warfare campaign consisted of two mutually supporting activities. First, the Taliban employed military power, early on by what in effect were guerrilla-style attacks but soon increasingly through the use of Improvised Explosive Devices (IEDs) placed at convenient locations, in particular along roads, in vehicles, or used in suicide attacks. The IED campaigns had the dual objective of limiting the freedom of movement of the international military forces and at the same time intimidating the foreign soldiers, if they could not be defeated outright.[68]

Pakistani military support, whether official or non-official, was particularly conspicuous in the IED campaign. As late as 2011, IED specialists in southern Afghanistan were still often of Punjabi origin. Locals believed that they were Pakistani Army specialists. When killed, the IED specialist would have to be replaced, so a replacement IED specialist was sent from the Taliban leadership. There was accordingly a degree of central control over the IED effort, which again suggests Pakistani involvement.[69] The Taliban had an IED development centre in Pakistan. The Taliban confirmed that Iraqi insurgents assisted them with IEDs, but ISAF assessed that both Iranian and Pakistani support played a major role.[70]

Since the Taliban knew that ISAF's rules of engagements did not permit the killing of minors, the Taliban developed a strategy of employing children as emplacers of IEDs.[71] In effect, this was yet another form of hybrid warfare tactics, since any killings of children by ISAF could be used for propaganda purposes.

The coalition presented numerous targets for the Taliban. British Royal Marines with Lima Company, 42 Commando, patrol during Operation Sond Chara, in Helmand Province, 25 December 2008. (Photo: U.S. Marine Corps Corporal John Scott Rafoss)

Terrorist Power Projection against the ISAF and ANSF

At the same time, the Taliban employed what can best be termed terrorist power, through the use of suicide bombers against international or Afghan military targets. Sometimes they were particularly effective, such as when on 15 January 2006 the director of the Canadian Provincial Reconstruction Team (PRT), senior diplomat Glynn Berry, was killed in Kandahar City.[72] Tactics developed in which one or more suicide bombers were used to spearhead an assault which then was followed up with guerilla-style forces (a tactics incidentally first development in Chechnya).[73] Results could be spectacular, such as when the Taliban attacked Sarpoza Prison on the outskirts of Kandahar City on 13 June 2008 with a vehicle borne IED (VBIED), a suicide bomber, and a rapid full scale attack by Taliban fighters on motorcycles. Some 400 imprisoned Taliban fighters were released, then removed in buses which the Taliban had waiting outside.[74]

The purpose of the terror campaign was to intimidate the ISAF coalition into withdrawing its forces. A further objective was to create success stories which could be used for propaganda purposes (see below).

Terrorist Power Projection against the Afghan Population

The Taliban also engaged in terror campaigns directed specifically against the Afghan population. This can be seen as a continuation of the policies used by the Taliban in the 1990s (see above). Terrorist power was used to intimidate the population into defecting from the government supported by international forces and the ANSF. Shadow government structures (often far better organized than the governing structures used when the Taliban in fact ruled major parts of Afghanistan pre-2001) were set up to exert control over the population. Examples of the use of terrorist power include the killings of collaborators (government workers and ordinary Afghans who reported the location of Taliban units or IEDs to the international military forces) and what the Taliban in religious terms labelled apostates, that is, Muslims who did not subscribe to the extremist version of Islam adopted by the Taliban. The Taliban would then execute, often by beheading, a number of locals for cooperating with foreign troops, displaying the corpses in public as a warning to others.[75] These methods had a major impact on the Afghan rural population. Cases were noted when Afghan National Police (ANP) units failed to engage the Taliban, since they knew that they or their families then would face the prospect of Taliban reprisals.[76]

In a similar manner, the Taliban regularly attempted to persuade people from voting in the national elections. A common method to influence voters not to participate was to cut off the index finger of those who went to the polls, who were easily recognizable since dipping the finger in black ink was part of the election process.[77] The campaign served a dual purpose. First, it terrorized the population into adopting the extremist version of Islam which served as the Taliban movement's ideology, since the Taliban considered democratic elections an affront to Islam. Second, the mutilations eroded trust in the Afghan government.

Another example of how the Taliban imposed their will by terrorist power was the strategy to force telecom operators to close cellular telephone networks at night. The Taliban believed that the international military forces used cellular phone signals to track and launch attacks against them. This was probably a correct assessment since cell phones periodically send signals to the network even when they are not making calls and such signals can be monitored by signals intelligence, satellites, or other means. But the Taliban also feared that ordinary Afghans on the side of the government might observe them and wished to prevent such collaborators from privately calling in to report Taliban movements. ISAF set up a call centre for this very purpose in 2007. Since most Taliban movements took place at night for reasons of security, this was the time to shut down the telephone networks. For this reason, the Taliban began to blow up telecommunications towers following threats to telephone operators warning them to shut down the towers at night or face attack. When telephone service providers responded by following the Taliban movement's orders, the Taliban not only ensured their own security, they also made a huge impact on the Afghan population, eroding their will to resist Taliban control by showing them by example that it was the Taliban movement, not the government forces, which set the agenda.[78] This successful intimidation campaign enabled the Taliban to impose a strategic, delegitimizing blow to the authority of the government.

A similar delegitimizing effect was achieved by the widespread assassinations of government leaders, high-ranking members of the clergy on the side of the government, and women in public service or girls' schools. While government leaders and women in public service were primarily targeted for political reasons and to intimidate the population, the assassination of pro-government clergy had the added effect of reducing their influence with the population. Those who were not killed had to remain in Afghan National Army (ANA) compounds from which they primarily preached by radio, not in person, which severely limited their impact and cleared the field for Taliban clergy to win the battle for souls.[79]

Media Power Projection against the Afghan Population

In the battle for souls, the Taliban also exercised its media power. This showed itself as proclamations and videos distributed online and by other means. The Taliban also used night letters, which were leaflets distributed at night, thus serving as a tangible reminder that the Taliban had a presence seemingly everywhere.[80] In particular the night letters were, due to the widespread illiteracy in Afghanistan, often read out aloud by a mullah or elder, which in itself increased the impact of the message. Media power fundamentally consisted of the dissemination of threats to collaborators and propaganda, which not only resulted in the winning of hearts and minds but also in the intimidation of the general public, who realized then, if not before, that when the foreigners eventually withdrew, the Taliban would remain.

Examples of intimidating propaganda included the video recording of public execution by stoning in August 2010 of a couple in Kunduz who in the eyes of the Taliban had committed adultery, the recording of which was subsequently distributed through the Internet.[81]

Power Projection through Organized Crime

The Taliban also enlisted, in a manner, the help of organized crime.[82] The Taliban often encouraged the activities of local bandit gangs in areas where the Taliban movement had not yet established, but was working to gain, a presence. Not only did this facilitate Taliban activities by causing confusion and presenting additional targets to the international military forces or ANSF, the activities of bandit gangs also legitimized the subsequent imposition of Taliban justice and its harsh methods. In effect, the Taliban first encouraged the growth of crime, then stepped in to suppress it. Many bandit gangs would indeed find the arguments to join the Taliban movement persuasive at this time, in particular if they already had used the Taliban name to discourage police or local communities from resisting.[83]

The International Theatre: Hybrid Threats

Diplomatic Power Projection against the ISAF Member States

Internationally, the Taliban primarily focused on diplomatic power projection. A major aim was to negotiate the withdrawal of the international coalition, with threats if necessary, so that the Taliban could return to power. For this task, the Taliban relied on diplomatic power, with negotiations conducted through friendly Muslim countries such as Pakistan, Saudi Arabia, the United Arab Emirates, and Qatar. These countries were not chosen by random; only Pakistan, Saudi Arabia, and the United Arab Emirates, in this order, had recognized the Taliban Emirate of Afghanistan in May 1997.[84]

We have seen that the diplomatic process against ISAF member states can be said to have begun in September 2009 in Dubai, United Arab Emirates. At the request of the Taliban, German intelligence then held a first meeting with a Taliban delegation. A further eight meetings had to take place, before the Germans brought in American representatives so that real negotiations could get underway. This first U.S.-Taliban meeting took place outside Munich in Germany on 28 November 2010, with the participation of a Qatari representative whom the Taliban representatives trusted. A second meeting accordingly took place in Qatar's capital Doha on 15 February 2011. The third meeting took place in Munich on 7–8 May 2011. Through this series of meetings, the Taliban aimed to persuade the United States to lift sanctions, release high-level Taliban prisoners, and to allow the opening of a Taliban representative office in a Muslim country.[85]

These meetings all took place in secret, and at the time there was little chance for the Taliban to gain a negotiated American withdrawal. However, the Taliban diplomatic campaign eventually paid off in the form of a more public, international diplomatic presence, aimed more at the worldwide Muslim community than at the West.

Diplomatic Power Projection against the Worldwide Muslim Community

Toward the worldwide Muslim community, it was important for the Taliban leadership to appear as a responsible and religiously legitimate party. The Taliban did not mind meeting with the Kabul government, as long as they met as equals. This was accomplished during 24–27 September 2008, when Saudi King Abdullah hosted talks with the Taliban in the holy city of Mecca.[86]

However, it took some time before suitable conditions for further meetings could be agreed, not least because of difficulties for outside observers to ascertain whether the alleged Taliban representatives who turned up from time to time really represented Mullah Omar. In June 2013, formal peace talks between the Afghan government and the Taliban were finally announced, to take place in Doha. However, the Qatari leaders were somewhat too hospitable to their Taliban guests, allowing them to open a formal representative office, and the talks were cancelled in a row over the Taliban displaying their flag and presenting themselves as the legitimate rulers of the Islamic Emirate, that is, the state of Afghanistan. The Doha office was closed within 24 hours of its opening, amid speculations that negotiations would reopen in Turkey or Saudi Arabia.[87]

However, the Taliban had achieved their aim to appear as a responsible and legitimate party. Besides, U.S. President Barack Obama had by then announced the planned drawdown of American military forces in Afghanistan, so for the Taliban leadership, it was only a question of time before they could make a move for real power. When in early 2014, Taliban leaders met representatives of the Afghan government in Dubai, United Arab Emirates, and in Riyadh, Saudi Arabia, they refused to negotiate a peace agreement.[88] This led to discussions on whether the Taliban representatives had been genuine emissaries of Mullah Omar or frauds; however, there was at this time no reason for the Taliban movement to negotiate further, since they had already achieved their key diplomatic aim of being seen as a legitimate party.

Media Power Projection against the ISAF Member States and the Worldwide Muslim Community

In conjunction with the application of diplomatic power, the Taliban movement also made good use of media power projection. The media campaign was aimed simultaneously at the ISAF member states and the worldwide Muslim community. Its purpose was to show the might of the Taliban, the hopelessness of continued war against them, and their legitimacy vis-à-vis the worldwide Muslim community.

Already in the 1990s, the Taliban had run a series of web sites, and this practice continued from the sanctuaries in Pakistan. Taliban web sites primarily published statements of the Leadership Council of the Islamic Emirate of Afghanistan, that is, the Taliban government, but they also published articles, weekly analyses, interviews, and reports, as well as a continuing list of news from the front. For an example of the latter, see Table 6. The emphasis was on enemies killed, in particular foreigners, ANA troops, and Arbakis (self-defence militias on the side of the government), and installations attacked.

Table 6: Sample text from Taliban web site, http://shahamat-english.com/, 11 May 2014.

11/05	Enemy vehicle blown up in Kunduz
11/05	Enemy base struck with missile strikes in Logar
11/05	Arbakis come under attack in Kunduz
11/05	Base in Logar comes under artillery rounds
11/05	46 killed, many injured in Ghazni operation
11/05	6 killed in gunfight in Nangarhar
11/05	6 Arbakis killed in Wardak
11/05	Commander along with 2 police captured in Kabul
10/05	5 enemy soldiers killed, 4 injured in Ghazni
10/05	Enemy security post destroyed in Laghman
10/05	Army installations attacked in Kabul
10/05	Enemy check point attacked
10/05	Mortar shells hit post; Arbaki killed
10/05	Clash occurs as enemy attacked in Paktika
10/05	Arbaki commander, 2 gunmen killed in Paktika
10/05	Arbaki militias suffer deadly losses in Kunduz
10/05	6 killed, two armored tanks destroyed in Kunduz
10/05	14 killed, 22 vehicles destroyed as convoy ambushed
10/05	Double martyrdom attack causes US-nato invaders heavy losses
10/05	5 puppets killed and wounded, vehicle and equipment seized
10/05	Check post attacked, 3 police killed in Marjah
10/05	3 police and ANA trooper killed in clash
10/05	5 ANA and 3 Arbakis killed in Gerishk, equipment seized
10/05	Roadside bomb rips through police truck, kills and wounds 4
10/05	Chora firefight leaves 2 puppets wounded

The Taliban movement also published a glossy, professionally produced electronic news magazine in English, with news from the front, lists of destroyed enemy aircraft, statistics of attacks, articles, interviews, and so on. This was *Islamic Emirate Afghanistan In Fight*, a publication with many colour photographs, including of killed and wounded enemy soldiers and destroyed enemy vehicles. The magazine was most likely published and distributed from Pakistan.

The Taliban also discovered, and made good use of, Twitter. As a tool for the dissemination of brief propaganda nuggets in English, Twitter eventually began to rival the Taliban web sites. The Taliban tweets focused on news from the front, with the customary emphasis on enemies killed and installations attacked. For a few examples of Taliban tweets, see Table 7.

Table 7: Sample Taliban tweets from https://twitter.com/ABalkhi, 7 May 2014

Abdulqahar Balkhi @ABalkhi A martyrdom seeker detonated car bomb on dismounted foreign troops in front of Maiwand district HQ building (#Kandahar) 3:30pm today...
Abdulqahar Balkhi @ABalkhi cont: as other troops gathered to evacuate the casualties around destroyed tank, another martyrdom seeker approached & detonated motorbike...
Abdulqahar Balkhi @ABalkhi cont: blasts killed more than 15 invaders & wounded many on final day of #KbWaleed operations, area cordoned off from public #Afghanistan
Abdulqahar Balkhi @ABalkhi A US terrorist along with Arbaki lapdog were killed, 3 US invaders wounded in missile strike on Shilgar district HQ (#Ghazni) 10am Wed.

Terrorist Power Projection against ISAF Soldiers' Family Members

While the Taliban media campaign did have the objective to influence the population in the ISAF member states, the Taliban no doubt realized that few ordinary Westerners would read their magazines, announcements, or tweets. Something more tangible was accordingly needed to influence public opinion in the ISAF member states. For this purpose, on a number of occasions apparent Taliban agents issued threats by telephone or Short Message Service (SMS) text messages to the family members of ISAF soldiers serving in Afghanistan. Some were threats that family members would be murdered, unless the soldier left Afghanistan, while others assured that the ISAF soldier would be the one killed, unless his or her family brought its offspring back home. There was little doubt that the threats were meant to intimidate the individual into resigning from service in Afghanistan. Some calls emanated from the area of operations in Afghanistan, while others originated within the ISAF member state, likely within the Afghan refugee diaspora. This showed the apparent worldwide reach of the Taliban movement. Less obvious but possibly equally serious, was that the telephone and SMS threats were directed to the private telephones of family members, which could only have been identified by somebody taking note of the private calls from ISAF garrisons to the place of origin of the troops. This showed that the Taliban had been able to infiltrate at least some of the Afghan telecom companies providing roaming services.[89]

Among the various types of international hybrid threats projection employed by the Taliban, this was the only one which was not exclusively directed and executed from Pakistan. Threatening telephone calls or text messages also emanated from within the ISAF member states, proving that the Taliban had supporters within the Afghan diaspora or among other groups overseas.

Terrorist Power Projection in the Form of Attacks Abroad

As far as is known, none of the telephone threats resulted in an actual attack. Indeed, a conspicuous characteristic of the terrorist power projection abroad of the Afghan Taliban movement was that the Taliban neither planned, nor carried out through opportunistic means, terrorist attacks *outside* Afghanistan. This did not happen during the 1990s, nor after the Taliban withdrawal into Pakistan. International terrorism would seem to have been a certain means to intimidate a foreign population into forcing a withdrawal of its military forces from Afghanistan. Yet no such attacks were carried out by the Afghan Taliban movement (although they certainly were carried out, for reasons of their own, by the Taliban movement's allies among Al-Qaida and other international terrorist groups).

The reason for this curious absence of international terrorist power projection can presumably be seen in two characteristics of the Afghan war. First, the Afghan Taliban movement had no history of engaging in terrorism abroad and many of its leaders had little interest in events elsewhere. Second, from 18 June 2004, when the first known American drone attacks was carried out,[90] a balance of terror emerged between the United States and the Taliban movement. As long as the Afghan Taliban movement did not sponsor international terrorism, the United States did not direct any drone attacks against the senior Afghan Taliban leaders in Pakistan. Whether this was a deliberate agreement with the Americans, if so no doubt negotiated with the help of Pakistani mediators, or merely an assumption on the part of the Taliban leadership remains unknown. Implicit in the understanding must have been the American realization that one eventually would need to have somebody to negotiate with in the Taliban leadership. Whether this conclusion is correct remains unknown to outside observers. Yet the fact remains that the Taliban leadership did not sponsor international terrorism, and no American drone attacks were aimed against the senior Taliban leaders in their well-known and easily recognizable compounds in a suburb of the Pakistani city of Quetta. The Afghan Taliban leadership, in a situation quite different from that of Al-Qaida, had little or nothing to fear from U.S. drone or special forces strikes until 2016, when Mullah Akhtar Muhammad Mansur was killed in a drone attack. The drone was American, but Mullah Mansur was then involved in a power struggle with other senior Taliban and Pakistani government leaders. The killing of Mansur by a U.S. drone was an exceptional event, which presumably is best understood as U.S. involvement in the power struggle with the intention to make sure that the Taliban leader who emerged as winner was one who was acceptable to Pakistan and also might become a future negotiating partner.[91]

Concluding Remarks on the Afghan Taliban's Hybrid Threats Power

The Taliban leadership had a *long-term strategy* to gain political power and impose a strict form of Islam in Afghanistan. When faced with the inability to defeat the coalition by regular military means, the long-term strategy hardened into an *intention* to fight with whatever tactics and strategies that were available. Although not conclusively proven, it seems likely that a *master plan* on how to oppose the coalition and the government of Afghanistan through a combination of particularly military power and terrorist power was worked out with the assistance of former or serving ISI officers. The actual details – the *operations plan* – grew out of developments in Afghanistan and elsewhere, in particular the limited number of foreign troops that were sent to Afghanistan. The Light Footprint policy, that is, the lack of boots on the ground, enabled the Taliban movement to reassert power in parts of the country. The *execution* phase of the operations plan began with full force only from 2005, since, despite incursions into Afghanistan, the Taliban were, as noted, earlier not under serious military pressure there or elsewhere.

This operations plan certainly included aspects of hybrid warfare and hybrid threats. Whether the Taliban actually used such terms is a moot point; events show that the concepts of hybrid warfare and threats were known and well understood by them. The Afghan Taliban leaders accordingly developed a hybrid threats capability, which they subsequently used as part of the tactics and strategies of the movement.

There is no denying that the Afghan Taliban movement enjoyed a certain level of success in its hybrid warfare campaigns. Most successes derived from the movement's capability to create and sustain a domestic hybrid capability. While the Taliban hybrid warfare capability was not in itself sufficient to defeat the international coalition, it certainly helped to create a sense of defeatism which ultimately led to President Obama's 22 June 2011 decision to end the American-led military presence in Afghanistan by 2014.[92] But this defeatism was not the result of the Taliban movement's attempts to intimidate the foreign militaries or their constituencies abroad. Instead, it derived directly from the Taliban ability to intimidate the Afghan population into turning away from the foreign military presence and the government of Afghanistan, an effect much facilitated by the general ineptitude and widespread corruption of the latter during these crucial years.

Then why did the Afghan Taliban movement neither plan, nor carry out through opportunistic means, terrorist attacks outside Afghanistan? International terrorism would seem to have been a certain means to intimidate an enemy population into forcing a withdrawal of its military forces from Afghanistan, yet no such attacks were carried out by the Afghan Taliban movement – and the behaviour of the Taliban toward the Afghan population shows that it was not reluctant to engage in violence that decided the issue. The reasons for this lack of foreign terrorism were no doubt two. First, the Afghan Taliban had no history of engaging in terrorism abroad. Second, a balance of terror emerged between the Taliban and the U.S.-led coalition. As long as the Afghan Taliban movement did not sponsor international terrorism, no drone attacks targeted senior Afghan Taliban leaders in Pakistan.

This balance of terror also illustrates the phenomenon that successful insurgencies tend to share two common features: access to sanctuaries in a neighbouring country and access to material support and financing from outside the conflict zone, either in the neighbouring country or from a diaspora population abroad. In 1961, the aforementioned Roger Trinquier, the experienced French counterinsurgency and counterterrorism practitioner, concluded that the best strategy to confront such an insurgency was a secret war against the neighbouring country, through the creation of a clandestine guerrilla force on its territory to strike the insurgent sanctuaries and serve as leverage until the material support ceased.[93] The armed drone program, which was led by the civilian Central Intelligence Agency (CIA) and utilized a combination of military and terrorist power, was in effect a high-tech version of such a clandestine force, which in the context of the present paper easily qualifies as a hybrid threats response to a hybrid threat.

There could be no purely military solution to the problem of Taliban and foreign fighters as long as they retained sanctuaries in Pakistan.[94] History abounds in cases in which guerrilla groups could not be defeated, as long as they were granted sanctuaries in neighbouring countries. A military solution could certainly have been found – if the coalition had been prepared to follow the enemy into their sanctuaries in Pakistan. However, the countries that constituted ISAF were unwilling to do so without Pakistani cooperation, and such was never likely to be forthcoming since Pakistan was sensitive about its territorial inviolability and integrity. The problem of the inviolability of the Pakistani sanctuaries of the Taliban became evident already when U.S. conventional troops launched the only major ground offensive in the 2001–2002 war against the Taliban. This was Operation Anaconda, commanded by Major General Franklin Hagenbeck and commenced on 1 March 2002 against what was reported to be a concentration of several hundred Taliban and Al-Qaida troops south of Gardez in Paktia province.[95] This was the first time when U.S. and coalition conventional forces were at the forefront of ground combat. Operation Anaconda was declared over on 18 March 2002. As before, the Taliban and Al-Qaida fighters simply dispersed and withdrew, many of them into Pakistan, when the battle turned against them. Major General Hagenbeck after the operation indicated the need to engage in hot pursuits into Pakistan, but he was on 25 March overruled by then Secretary of Defense Donald H. Rumsfeld.[96] As a direct result of Rumsfeld's decision, the Taliban and allied non-Afghan terrorist groups established bases in Pakistan, the Taliban particularly in and around Quetta and the Al-Qaida and other foreign fighters in primarily Waziristan.

How could the coalition reach and neutralize these bases? By military means, it could not, since no coalition soldiers were permitted to engage in hot pursuit into Pakistani territory. Drone warfare became the solution, and the CIA's clandestine Predator and Reaper armed drone program inflicted significant losses on terrorists and insurgents in Waziristan.[97]

The drone campaign had a strategic effect that went far beyond the killing of insurgent leaders and the disruption of insurgent networks and activities. First, data-driven as opposed to anecdotal research shows that drone strikes were associated with decreases in the incidence and lethality of terrorist attacks. They were also associated with decreases in particularly lethal terrorist tactics, including suicide and IED attacks.[98] A primary reason for this was the disruption mechanism of drone strikes. Strikes disrupted and reduced the ability of terrorists in the safe havens to operate in a cohesive and effective manner. The havens were simply not safe anymore, and the terrorists found it increasingly difficult to exercise sovereign control over their sanctuaries. Besides, the drone strikes resulted in the deaths of many terrorist leaders. This too reduced the ability of the terrorists to engage in violence elsewhere, since the decapitation of the terrorist leadership reduced its ability to plan and carry out acts of terrorism. In effect, drone attacks terrorized the terrorists, forcing them to change their activities so as not expose themselves needlessly to strikes. Besides, data indicate that drone strikes seemed to reduce terrorist activity not only in their safe havens but in their immediate neighbourhoods as well.[99] It was thus hardly surprising that Pakistan's military leadership early on tacitly agreed to the drone campaign in Waziristan, a territory which by then was beyond the control of the Pakistani military, even though it resulted in political frictions.[100]

There is thus little doubt that drone strikes aimed at the Taliban Leadership Shura in Quetta would have made an impact on the Taliban movement, had such strikes taken place. However, this particular method of hybrid warfare was not (with the one exception noted above) used by the United States against the Taliban leaders, nor did the latter respond with terrorist attacks overseas. A hybrid threat, drone warfare, was accordingly successfully used to counter another hybrid threat, that of international terrorism.

4

COUNTERING HYBRID THREATS

A successful response to hybrid threats requires a whole-of-government perspective within the public sector and preferably also a whole-of-society approach. Countermeasures against hybrid threats become more difficult to set into motion if the relevant authorities are unable to recognize the nature and common origin of the threat. A partitioned, cellular security architecture is highly unsuitable for responding to hybrid threats. No ministry, intelligence or security service, or other institution can be expected to be able to act in its own right against all of them. Complex systems require complex and comprehensive inter and intra-ministerial coordination. A comparison should be made here with other types of crisis management. If society's responsibility and resources for responding to crises are spread across many actors, collaboration between them to prepare, protect, and rebuild society in the event of severe events becomes a major challenge. A coordinated approach shared by security authorities, private businesses, civil society, and policymakers minimizes risks and offers better hope for success.

International cooperation is helpful, too. Such cooperation may be able to alleviate the negative consequences of a hostile actor's hybrid threats operation. Furthermore, international intelligence cooperation among allies is particularly important for identifying covert hybrid threats actors. Allies need to share intelligence on these actors, and on the threat itself. There are, no doubt, lessons to be learned from counterterrorism cooperation in this regard. However, a persistent problem is that countries often remain unwilling to share information that may expose own weaknesses, which for obvious reasons is what hybrid threats is all about. In comparison, the frequent unwillingness to agree on terminology within EU and NATO structures already alluded to may well be of less significance.

A hostile actor's use of non-state actors as proxies poses additional problems, but this phenomenon is so prevalent that it cannot be ignored. We have seen how non-state actors may have complex relationships with the state actors on which behalf they operate. The non-state actor may be a dependent, an ally, or a rival. Some non-state actors were established by state actors, even though they later went separate ways. The non-state actor and state actor may share objectives, or the arrangement may be one in which the non-state actor is merely hired to do a job. Relationships may be long-term, short-term, or even limited to temporary exploitation. The non-state actor may be compelled to act on behalf of the state actor, or the relationship may be a voluntary one. In each case, the cooperation may be overt or covert. Most non-state actors have independent agendas, even if they for various reasons also carry out activities based on the sponsoring state actor's agenda.

In most cases, the key reason for using non-state actors as proxies is plausible deniability. This holds true even for overt relationships, since even then the state actor can distance itself from the activities of the non-state actor. However, the employment of non-state actors as proxies raises the issue of the principal-agent relationship. While the actions of the non-state actor may be deniable, many non-state actors are difficult to control. Organised crime actors, in particular, are for hire, so anybody can use them. However, they constitute a blunt instrument and deniability is easily exposed, as was shown by the Mamayev and Chatayev cases. Moreover, not every case involving the employment of organized crime groups constitutes a hybrid threat. The Mamayev

Taliban soldiers inside the Hamid Karzai International Airport after the U.S. departure from Afghanistan. Hybrid threats power projection helped them to achieve victory. (Photo Free Malaysia Today)

Taliban fighters patrol in a former Afghan police technical. (Sidiqullah Khan/AP)

case illustrates how simple cases of hiring organized crime actors for violent activities may not, in effect, qualify as hybrid threats operations. It never reached the strategic threshold to affect at least two dimensions (domains) of power and accordingly could be handled (defended against) solely within the realm of the Ministry of Justice.

Finally, a word of caution. We have seen that hybrid threats attacks typically come from unexpected directions, and that deception always plays a major role. Yet, not every security incident is a hybrid threats operation. Do not mistake our own errors or lack of adequate planning for enemy action. But also do not assume that attacks are unthinkable. We have seen that even supposedly loyal allies have their own agendas. The Pentagon project's deployment of anti-vax media power against the Philippines comes to mind, as well as Georgia's recruitment in friendly countries of organized crime actors to carry out terrorist attacks against Russia. As noted in the introduction, in hybrid threats operations, nothing is what it seems. Prepare for the unexpected.

BIBLIOGRAPHY

Official Sources

Cohen, William S., [U.S.] Secretary of Defense. *Report of the Quadrennial Defense Review*, May 1997

Délégation des Commissions de gestion des Chambres fédérales (Confédération suisse). Affaire Crypto AG: Rapport de la Délégation des Commissions de gestion des Chambres fédérales, 2 November 2020

Doklad Gosudarstvennoy Komissii Chechenskoy Respubliki Ichkeriya o rezul'tatakh rassledovaniya intsidenta v ushchel'e Lopota Respubliki Gruziya, 29 August 2012 (http://chechenpress.org/news/3903-doklad-goskomissii-chri-o-rezultatakh-rassledovaniya-intsidenta-v-ushchele-lopota.html). Report dated 3 May 2013

Energeticheskaya strategiya Rossii na period do 2020 goda ('Energy Strategy of Russia to the Year 2020'), Government of the Russian Federation Decree No. 1234-r, 28 August 2003. Approved on 23 May 2003 and confirmed by the Russian government on 28 August 2003

European Commission. Joint Framework on Countering Hybrid Threats: A European Union Response. Joint Communication to the European Parliament and the Council, 6 April 2016 (JOIN(2016) 18 final; https://eur-lex.europa.eu/legal-content/EN/TXT/PDF/?uri=CELEX:52016JC0018)

European Commission. Joint report to the European Parliament and the Council on the Implementation of the Joint Framework on Countering Hybrid Threats – a European Union Response, 19 July 2017 (JOIN(2017) 30 final; https://ec.europa.eu/docsroom/documents/24601)

European Commission. Joint Communication to the European Parliament, the European Council and the Council: Increasing Resilience and Bolstering Capabilities to Address Hybrid Threats, 13 June 2018 (JOIN(2018) 16 final; https://eur-lex.europa.eu/legal-content/EN/TXT/PDF/?uri=CELEX:52018JC0016)

European Commission and North Atlantic Treaty Organization. Common set of proposals for the implementation of the Joint Declaration by the President of the European Council, the President of the European Commission and the Secretary General of the North Atlantic Treaty Organization, 6 December 2016

European Parliament. Joint Motion for a Resolution on Russia, the Case of Alexei Navalny, the Military Build-up on Ukraine's Border and Russian Attacks in the Czech Republic (2021/2642(RSP)), 28 April 2021, Section 8 (https://www.europarl.europa.eu/doceo/document/RC-9-2021-0236_EN.html)

European Union. Countering Hybrid Threats. Factsheet, March 2022 (https://defence-industry-space.ec.europa.eu/eu-defence-industry/hybrid-threats_en)

European Union's High Representative for Foreign Affairs and Security Policy. EU Declaration. Press Release, 24 September 2021 (www.consilium.europa.eu/en/press/press-releases/2021/09/24/

declaration-by-the-high-representative-on-behalf-of-the-european-union-on-respect-for-the-eu-s-democratic-processes)

Försvarsmakten (Swedish Armed Forces). Årsrapport *Säkerhetstjänst 2011: Militära underrättelse- och säkerhetstjänsten, MUST*. Stockholm: Försvarsmakten, 2012

Gunnarsson, Gösta. *Rapport av den särskilde utredaren för granskning av hotbilden mot och säkerhetsskyddet kring statsminister Olof Palme*. Stockholm: SOU 1989

Joint Publication (JP) 1, Joint Warfare of the Armed Forces of the United States. Washington, DC: U.S. Government Printing Office, 10 January 1995

Joint Staff Working Document: EU Operational Protocol for Countering Hybrid Threats 'EU Playbook'. Council of the European Union, 5 July 2016. Available from web site, https://www.statewatch.org/media/documents/news/2016/jul/eu-com-countering-hybrid-threats-playbook-swd-227-16.pdf

Joint Strategy Review, Asymmetric Approaches to Warfare. Washington, DC: CJCS, 1999

Judicial proceedings (Sweden), Hovrätten för Nedre Norrland, dom 2021-04-01, mål B 82-21

Judicial proceedings (Sweden), Södertörns tingsrätt, dom 2015-02-26, mål B 13656-14

National Coordinator for Security and Counterterrorism (NCTV). *Chimaera: An Analysis of the 'Hybrid Threat' Phenomenon* . The Hague: NCTV, 2019

North Atlantic Treaty Organization (NATO). Capstone Concept, Hybrid Threats Description and Context, IMSM-0292-2010, 31 May 2010

North Atlantic Treaty Organization (NATO). Operation UNIFIED PROTECTOR Final Mission Stats, Fact Sheet, 2 November 2011

North Atlantic Treaty Organization (NATO). Countering Hybrid Threats, 7 May 2024 (https://www.nato.int/cps/en/natohq/topics_156338.htm)

Public Defender of Georgia's Report, 1 December 2014 (www.ombudsman.ge/en/reports/specialuri-angarishebi/report-of-the-public-council-at-the-public-defenders-office-of-georgia-on-the-special-operation-of-28-august-2012-near-the-village-of-lapankuri-lopota-gorge-georgia.page)

State Security Service of Georgia, Statement. 1 December 2017

Syria Justice and Accountability Centre (SJAC). 'Sweden's First Steps towards Justice Prove Controversial among Syrians'. SJAC web site, 9 March 2015 (http://syriaaccountability.org/updates/2015/03/09/swedensfirststepstowardsjusticeprovecontroversialamongsyrians)

United Nations Security Council Resolution 1973 (2011), adopted on 17 March 2011 (S/RES/1973 (2011)

U.S. Army Training and Doctrine Command (TRADOC). *Operational Environment 2024-2034: Large-Scale Combat Operations*. Fort Eustis, Virginia: TRADOC, 31 July 2024

U.S. Department of Defense (DoD). *The National Defense Strategy of The United States of America*. Washington, DC: Department of Defense, March 2005

U.S. Department of Defense (DoD). *DoD Dictionary of Military and Associated Terms*. Washington, DC: Department of Defense, March 2017

U.S. Department of Justice, Office of Public Affairs. 'U.S. Charges Five Chinese Military Hackers for Cyber Espionage Against U.S. Corporations and a Labor Organization for Commercial Advantage'. Press Release, 19 May 2014 (https://www.justice.gov/opa/pr/us-charges-five-chinese-military-hackers-cyber-espionage-against-us-corporations-and-labor)

U.S. Department of Justice, Office of Public Affairs. 'Computer Hacking Conspiracy Charges Unsealed Against Members of Syrian Electronic Army'. Press Release No. 16-329, 22 March 2016 (https://www.justice.gov/opa/pr/ computer-hacking-conspiracy-charges-unsealed-against-members-syrian-electronic-army/)

U.S. Department of Justice, U.S. Attorney's Office, Southern District of New York. 'Nine Iranians Charged with Conducting Massive Cyber Theft Campaign on Behalf of The Islamic Revolutionary Guard Corps'. Press Release No. 18-089, 23 March 2018, updated 26 March 2018 (https://www.justice.gov/usao-sdny/pr/nine-iranians-charged-conducting-massive-cyber-theft-campaign-behalf-islamic)

U.S. Department of Justice, Office of Public Affairs. 'Seven International Cyber Defendants, Including "Apt41" Actors, Charged in Connection with Computer Intrusion Campaigns against More Than 100 Victims Globally'. Press Release No. 20-942, updated 16 September 2020 (https://www.justice.gov/opa/pr/seven-international-cyber-defendants-including-apt41-actors-charged-connection-computer)

U.S. Department of State, *Active Measures: A Report on the Substance and Process of Anti-U.S. Disinformation and Propaganda Campaigns*. Washington, DC: Department of State, 1986

U.S. Department of State, *Soviet Influence Activities: A Report on Active Measures and Propaganda, 1986-87*. Washington, DC: Department of State, 1987

U.S. Department of the Treasury. Frequently Asked Questions Regarding the Re-Imposition of Sanctions Pursuant to the May 8, 2018 National Security Presidential Memorandum Relating to the Joint Comprehensive Plan of Action (JCPOA), 8 May 2018

U.S. Government Accountability Office (GAO). *Hybrid Warfare: Briefing to the Subcommittee on Terrorism, Unconventional Threats and Capabilities, 10 September 2010*. Washington, DC: GAO, GAO-10-1036R, 2010

Literature

Aaronson, Michael; Sverre Diessen; Yves de Kermabon; Mary Beth Long; and Michael Miklaucic, 'NATO Countering the Hybrid Threat'. *PRISM* 2: 4 (2011): pp.111–124.

Anon. 'Remembering Our Warriors: Babar "the Great"'. *Defence Journal* (Pakistan), April 2001.

Abdur Rahman. *The Life of Abdur Rahman, Amir of Afghanistan* (London: John Murray, 2 vols., 1900)

O'Bagy, Elizabeth. *The Free Syrian Army* (Washington, DC: Institute for the Study of War, 2013)

Boghardt, Thomas. 'Operation INFEKTION: Soviet Bloc Intelligence and Its AIDS Disinformation Campaign'. *Studies in Intelligence* 53:4 (December 2009): pp.1–24.

Boulter, Jack; and Michael Fredholm [von Essen]. 'Loyalty to None, Disloyalty to All'. *Journal for Intelligence, Propaganda and Security Studies* (JIPSS) 17: 2 (2023): pp.86–96.

Caro, Carlo J. V. 'Underwater Geopolitics: How China's Control of Undersea Cables and Data Flows Reshapes Global Power', *Real Clear Defense* web site, 26 November 2024 (https://www.realcleardefense.com/articles/2024/11/26/underwater_geopolitics_1074698.htm)

Clarke, Ryan; and Stuart Lee. 'The PIRA, D-Company, and the Crime-Terror Nexus'. *Terrorism and Political Violence* 20: 3 (2008): pp.376–395

Conrad, Gerhard; and Martin Specht. *Keine Lizenz zum Töten: 30 Jahre als BND-Mann und Geheimdiplomat* (Berlin: Econ, 2022)

Dam, Bette. *Expeditie Uruzgan: De weg van Hamid Karzai naar het paleis* (Amsterdam: De Arbeiderspers, 2009)

Davis, Anthony. 'How the Taliban Became a Military Force'. William Maley (ed.). *Fundamentalism Reborn? Afghanistan and the Taliban*. New York: New York University Press, 1998: pp.43–71

Davis, Anthony. 'Struggle for Recognition'. *Jane's Defence Weekly*, 4 October 2000

Davis, Anthony. 'Foreign Fighters Step Up Activity in Afghan Civil War'. *Jane's Intelligence Review* 13: 8 (August 2001): pp.14–17

Dengg, Anton; and Michael N. Schurian. 'Zum Begriff der Hybriden Bedrohungen'. Anton Dengg and Michael Schurian (eds). *Vernetzte Unsicherheit: Hybride Bedrohungen im 21. Jahrhundert* (Vienna: Landesverteidigungsakademie, 2015): pp.23–75

Dengg, Anton; and Michael N. Schurian 'On the Concept of Hybrid Threats'. Anton Dengg and Michael Schurian (eds). *Networked Insecurity: Hybrid Threats in the 21st Century* (Vienna: Landesverteidigungsakademie, 2016): pp.25–80

Dengg, Anton; and Michael Schurian (eds). *Vernetzte Unsicherheit: Hybride Bedrohungen im 21. Jahrhundert* (Vienna: Landesverteidigungsakademie, 2015)

Dengg, Anton; and Michael Schurian (eds). *Networked Insecurity: Hybrid Threats in the 21st Century* (Vienna: Landesverteidigungsakademie, 2016)

Dubovitskiy, Natan. 'Bez neba', *Russkiy pioner* 3 (45), April 2014: pp.104–107

Evenett, Simon; and Johannes Fritz. 'Revisiting the China–Japan Rare Earths dispute of 2010'. *VoxEU* web site, 19 July 2023 (https://cepr.org/voxeu/columns/revisiting-china-japan-rare-earths-dispute-2010)

FireEye. *Double Dragon: APT41, a Dual Espionage and Cyber Crime Operation* (Milpitas, California: FireEye, Inc., 2019)

FireEye. *'Ghostwriter' Influence Campaign: Unknown Actors Leverage Website Compromises and Fabricated Content to Push Narratives Aligned with Russian Security Interests* (Milpitas, California: FireEye, Inc., July 2020)

FireEye. *Ghostwriter Update: Cyber Espionage Group UNC1151 Likely Conducts Ghostwriter Influence Activity* (Milpitas, California: FireEye, Inc., April 2021)

Fitsanakis, Joseph. 'Analysis: Mullah Mansour's Killing Will Shape Future of Afghan War'. *IntelNews*, 24 May 2016 (https://intelnews.org/2016/05/24/011907/).

Forsberg, Carl. *Politics and Power in Kandahar* (Washington, DC: Institute for the Study of War, 2010)

Fredholm [von Essen], Michael. 'The New Face of Chechen Terrorism'. *Central Asia – Caucasus Analyst,* September 2003 (Johns Hopkins University)

Fredholm [von Essen], Michael. *Afghanistan and Central Asian Security* (Stockholm: Stockholm University, Asian Cultures and Modernity 1, 2002)

Fredholm [von Essen], Michael. *The World of Central Asian Oil and Gas: Power Politics, Market Forces, and Stealth Pipelines* (Stockholm: Stockholm University, Asian Cultures and Modernity 16, 2008)

Fredholm [von Essen], Michael. 'The Need for New Policies in Afghanistan: A European's Perspective'. *Himalayan and Central Asian Studies* 15: 1–2 (2011)

Fredholm [von Essen], Michael. 'Kashmir, Afghanistan, India, and Beyond: A Taxonomy of Islamic Extremism and Terrorism in Pakistan', *Himalayan and Central Asian Studies* 15: 3 (2011), pp.24–80

Fredholm [von Essen], Michael. 'Strategies of Energy and Security in Contemporary Eurasia: Vulnerabilities and Opportunities in Russia's Energy Relationships with Europe, Central Asia, and China'. Sreemati Ganguli (ed.). *Strategising Energy: An Asian Perspective* (New Delhi: KW Publishers, 2014): pp.163–202

Fredholm [von Essen], Michael. 'Power Projection by Pipeline: Russia, Sweden, and the Hybrid Threat from the Nord Stream Project, 2005-2009'. Anton Dengg and Michael Schurian (eds). *Vernetzte Unsicherheit: Hybride Bedrohungen im 21. Jahrhundert* (Vienna: Landesverteidigungsakademie, 2015): pp.263–332

Fredholm [von Essen], Michael. 'The Hybrid Threat Capability of the Afghan Taliban Movement, 2001-2014'. Anton Dengg and Michael Schurian (eds). *Vernetzte Unsicherheit: Hybride Bedrohungen im 21. Jahrhundert* (Vienna: Landesverteidigungsakademie, 2015): pp.313–346

Fredholm [von Essen], Michael. *Transnational Organized Crime and Jihadist Terrorism: Russian-Speaking Networks in Western Europe* (London: Routledge, 2016)

Fredholm von Essen, Michael. *Hybrid Threats, the Gerasimov Doctrine, Nonlinear Warfare – or Indirect and Asymmetric Operations?* (Stockholm: IRI, 2017)

Fredholm [von Essen], Michael. *Afghanistan Beyond the Fog of War: Persistent Failure of a Rentier State* (Copenhagen: NIAS Press, 2018)

Fredholm [von Essen], Michael. 'Soviet Active Measures in West, Southeast, and East Asia with regard to Afghanistan, 1980-1982'. *Journal for Intelligence, Propaganda and Security Studies* (JIPSS) 13: 1 (2019): pp.56–74

Fredholm [von Essen], Michael. *Hemligstämplat: Svensk underrättelsetjänst från Erlander till Bildt* (Stockholm: Medström, 2020)

Fredholm [von Essen], Michael. 'The Fog of War Again Descends on Afghanistan'. *NIAS Press Blog*, 10 May 2020 (https://www.niaspress.dk)

Gasztold, Przemysław. 'Polish Military Intelligence and Its Secret Relationship with the Abu Nidal Organization'. Adrian Hänni, Thomas Riegler, and Przemysław Gasztold (eds). *Terrorism in the Cold War* 1: *State Support in Eastern Europe and the Soviet Sphere of Influence* (London: I.B. Tauris, 2020): pp.85–106

Gerasimov, Valeriy. 'Tsennost' nauki v predvidenii: Novyye vyzovy trebuyut pereosmysleniya form i sposobov vedeniya boyevykh deystviy'. *Voyenno-Promyshlennyy Kuryer* 8 (476; 27 February 2013)

Gerasimov, Valeriy. 'Mir na granyakh voyny: Malo uchityvat' segodnyashniye vyzovy, nado prognozirovat' budushiye'. *Voyenno-Promyshlennyy Kuryer* 10 (674), 15 March 2017

Giustozzi, Antonio. 'Military Adaptation by the Taliban, 2002–2011'. Theo Farrell, Frans Osinga, and James A. Russell (eds). *Military Adaptation in Afghanistan* (Stanford: Stanford University Press, 2013): pp.242–262

Giustozzi, Antonio. *Turmoil within the Taliban: A Crisis of Growth?* Central Asia Program, George Washington University: Central Asia Policy Brief 7, 2013.

Giustozzi, Antonio. *The Taliban and the 2014 Elections in Afghanistan* (Washington, DC: United States Institute of Peace, 2014)

Gohari, M. J. *The Taliban: Ascent to Power* (Oxford: Oxford Logos Society, 1999)

Gopal, Anand; Mansur Khan Mahsud; and Brian Fishman. *The Battle for Pakistan: Militancy and Conflict in North Waziristan* (Washington, DC: New America Foundation, 2010)

Grayson, George; and Samuel Logan. *The Executioner's Men, Los Zetas, Rogue Soldiers, Criminal Entrepreneurs, and the Shadow State They Created* (New Brunswick, New Jersey: Transaction Publishers, 2012)

Hammer, Carl [Michael Fredholm von Essen]. *Tide of Terror: America, Islamic Extremism, and the War on Terror* (Boulder, Colorado: Paladin Press, 2003)

Hernández, Joel. 'Terrorism, Drug Trafficking, and the Globalization of Supply'. *Perspectives on Terrorism* 7: 4 (2013): pp.41–61

Hjort, Magnus. *Den farliga fredsrörelsen: Säkerhetstjänsternas* övervakning *av fredsorganisationer, värnpliktsvägrare och FNL-grupper 1945–1990* (Stockholm: SOU 2002): p.90

Hoffman, Frank G. *Conflict in the 21st Century: The Rise of Hybrid Wars* (Arlington, Virginia: Potomac Institute for Policy Studies, 2007)

Hoffman, Frank G. 'Hybrid Warfare and Challenges'. *Joint Force Quarterly (JFQ)* 52 (2009): pp.34–39

Holliday, Joseph. *Syria's Armed Opposition* (Washington, DC: Institute for the Study of War, 2012)

Holliday, Joseph. *Syria's Maturing Insurgency* (Washington, DC: Institute for the Study of War, 2012)

Human Rights Watch (HRW). *Fueling Afghanistan's War* (HRW Press Backgrounder, 2001)

Hurska, Alla. 'Russian Attacks on Ukrainian Critical Infrastructure Become Hybrid Threat to Europe', *Eurasia Daily Monitor* 21: 74 (14 May 2024) (https://jamestown.org/program/russian-attacks-on-ukrainian-critical-infrastructure-become-hybrid-threat-to-europe/)

Jacquard, Roland. *Les archives secrètes d'Al-Qaida: Révélations sur les héritiers de Ben Laden* (Paris: Jean Picollec, 2002)

Jamieson, Alison. 'Antimafia Efforts in Italy, 1992-1997'. *Studies in Conflict & Terrorism* 21: 3 (1998): pp.233–260

Jamieson, Alison. *The Antimafia: Italy's Fight against Organized Crime* (London: Macmillan, 1999)

Johnson, A. Ross *Radio Free Europe and Radio Liberty: The CIA Years and Beyond* (Washington, DC: Woodrow Wilson Center Press with Stanford University Press, 2010)

Johnson, Thomas H. 'The Taliban Insurgency and an Analysis of *Shabnamah* (Night Letters)'. *Small Wars and Insurgencies* 18: 3 (September 2007): pp.317–344

Johnston, Patrick B.; and Anoop K. Sarbahi. *The Impact of U.S. Drone Strikes on Terrorism in Pakistan and Afghanistan*. Paper, RAND Corporation and Stanford University, 11 February 2014

Jokinen, Janne; Magnus Normark; and Michael Fredholm [von Essen]. *Hybrid Threats from Non-State Actors: A Taxonomy*. Helsinki: The European Centre of Excellence for Countering Hybrid Threats (Hybrid CoE), Hybrid CoE Research Report 6, June 2022.

Katzman, Kenneth. *Afghanistan: Post-Taliban Governance, Security, and U.S. Policy* (Washington, DC: Congressional Research Service, 21 September 2012)

Kaznacheev, Alexander. *Inside a Soviet Embassy: Experiences of a Russian Diplomat in Burma* (Philadelphia: J. B. Lippincott, 1962)

King, Amy; and Shiro Armstrong. 'Did China Really Ban Rare Earth Metals Exports to Japan?' *East Asia Forum* web site, 18 August 2013 (https://eastasiaforum.org/2013/08/18/did-china-really-ban-rare-earth-metals-exports-to-japan/)

Klein, Margarete. *Private Military Companies; A Growing Instrument in Russia's Foreign and Security Policy Toolbox*. Helsinki: European Centre of Excellence for Countering Hybrid Threats, Hybrid CoE Strategic Analysis 17, June 2019.

Kofman, Michael; Katya Migacheva; Brian Nichiporuk; Andrew Radin; Olesya Tkacheva; and Jenny Oberholtzer. *Lessons from Russia's Operations in Crimea and Eastern Ukraine* (Santa Monica, California: RAND, 2017)

Mack, Andrew. 'Why Big Nations Lose Small Wars: The Politics of Asymmetric Conflict'. *World Politics* 27: 2 (1975): pp.175–200

Magnus, Ralph H.; and Eden Naby. *Afghanistan: Mullah, Marx, and Mujahid* (Boulder, Colorado: Westview, 1998)

Maley, William (ed.). *Fundamentalism Reborn? Afghanistan and the Taliban* (New York: New York University Press, 1998)

Mandiant. *APT1: Exposing One of China's Cyber Espionage Units* (np: Mandiant, nd (2013))

Metz, Steven. 'Strategic Asymmetry'. *Military Review*, July-August 2001: pp.23–31

Mitrokhin, Vasiliy (ed.). *KGB Lexicon: The Soviet Intelligence Officer's Handbook* (London: Frank Cass, 2002)

Musharraf, Pervez. *In the Line of Fire: A Memoir* (London: Simon & Schuster, 2006)

Nord Stream AG. *Bemötande av synpunkter m.m. från den publika remissrundan* (Virum: Ramboll Oil & Gas, on behalf of Nord Stream AG, September 2009)

Nord Stream AG. *Sammanfattning av projektet* (Stockholm: Nord Stream, 30 September 2009)

Nord Stream AG. *Secure Energy for Europe: The Nord Stream Pipeline Project 2005-2012* (Zug: Nord Stream AG, 2013)

Peters, Gretchen. *Crime and Insurgency in the Tribal Areas of Afghanistan and Pakistan* (West Point: Harmony Program, Combating Terrorism Center, 2010)

Rashid, Ahmed. 'Pakistan and the Taliban'. William Maley (ed.). *Fundamentalism Reborn? Afghanistan and the Taliban* (New York: New York University Press, 1998): pp.72–89

Rashid, Ahmed. 'Heart of Darkness'. *Far Eastern Economic Review,* 5 August 1999: pp.8–12

Rashid, Ahmed. 'The Taliban: Exporting Extremism'. *Foreign Affairs,* November/December 1999: pp.22–35

Rashid, Ahmed. *Taliban: Islam, Oil and the New Great Game in Central Asia* (London: I. B. Tauris, 2000)

Rashid, Ahmed. *Jihad: The Rise of Militant Islam in Central Asia* (New Haven: Yale University Press, 2002)

Rashid, Ahmed. 'The Truth behind America's Taliban Talks'. *Financial Times*, 29 June 2011 (http://blogs.ft.com)

Rassler, Don; and Vahid Brown. *The Haqqani Nexus and the Evolution of al-Qa'ida* (West Point: Harmony Program, Combating Terrorism Center, 2011)

Ray, Jayanta Kumar. *India's Foreign Relations, 1947-2007* (New Delhi: Routledge, 2011)

Roggio, Bill, and Alexander Mayer. *Charting the Data for US Airstrikes in Pakistan, 2004–2010* (www.longwarjournal.org)

Saikal, Amin. 'The Rabbani Government, 1992–1996'. William Maley (ed.). *Fundamentalism Reborn? Afghanistan and the Taliban* (New York: New York University Press, 1998): pp.29–42

Smirnov, Alexej. *Det första stora kriget* (Stockholm: Medströms Bokförlag, 2009)

Stanford Internet Observatory. *Unheard Voice: Evaluating Five Years of Pro-Western Covert Influence Operations* (Stanford, California: Graphika and Stanford Internet Observatory, 24 August 2022)

Terazawa, Tatsuya. 'How Japan Solved Its Rare Earth Minerals Dependency Issue'. *World Economic Forum* web site, 13 October 2023 (https://www.weforum.org/stories/2023/10/japan-rare-earth-minerals/)

Thomas, Timothy L. 'Deciphering Asymmetry's Word Game'. *Military Review*, July-August 2001: pp.32–37

Thomas, Timothy L. *Russia Military Strategy: Impacting 21st Century Reform and Geopolitics* (Fort Leavenworth, Kansas: Foreign Military Studies Office (FMSO), 2015)

Thomas, Timothy L. 'Russia's Military Strategy and Ukraine: Indirect, Asymmetric—and Putin-Led'. *Journal of Slavic Military Studies* 28 (2015): pp.445–461

Thoumi, Francisco E. 'Colombian Organized Crime: From Drug Trafficking to Parastatal Bands and Widespread Corruption'. Dina Siegel and Henk van de Bunt (eds). *Traditional Organized Crime in the Modern World: Responses to Socioeconomic Change* (New York: Springer, 2012): pp.131–148

Trinquier, Roger. *Modern Warfare: A French View of Counterinsurgency* (Westport, Connecticut: Praeger Security International, 2006). First published in French in 1961 as *La guerre moderne*.

Treverton, Gregory F.; Andrew Thvedt; Alicia R. Chen; Kathy Lee; and Madeline McCue. *Addressing Hybrid Threats* (Stockholm: Center for Asymmetric Threat Studies (CATS), Swedish Defence University/ Helsinki: European Centre of Excellence for Countering Hybrid Threats (Hybrid CoE), 2018)

Newspaper Reports

'Aleppo Syria: Global Shows of Solidarity over Aleppo'. BBC News, 15 December 2016 (https://www.bbc.com/news/world-middle-east-38327586)

Araullo, Kenneth. 'Reinsurers Grapple with Hybrid Cyber Threat Complexity – CyberCube'. *Reinsurance Business* web site, 29 November 2024 (https://www.insurancebusinessmag.com/us/news/reinsurance/reinsurers-grapple-with-hybrid-cyber-threat-complexity--cybercube-516025.aspx)

Bing, Chris; and Joel Schechtman. 'Pentagon Ran Secret Anti-Vax Campaign to Undermine China during Pandemic'. Reuters, 14 June 2024 (https://www.reuters.com/investigates/special-report/usa-covid-propaganda/)

Borger, Julian; and Martin Chulov. 'Al-Jazeera Footage Captures "Western Troops on the Ground" in Libya'. *The Guardian*, 30 May 2011 (https://www.theguardian.com/world/2011/may/30/western-troops-on-ground-libya)

'Crack SAS Troops Hunt Gaddafi Weapons inside Libya'. *The Mirror*, 20 March 2011 (https://www.mirror.co.uk/news/uk-news/crack-sas-troops-hunt-gaddafi-117405)

Fielding, Nick; and Ian Cobain. 'Revealed: US Spy Operation That Manipulates Social Media'. *The Guardian*, 17 March 2011 (https://amp.theguardian.com/technology/2011/mar/17/us-spy-operation-social-networks)

'Germany warns Russia over cyberattacks ahead of election'. *Deutsche Welle*, 6 September 2021 (www.dw.com/en/germany-warns-russia-over-cyberattacks-ahead-of-election/a-59101191)

Gutterman, Steve. 'Putin Puts Troops in Western Russia on Alert in Drill'. Reuters, 26 February 2014 (https://www.reuters.com/article/us-ukraine-crisis-russia-military-idUSBREA1P0RW20140226/)

Moreau, Ron. 'Taliban Forces Desperate to Hear from Their Absent Leader, Mullah Omar'. *The Daily Beast*, 1 May 2013

Modderkolk, Huib. 'Sabotage in Iran: Een missie in duisternis'. *De Volksrant*, 8 January 2024

'NATO Says Russian Hybrid Attack Intensify on Members' Territories'. Reuters, 2 May 2024 (https://www.reuters.com/world/europe/nato-says-russian-hybrid-attack-intensify-members-territories-2024-05-02/)

Norton, Ben. 'Leaked Docs Expose Massive Syria Propaganda Operation by Western Govt Contractors & Media'. *Consortium News*, 12 October 2020 (https://consortiumnews.com/2020/10/12/leaked-docs-expose-massive-syria-propaganda-operation-by-western-govt-contractors-media/)

Pancevski, Bojan. 'U.S. Officials Say Huawei Can Covertly Access Telecom Networks'. *Wall Street Journal*, 12 February 2020 (https://www.wsj.com/articles/u-s-officials-say-huawei-can-covertly-access-telecom-networks-11581452256)

Peel, Michael. 'Swift to Comply with US Sanctions on Iran in Blow to EU'. *Financial Times*, 5 November 2018 (ft.com/content/8f16f8aa-e104-11e8-8e70-5e22a430c1ad)

Pirro, Deirdre. 'The Olive Tree of Peace: The Massacre in Via dei Georgofili'. *The Florentine* 164 (24 May 2012)

Newman, Lily Hay. "Ghostwriter' Looks Like a Purely Russian Op – Except It's Not'. *Wired*, 16 November 2021 (www.wired.com/story/ghostwriter-hackers-belarus-russia-misinformationo)

Regan, Tom. 'When Contemplating War, Beware of Babies in Incubators'. *Christian Science Monitor*, 6 September 2002 (https://www.csmonitor.com/2002/0906/p25s02-cogn.html)

'Russische Gruppe »Ghostwriter« attackiert offenbar Parlamentarier'. *Der Spiegel*, 26 March 2021 (www.spiegel.de/politik/deutschland/russischer-hack-erneute-attacke-hack-auf-bundestag-sieben-abgeordnete-betroffen-a-75e1adbe-4462-4e30-bd94-96796aed6b8a)

Selyukh, Alina. 'Hackers Send Fake Market-moving AP Tweet on White House Explosions'. Reuters, 23 April 2013 (https://www.reuters.com/article/net-us-usa-whitehouse-ap-idUSBRE93M12Y20130423)

'Undersea "Hybrid Warfare" Threatens Security of 1bn, NATO Commander Warns'. *The Guardian*, 16 April 2024 (https://www.theguardian.com/world/2024/apr/16/undersea-hybrid-warfare-threatens-security-of-1bn-nato-commander-warns)

Untersinger, Martin. 'Ghostwriter, des pirates informatiques prorusses qui s'invitent dans la guerre en Ukraine'. *Le Monde*, 28 May 2022 (www.lemonde.fr/pixels/article/2022/04/28/ghostwriter-des-pirates-informatiques-prorusses-qui-s-invitent-dans-la-guerre-en-ukraine_6124044_4408996.html)

'US Mainland Ultra-vulnerable to China, Russia Hybrid Attacks'. *Asia Times*, 5 August 2024 (https://asiatimes.com/2024/08/us-mainland-ultra-vulnerable-to-china-russia-hybrid-attacks/)

'Yoon Urges Readiness for NK's 'Hybrid Warfare'', *The Korea Herald*, 19 August 2024 (https://www.koreaherald.com/view.php?ud=20240819050516)

ENDNOTES

Introduction

1 'Undersea "Hybrid Warfare" Threatens Security of 1bn, NATO Commander Warns', *The Guardian*, 16 April 2024 (https://www.theguardian.com/world/2024/apr/16/undersea-hybrid-warfare-threatens-security-of-1bn-nato-commander-warns).

2 'NATO Says Russian Hybrid Attack Intensify on Members' Territories', Reuters, 2 May 2024 (https://www.reuters.com/world/europe/nato-says-russian-hybrid-attack-intensify-members-territories-2024-05-02/).

3 Alla Hurska, 'Russian Attacks on Ukrainian Critical Infrastructure Become Hybrid Threat to Europe', *Eurasia Daily Monitor* 21: 74 (14 May 2024) (https://jamestown.org/program/russian-attacks-on-ukrainian-critical-infrastructure-become-hybrid-threat-to-europe/).

4 U.S. Army Training and Doctrine Command (TRADOC), *Operational Environment 2024-2034: Large-Scale Combat Operations* (Fort Eustis, Virginia: TRADOC, 31 July 2024), pp.4, 20.

5 'US Mainland Ultra-vulnerable to China, Russia Hybrid Attacks', *Asia Times*, 5 August 2024 (https://asiatimes.com/2024/08/us-mainland-ultra-vulnerable-to-china-russia-hybrid-attacks/).

6 'Yoon Urges Readiness for NK's 'Hybrid Warfare'', *The Korea Herald*, 19 August 2024 (https://www.koreaherald.com/view.php?ud=20240819050516).

7 Kenneth Araullo, 'Reinsurers Grapple with Hybrid Cyber Threat Complexity – CyberCube', *Reinsurance Business* web site, 29 November 2024 (https://www.insurancebusinessmag.com/us/news/reinsurance/reinsurers-grapple-with-hybrid-cyber-threat-complexity--cybercube-516025.aspx).

8 Comment during the Publication Event of the Non-State Actor Report, European Centre of Excellence for Countering Hybrid Threats (Hybrid CoE), Helsinki, 9 June 2022. In short, the representative implied that we must do unto them before they do unto us. And, interestingly, that the Western world indeed already is doing exactly this.

Chapter 1

1 A notable exception being Andrew Mack, 'Why Big Nations Lose Small Wars: The Politics of Asymmetric Conflict', *World Politics* 27: 2 (1975): pp.175–200.

2 Joint Publication (JP) 1, *Joint Warfare of the Armed Forces of the United States* (Washington, DC: US Government Printing Office, 10 January 1995), pp.IV-10 and IV-11.

3 Secretary of Defense William S. Cohen, *Report of the Quadrennial Defense Review*, May 1997, Section II.

4 *Joint Strategy Review, Asymmetric Approaches to Warfare* (Washington, DC: CJCS, 1999), p.2.

5 Timothy L. Thomas, 'Deciphering Asymmetry's Word Game', *Military Review*, July-August 2001, pp.32–37, on p.32.

6 Steven Metz, 'Strategic Asymmetry', *Military Review*, July-August 2001, pp.23–31, on pp.24, 31.

7 Frank G. Hoffman, *Conflict in the 21st Century: The Rise of Hybrid Wars* (Arlington, Virginia: Potomac Institute for Policy Studies, 2007), p.28.

8 Hoffman, *Conflict in the 21st Century*, p.28.

9 Hoffman, *Conflict in the 21st Century*, p.7.

10 Frank G. Hoffman, 'Hybrid Warfare and Challenges', *Joint Force Quarterly (JFQ)* 52 (2009), pp.34–39, on p.35.

11 U.S. Department of Defense. *The National Defense Strategy of The United States of America* (Washington, DC: Department of Defense, March 2005), p.2.

12 Hoffman, *Conflict in the 21st Century*, p.8.

13 Hoffman, *Conflict in the 21st Century*, pp.26–27.

14 United States Government Accountability Office (GAO), *Hybrid Warfare: Briefing to the Subcommittee on Terrorism, Unconventional Threats and Capabilities, 10 September 2010* (Washington, DC: GAO, GAO-10-1036R, 2010), p.1.

15 GAO, *Hybrid Warfare*, p.2.

16 GAO, *Hybrid Warfare*, p.2.

17 GAO, *Hybrid Warfare*, p.14.

18 GAO, *Hybrid Warfare*, p.18.

19 Cited in GAO, *Hybrid Warfare*, p.15.

20 North Atlantic Treaty Organization (NATO). Capstone Concept, Hybrid Threats Description and Context, IMSM-0292-2010, 31 May 2010. Cited in Michael Aaronson, Sverre Diessen, Yves de Kermabon, Mary Beth Long, and Michael Miklaucic, 'NATO Countering the Hybrid Threat', *PRISM* 2: 4 (2011), pp.111–124, on p.115.

21 Aaronson et al, 'NATO Countering the Hybrid Threat', p.115.

22 Valeriy Gerasimov, 'Tsennost' nauki v predvidenii: Novyye vyzovy trebuyut pereosmysleniya form i sposobov vedeniya boyevykh deystviy', *Voyenno-Promyshlennyy Kuryer* 8 (476; 27 February 2013), pp.1, 2–3.

23 Michael Fredholm von Essen, *Hybrid Threats, the Gerasimov Doctrine, Nonlinear Warfare – or Indirect and Asymmetric Operations?* (Stockholm: IRI, 2017).

24 Natan Dubovitskiy, 'Bez neba', *Russkiy pioner* 3 (45), April 2014, pp.104–107. The story, dated 12 March 2014, is available online at http://ruspioner.ru/honest/m/single/4131.

25 Timothy L. Thomas, 'Russia's Military Strategy and Ukraine: Indirect, Asymmetric—and Putin-Led', *Journal of Slavic Military Studies* 28 (2015), pp.445–461; Timothy L. Thomas, *Russia Military Strategy: Impacting 21st Century Reform and Geopolitics* (Fort Leavenworth, Kansas: Foreign Military Studies Office (FMSO), 2015), p.37.

26 Valeriy Gerasimov, 'Mir na granyakh voyny: Malo uchityvat' segodnyashniye vyzovy, nado prognozirovat' budushiye', *Voyenno-Promyshlennyy Kuryer* 10 (674), 15 March 2017.

27 Vasiliy Mitrokhin (ed.), *KGB Lexicon: The Soviet Intelligence Officer's Handbook* (London: Frank Cass, 2002), p.13.

28 Anton Dengg and Michael N. Schurian, 'Zum Begriff der Hybriden Bedrohungen', Anton Dengg and Michael Schurian (eds), *Vernetzte Unsicherheit: Hybride Bedrohungen im 21. Jahrhundert* (Vienna: Landesverteidigungsakademie, 2015), pp.23–75, on pp.29–39, 43–46; Anton Dengg and Michael N. Schurian, 'On the Concept of Hybrid Threats', Anton Dengg and Michael Schurian (eds), *Networked Insecurity: Hybrid Threats in the 21st Century* (Vienna: Landesverteidigungsakademie, 2016), pp.25–80, on pp.31–41, 46–48.

29 Dengg and Schurian (*Vernetzte Unsicherheit*), p.25.

30 Since no agency then formally worked with non-military hybrid threats, the invitation arrived in a somewhat roundabout way through the Swedish unit of the EU Police Mission in Afghanistan (EUPOL Afghanistan), from which it reached the head of the Swedish National Centre for Terrorist Threat Assessment (NCT), who commissioned the present author to participate in the Austrian project as Sweden's representative. In 2014, the NCT handed over the project to the Swedish Police Authority which the present author represented from this year until 2016, when the project's final English-language report was published. In addition, this author contributed several case studies to the Austrian report, which he wrote in a semi-private capacity and as part of academic research.

31 Dengg and Schurian, *Vernetzte Unsicherheit*, p.37. See also the English-language edition later published as Dengg and Schurian, *Networked Insecurity*, pp.38–39.

32 Dengg and Schurian, *Vernetzte Unsicherheit*, pp.55–56.

33 European Commission, Joint Framework on Countering Hybrid Threats: A European Union Response, Joint Communication to the European Parliament and the Council, 6 April 2016 (JOIN(2016) 18 final; https://eur-lex.europa.eu/legal-content/EN/TXT/PDF/?uri=CELEX:52016JC0018).

34 European Commission, Joint Framework on Countering Hybrid Threats, p.2.

35 European Commission, Joint report to the European Parliament and the Council on the Implementation of the Joint Framework on Countering Hybrid Threats – a European Union Response, 19 July 2017 (JOIN(2017) 30 final; https://ec.europa.eu/docsroom/documents/24601), p.4.

36 European Commission, Joint report to the European Parliament and the Council on the Implementation of the Joint Framework on Countering Hybrid Threats, p.15.

37 Joint Staff Working Document: EU Operational Protocol for Countering Hybrid Threats 'EU Playbook', Council of the European Union, 5 July 2016, Available from web site, https://www.statewatch.org/media/documents/news/2016/jul/eu-com-countering-hybrid-threats-playbook-swd-227-16.pdf.

38 Gerhard Conrad and Martin Specht, *Keine Lizenz zum Töten: 30 Jahre als BND-Mann und Geheimdiplomat* (Berlin: Econ, 2022), pp.299–300.

39 European Commission, Joint Framework on Countering Hybrid Threats, p.2.

40 National Coordinator for Security and Counterterrorism (NCTV). *Chimaera: An Analysis of the 'Hybrid Threat' Phenomenon* (The Hague: NCTV, 2019), 6. The report was originally written in the autumn of 2016, but then classified as RESTRICTED.

41 Conrad and Specht, *Keine Lizenz zum Töten*, pp.299–300.

42 NATO, Countering Hybrid Threats, 7 May 2024. (https://www.nato.int/cps/en/natohq/topics_156338.htm).

43 European Commission, Joint Communication to the European Parliament, the European Council and the Council: Increasing Resilience and Bolstering Capabilities to Address Hybrid Threats, 13 June 2018 (JOIN(2018) 16 final; https://eur-lex.europa.eu/legal-content/EN/TXT/PDF/?uri=CELEX:52018JC0016), p.1.

44 Common set of proposals for the implementation of the Joint Declaration by the President of the European Council, the President of the European Commission and the Secretary General of the North Atlantic Treaty Organization, 6 December 2016.

45 Hybrid CoE web site (https://www.hybridcoe.fi/hybrid-threats-as-a-phenomenon/), as accessed on 12 December 2024.

46 Abdur Rahman, *The Life of Abdur Rahman, Amir of Afghanistan* 2 (London: John Murray, 1900), pp.239–240.

47 Roger Trinquier, *Modern Warfare: A French View of Counterinsurgency* (Westport, Connecticut: Praeger Security International, 2006), p.5. First published in French in 1961.

48 Trinquier, *Modern Warfare*, p.5.

49 Trinquier, *Modern Warfare*, pp.5, 7.

50 Trinquier, *Modern Warfare*, p.23.

51 Trinquier, *Modern Warfare*, pp.20–21.

52 Trinquier, *Modern Warfare*, pp.77, 80–84.

Chapter 2

1 Michael Fredholm von Essen, *Transnational Organized Crime and Jihadist Terrorism: Russian-Speaking Networks in Western Europe* (London: Routledge, 2016), pp.30–33; Michael Fredholm von Essen, 'The Hybrid Threat Capability of the Afghan Taliban Movement, 2001-2014', Anton Dengg and Michael Schurian (eds), *Vernetzte Unsicherheit: Hybride Bedrohungen im 21. Jahrhundert* (Vienna: Landesverteidigungsakademie, 2015), pp.313–346. On the PKK, see below.

2 European Union, Countering Hybrid Threats, Factsheet, March 2022 (https://defence-industry-space.ec.europa.eu/eu-defence-industry/hybrid-threats_en).

3 Some of the case studies in this book were prepared by the present author for inclusion in Janne Jokinen, Magnus Normark, and Michael Fredholm von Essen, *Hybrid Threats from Non-State Actors: A Taxonomy* (Helsinki: The European Centre of Excellence for Countering Hybrid Threats (Hybrid CoE), Hybrid CoE Research Report 6, June 2022.

4 U.S. Department of Defense (DoD), *DoD Dictionary of Military and Associated Terms* (Washington, DC: DoD, March 2017), pp.37, 58, 180.

5 Steve Gutterman, 'Putin Puts Troops in Western Russia on Alert in Drill', Reuters, 26 February 2014 (https://www.reuters.com/article/us-ukraine-crisis-russia-military-idUSBREA1P0RW20140226/).

6 Gregory F. Treverton, Andrew Thvedt, Alicia R. Chen, Kathy Lee, and Madeline McCue, *Addressing Hybrid Threats* (Stockholm: Center for Asymmetric Threat Studies (CATS), Swedish Defence University/Helsinki: European Centre of Excellence for Countering Hybrid Threats (Hybrid CoE), 2018), pp.16–20.

7 Treverton et al., *Addressing Hybrid Threats*, p.18.

8 Michael Kofman, Katya Migacheva, Brian Nichiporuk, Andrew Radin, Olesya Tkacheva, and Jenny Oberholtzer, *Lessons from Russia's Operations in Crimea and Eastern Ukraine* (Santa Monica, California: RAND, 2017), pp.5–6.

9 North Atlantic Treaty Organization (NATO), Operation UNIFIED PROTECTOR Final Mission Stats, Fact Sheet, 2 November 2011.

10 United Nations Security Council Resolution 1973 (2011), adopted on 17 March 2011 (S/RES/1973 (2011), p.3.

11 Julian Borger and Martin Chulov, 'Al-Jazeera Footage Captures "Western Troops on the Ground" in Libya', *The Guardian*, 30 May 2011 (https://www.theguardian.com/world/2011/may/30/western-troops-on-ground-libya).

12 'Crack SAS Troops Hunt Gaddafi Weapons inside Libya', *The Mirror*, 20 March 2011 (https://www.mirror.co.uk/news/uk-news/crack-sas-troops-hunt-gaddafi-117405).

13 Borger and Chulov, 'Al-Jazeera Footage Captures "Western Troops on the Ground" in Libya'.

14 Huib Modderkolk, 'Sabotage in Iran: Een missie in duisternis', *De Volksrant*, 8 January 2024.

15 U.S. Department of Justice, U.S. Attorney's Office, Southern District of New York, 'Nine Iranians Charged With Conducting Massive Cyber Theft Campaign On Behalf Of The Islamic Revolutionary Guard Corps', Press Release No. 18-089, 23 March 2018, updated 26 March 2018 (https://www.justice.gov/usao-sdny/pr/nine-iranians-charged-conducting-massive-cyber-theft-campaign-behalf-islamic).

16 FireEye, *Double Dragon: APT41, a Dual Espionage and Cyber Crime Operation* (Milpitas, California: FireEye, Inc., 2019); U.S. Department of Justice, Office of Public Affairs, 'Seven International Cyber Defendants, Including "Apt41" Actors, Charged in Connection with Computer Intrusion Campaigns against More Than 100 Victims Globally', Press Release No. 20-942, updated 16 September 2020 (https://www.justice.gov/opa/pr/seven-international-cyber-defendants-including-apt41-actors-charged-connection-computer).

17 Mandiant, *APT1: Exposing One of China's Cyber Espionage Units* (np: Mandiant, nd (2013)).

18 U.S. Department of Justice, Office of Public Affairs, 'U.S. Charges Five Chinese Military Hackers for Cyber Espionage Against U.S. Corporations and a Labor Organization for Commercial Advantage', Press Release, 19 May 2014 (https://www.justice.gov/opa/pr/us-charges-five-chinese-military-hackers-cyber-espionage-against-us-corporations-and-labor).

19 Ryan Clarke and Stuart Lee, 'The PIRA, D-Company, and the Crime-Terror Nexus', *Terrorism and Political Violence* 20: 3 (2008), pp.376–395, on pp.385–391; Fredholm von Essen, *Transnational Organized Crime and Jihadist Terrorism*, 28. On ISI and LeT, see also Michael Fredholm von Essen, 'Kashmir, Afghanistan, India, and Beyond: A Taxonomy of Islamic Extremism and Terrorism in Pakistan', *Himalayan and Central Asian Studies* 15: 3 (2011), pp.24–80.

20 Judicial proceedings, Hovrätten för Nedre Norrland, dom 2021-04-01, mål B 82-21.

21 Margarete Klein, *Private Military Companies; A Growing Instrument in Russia's Foreign and Security Policy Toolbox* (Helsinki: European Centre of Excellence for Countering Hybrid Threats, Hybrid CoE Strategic Analysis 17, June 2019).

22 Joseph Holliday, *Syria's Armed Opposition* (Washington, DC: Institute for the Study of War, 2012), p.14.

23 Joseph Holliday, *Syria's Maturing Insurgency* (Washington, DC: Institute for the Study of War, 2012), p.9; Elizabeth O'Bagy, *The Free Syrian Army* (Washington, DC: Institute for the Study of War, 2013), p.11.

24 Judicial proceedings, Södertörns tingsrätt, dom 2015-02-26, mål B 13656-14.

25 Syria Justice and Accountability Centre (SJAC), 'Sweden's First Steps towards Justice Prove Controversial among Syrians', SJAC web site, 9 March 2015 (http://syriaaccountability.org/updates/2015/03/09/swedensfirststepstowardsjusticeprovecontroversialamongsyrians).

26 Michael Fredholm von Essen, *Afghanistan Beyond the Fog of War: Persistent Failure of a Rentier State* (Copenhagen: NIAS Press, 2018), pp.157–158.

27 Fredholm von Essen, *Transnational Organized Crime and Jihadist Terrorism*, pp.175–178, with references, most importantly Public Defender of Georgia's final report published on 1 December 2014 (www.ombudsman.ge/en/reports/specialuri-angarishebi/report-of-the-public-council-at-the-public-defenders-office-of-georgia-on-the-special-operation-of-28-august-2012-near-the-village-of-lapankuri-lopota-gorge-georgia.page).

28 Doklad Gosudarstvennoy Komissii Chechenskoy Respubliki Ichkeriya o rezul'tatakh rassledovaniya intsidenta v ushchel'e Lopota Respubliki Gruziya, 29 August 2012 (http://chechenpress.org/news/3903-doklad-goskomissii-chri-o-rezultatakh-rassledovaniya-intsidenta-v-ushchele-lopota.html). Report dated 3 May 2013.

29 Statement of the State Security Service of Georgia, 1 December 2017.

30 Przemysław Gasztold, 'Polish Military Intelligence and Its Secret Relationship with the Abu Nidal Organization', Adrian Hänni, Thomas Riegler, and Przemysław Gasztold (eds), *Terrorism in the Cold War* 1: *State Support in Eastern Europe and the Soviet Sphere of Influence* (London: I.B. Tauris, 2020), pp.85–106.

31 *Energeticheskaya strategiya Rossii na period do 2020 goda* ('Energy Strategy of Russia to the Year 2020'), Government of the Russian Federation Decree No. 1234-r, 28 August 2003. Approved on 23 May 2003 and confirmed by the Russian government on 28 August 2003.

32 *Russian Petroleum Investor* 14: 10 (November/December 2005), pp.46, 51.

33 NEGP Press Release, 9 December 2005 (www.negp.info; defunct); *Russian Petroleum Investor* 15: 2 (February 2006), p.12. The project was then known as NEGP.

34 *Russian Petroleum Investor* 15: 2 (February 2006), 10; *Russian Petroleum Investor* 15: 6 (June/July 2006), p.26.

35 Sweden was one such country. For details, see Michael Fredholm von Essen, 'Power Projection by Pipeline: Russia, Sweden, and the Hybrid Threat from the Nord Stream Project, 2005-2009', Anton Dengg and Michael Schurian (eds), *Vernetzte Unsicherheit: Hybride Bedrohungen im 21. Jahrhundert* (Vienna: Landesverteidigungsakademie, 2015), pp.263–332, with references.

36 *Helsingin Sanomat* (Finland), 15 August 2008 (www.hs.fi).

37 United Nations Convention on the Law of the Sea of 10 December 1982, Article 79.

38 Convention on Environmental Impact Assessment in a Transboundary Context, signed at Espoo, Finland, on 25 February 1991.

39 Swedish television station TV4 investigative news program *Kalla fakta*, 15 February 2009 (www.tv4.se).

40 *Kalla fakta*, 15 February 2009. See also Nord Stream, *Secure Energy for Europe: The Nord Stream Pipeline Project 2005-2012* (Zug: Nord Stream, 2013), p.129.

41 Nord Stream, *Secure Energy for Europe*, p.121.

42 Nord Stream AG, *Bemötande av synpunkter m.m. från den publika remissrundan* (Virum: Ramboll Oil & Gas, on behalf of Nord Stream AG, September 2009), p.121.

43 *Kalla fakta*, 15 February 2009.

44 *Kalla fakta*, 15 February 2009; Kristoffer Morén, in *Baltic Worlds* 4, 2010, p.15.

45 *Resumé*, 9 July 2008 (www.resume.se); *Kalla fakta*, 15 February 2009; *Nyhetskanalen*, 15 February 2009 (http://nyhetskanalen.se); *Dagens Nyheter* (Sweden), 15 February 2009.

46 Nord Stream, *Sammanfattning av projektet* (Stockholm: Nord Stream, 30 September 2009), p.5.

47 Nord Stream, *Secure Energy for Europe*, p.71.

48 Alexej Smirnov, *Det första stora kriget* (Stockholm: Medströms Bokförlag, 2009).

49 Hill and Knowlton web site, www.hillandknowlton.co.uk. The web site mentioned the firm's successful work for Nord Stream but did not offer access to details with regard to the project.

50 AMEC Communication Effectiveness Awards (http://amecorg.com/wp-content/uploads/2011/08/amec_awards_2010_winners.pdf).

51 Nord Stream, *Secure Energy for Europe*, pp.76, 133, 141, 240. By late May 2012, Nord Stream announced plans for a third and fourth line. Ibid., p.75.

52 Nord Stream, *Sammanfattning av projektet*, p.6. In fact, this was the total cost of the environmental studies, route surveys, and technical planning and many of these would in any case have been necessary for the project. Nord Stream, *Secure Energy for Europe*, pp.43, 58, 72.

53 For further details on these goals, see Fredholm von Essen, 'Power Projection by Pipeline', pp.263–332.

54 For the origin of the TAPI project, see Michael Fredholm von Essen, *The World of Central Asian Oil and Gas: Power Politics, Market Forces, and Stealth Pipelines* (Stockholm: Stockholm University, Asian Cultures and Modernity 16, 2008), p.58.

55 Tatsuya Terazawa, 'How Japan Solved Its Rare Earth Minerals Dependency Issue', *World Economic Forum* web site, 13 October 2023 (https://www.weforum.org/stories/2023/10/japan-rare-earth-minerals/).

56 Amy King and Shiro Armstrong, 'Did China Really Ban Rare Earth Metals Exports to Japan?' *East Asia Forum* web site, 18 August 2013 (https://eastasiaforum.org/2013/08/18/did-china-really-ban-rare-earth-metals-exports-to-japan/); Simon Evenett and Johannes Fritz, 'Revisiting the China–Japan Rare Earths dispute of 2010', *VoxEU* web site, 19 July 2023 (https://cepr.org/voxeu/columns/revisiting-china-japan-rare-earths-dispute-2010).

57 Terazawa, 'How Japan Solved Its Rare Earth Minerals Dependency Issue'.

58 Japan's dependence on the United States was in fact yet more serious. In 1940, Japan was also 66.9% dependent on American iron imports, and 66.2% dependent on American machine tools. As for oil, 24.9% of imports came from the Dutch East Indies and only 8.8% from other sources.

59 Michael Fredholm von Essen, 'Strategies of Energy and Security in Contemporary Eurasia: Vulnerabilities and Opportunities in Russia's Energy Relationships with Europe, Central Asia, and China', Sreemati Ganguli (ed.), *Strategising Energy: An Asian Perspective* (New Delhi: KW Publishers, 2014), pp.163–202, on p.196.

60 SWIFT Press Release, 15 March 2012 (SWIFT ist nach Beschluss des EU-Rats angewiesen, von Sanktionen betroffene iranische Banken von seinen Services auszuschließen).

61 U.S. Department of the Treasury, Frequently Asked Questions Regarding the Re-Imposition of Sanctions Pursuant to the May 8, 2018 National Security Presidential Memorandum Relating to the Joint Comprehensive Plan of Action (JCPOA), 8 May 2018, p.3. The same threat was repeated in the 6 August 2018 update of the document.

62 Iran Threat Reduction and Syria Human Rights Act of 2012, Public Law pp.112–158.

63 Michael Peel, 'Swift to Comply with US Sanctions on Iran in Blow to EU', *Financial Times*, 5 November 2018 (ft.com/content/8f16f8aa-e104-11e8-8e70-5e22a430c1ad).

64 SWIFT web site (https://www.swift.com/about-us/legal/compliance-0/swift-and-sanctions/).

65 See, e.g., European Parliament, Joint Motion for a Resolution on Russia, the Case of Alexei Navalny, the Military Build-up on Ukraine's Border and Russian Attacks in the Czech Republic (2021/2642(RSP)), 28 April 2021, Section 8 (https://www.europarl.europa.eu/doceo/document/RC-9-2021-0236_EN.html).

66 Alina Selyukh, 'Hackers Send Fake Market-moving AP Tweet on White House Explosions', Reuters, 23 April 2013 (https://www.reuters.com/article/net-us-usa-whitehouse-ap-idUSBRE93M12Y20130423); U.S. Department of Justice, Office of Public Affairs, 'Computer Hacking Conspiracy Charges Unsealed Against Members of Syrian Electronic Army', Press Release No. 16-329, 22 March 2016 (https://www.justice.gov/opa/pr/ computer-hacking-conspiracy-charges-unsealed-against-members- syrian-electronic-army/).

67 For full details on the Pakistani involvement in the establishment of the Afghan Taliban, which was noted by diplomats at the time, see Fredholm von Essen, *Afghanistan Beyond the Fog of War*, pp.192–202.

68 U.S. Department of State, 'Afghanistan: Taliban Rep Won't Seek UN Seat For Now', Cable, 13 December 1996, Confidential. Declassified and available from the National Security Archive (http://nsarchive.gwu.edu/non-state actorEBB/non-state actorEBB97).

69 AFP, 25 May 1997 (Pakistan, on 25 May); *The News International*, 27 May 1997 (Saudi Arabia, on 26 May); AFP, 28 May 1997 (UAE, last of the three). In turn, the Taliban government recognized the separatist government in the Russian republic of Chechnya in January 2000. Jane's Sentinel: Afghanistan, 1 June 2000.

70 Fredholm von Essen, 'Hybrid Threat Capability of the Afghan Taliban', pp.313–346.

71 Ahmed Rashid, 'The Truth behind America's Taliban Talks', *Financial Times*, 29 June 2011 (http://blogs.ft.com).

72 BBC News, 9 November 2018 (https://www.bbc.com/news/world-asia-46155189); Taliban communique, 13 November 2018.

73 Taliban communique, 21 February 2020.

74 Taliban communique, 29 February 2020; BBC News, 29 February 2020 (https://www.bbc.com/news/world-asia-51689443).

75 For details on the series of meetings, see Fredholm von Essen, ' Hybrid Threat Capability of the Afghan Taliban', pp.335–336, and Michael

Fredholm von Essen, 'The Fog of War Again Descends on Afghanistan', *NIAS Press Blog*, 10 May 2020 (https://www.niaspress.dk).

76 Michael Fredholm von Essen, *Hemligstämplat: Svensk underrättelsetjänst från Erlander till Bildt* (Stockholm: Medström, 2020), pp.187–196, with references.

77 Magnus Hjort, *Den farliga fredsrörelsen: Säkerhetstjänsternas övervakning av fredsorganisationer, värnpliktsvägrare och FNL-grupper 1945–1990* (Stockholm: SOU 2002:90), pp.326–327; Fredholm von Essen, *Hemligstämplat*, pp.213–214.

78 Délégation des Commissions de gestion des Chambres fédérales (Confédération suisse), Affaire Crypto AG: Rapport de la Délégation des Commissions de gestion des Chambres fédérales, 2 November 2020.

79 Bojan Pancevski, 'U.S. Officials Say Huawei Can Covertly Access Telecom Networks', *Wall Street Journal*, 12 February 2020 (https://www.wsj.com/articles/u-s-officials-say-huawei-can-covertly-access-telecom-networks-11581452256). Notably, no evidence on Huawei backdoors was released; only managed leaks to trusted journalists.

80 Carlo J. V. Caro, 'Underwater Geopolitics: How China's Control of Undersea Cables and Data Flows Reshapes Global Power', *Real Clear Defense* web site, 26 November 2024 (https://www.realcleardefense.com/articles/2024/11/26/underwater_geopolitics_1074698.html).

81 Tom Regan, 'When Contemplating War, Beware of Babies in Incubators', *Christian Science Monitor*, 6 September 2002 (https://www.csmonitor.com/2002/0906/p25s02-cogn.html).

82 Anthony Paphiti, Brig. (rtd), UK Army, key note speech on propaganda (as a component of hybrid warfare) and accountability, *Hybrid Threats and Asymmetric Warfare: What to do?*, conference, 14–15 November 2017, Swedish Defence University, Stockholm.

83 Ben Norton, 'Leaked Docs Expose Massive Syria Propaganda Operation by Western Govt Contractors & Media', *Consortium News*, 12 October 2020 (https://consortiumnews.com/2020/10/12/leaked-docs-expose-massive-syria-propaganda-operation-by-western-govt-contractors-media/).

84 'Aleppo Syria: Global Shows of Solidarity over Aleppo', BBC News, 15 December 2016 (https://www.bbc.com/news/world-middle-east-38327586).

85 See, e.g., CIA study on Trends and Developments in Soviet Active Measures, released at a hearing on Soviet active measures before the Permanent Select Committee on Intelligence, House of Representatives, Washington, D.C., 13-14 July 1982, pp.56–60, 61–69.

86 U.S. Department of State, *Active Measures: A Report on the Substance and Process of Anti-U.S. Disinformation and Propaganda Campaigns* (Washington, DC: Department of State, 1986); U.S. Department of State, *Soviet Influence Activities: A Report on Active Measures and Propaganda, 1986-87* (Washington, DC: Department of State, 1987).

87 Mitrokhin, *KGB Lexicon*, p.13.

88 For full details, see Michael Fredholm von Essen, 'Soviet Active Measures in West, Southeast, and East Asia with regard to Afghanistan, 1980-1982', *Journal for Intelligence, Propaganda and Security Studies* (JIPSS) 13: 1 (2019), pp.56–74.

89 Aleksandr Kaznacheyev, a Soviet diplomat who defected to the West in 1959, described how articles were received from the KGB in Moscow, sent to Soviet embassies abroad, translated, and planted into local newspapers, among them *Blitz*. The published articles were returned to Moscow through TASS channels. The Soviet press then republished the materials as if they were genuine foreign articles. Alexander Kaznacheev, *Inside a Soviet Embassy: Experiences of a Russian Diplomat in Burma* (Philadelphia: J. B. Lippincott, 1962), pp.172–173, 177.

90 Thomas Boghardt, 'Operation INFEKTION: Soviet Bloc Intelligence and Its AIDS Disinformation Campaign', *Studies in Intelligence* 53:4 (December 2009), pp.1–24, on p.4.

91 Jayanta Kumar Ray, *India's Foreign Relations, 1947-2007* (New Delhi: Routledge, 2011), p.649.

92 For details, see Fredholm von Essen, 'Soviet Active Measures in West, Southeast, and East Asia', pp.70–71.

93 Fredholm von Essen, 'Soviet Active Measures in West, Southeast, and East Asia', passim.

94 Jack Boulter and Michael Fredholm von Essen, 'Loyalty to None, Disloyalty to All', *Journal for Intelligence, Propaganda and Security Studies* (JIPSS) 17: 2 (2023), pp.86–96.

95 FireEye, *'Ghostwriter' Influence Campaign: Unknown Actors Leverage Website Compromises and Fabricated Content to Push Narratives Aligned with Russian Security Interests* (Milpitas, California: FireEye, Inc., July 2020); FireEye, *Ghostwriter Update: Cyber Espionage Group UNC1151 Likely Conducts Ghostwriter Influence Activity* (Milpitas, California: FireEye, Inc., April 2021). In October 2021, FireEye changed its corporate name to Mandiant. Google acquired Mandiant in September 2022.

96 Based on FireEye, *'Ghostwriter' Influence Campaign*, pp.8–9; FireEye, *Ghostwriter Update*, pp.6–7, 12.

97 'Russische Gruppe »Ghostwriter« attackiert offenbar Parlamentarier', *Der Spiegel*, 26 March 2021 (www.spiegel.de/politik/deutschland/russischer-hack-erneute-attacke-hack-auf-bundestag-sieben-abgeordnete-betroffen-a-75e1adbe-4462-4e30-bd94-96796aed6b8a).

98 'Germany warns Russia over cyberattacks ahead of election', *Deutsche Welle*, 6 September 2021 (www.dw.com/en/germany-warns-russia-over-cyberattacks-ahead-of-election/a-59101191).

99 EU's High Representative for Foreign Affairs and Security Policy, EU Declaration, Press Release, 24 September 2021 (www.consilium.europa.eu/en/press/press-releases/2021/09/24/declaration-by-the-high-representative-on-behalf-of-the-european-union-on-respect-for-the-eu-s-democratic-processes).

100 Lily Hay Newman, "Ghostwriter' Looks Like a Purely Russian Op – Except It's Not', *Wired*, 16 November 2021 (www.wired.com/story/ghostwriter-hackers-belarus-russia-misinformationo).

101 Martin Untersinger, 'Ghostwriter, des pirates informatiques prorusses qui s'invitent dans la guerre en Ukraine', *Le Monde*, 28 May 2022 (www.lemonde.fr/pixels/article/2022/04/28/ghostwriter-des-pirates-informatiques-prorusses-qui-s-invitent-dans-la-guerre-en-ukraine_6124044_4408996.html).

102 Nick Fielding and Ian Cobain, 'Revealed: US Spy Operation That Manipulates Social Media', *The Guardian*, 17 March 2011 (https://amp.theguardian.com/technology/2011/mar/17/us-spy-operation-social-networks).

103 Stanford Internet Observatory, *Unheard Voice: Evaluating Five Years of Pro-Western Covert Influence Operations* (Stanford, California: Graphika and Stanford Internet Observatory, 24 August 2022).

104 Chris Bing and Joel Schechtman, 'Pentagon Ran Secret Anti-Vax Campaign to Undermine China during Pandemic', Reuters, 14 June 2024 (https://www.reuters.com/investigates/special-report/usa-covid-propaganda/).

105 A. Ross Johnson, *Radio Free Europe and Radio Liberty: The CIA Years and Beyond* (Washington, DC: Woodrow Wilson Center Press with Stanford University Press, 2010).

106 See, e.g., the series of reports on Russian 'robotrolling' issued by NATO Strategic Communications (StratCom) Centre of Excellence in Latvia between 2017 and 2021 (https://stratcomcoe.org/).

Chapter 3

1 *Los Angeles Times*, 25 August 1989.

2 The alleged links between the Medellín Cartel and some of these events have been disputed. See, e.g., 'M-19 cambió drogas por armas', *El Pais* (Colombia), 26 September 2007 (original web site: www.elpais.com.co/paisonline/notas/Octubre062004/A206N2.html; currently at https://web.archive.org/web/20070927015332/http://www.elpais.com.co/paisonline/notas/Octubre062004/A206N2.html#)

3 Francisco E. Thoumi, 'Colombian Organized Crime: From Drug Trafficking to Parastatal Bands and Widespread Corruption', Dina Siegel and Henk van de Bunt (eds), *Traditional Organized Crime in the Modern World: Responses to Socioeconomic Change* (New York: Springer, 2012), pp.131–148, on p.137.

4 Alison Jamieson, 'Antimafia Efforts in Italy, 1992-1997', *Studies in Conflict & Terrorism* 21: 3 (1998), pp.233–260; Alison Jamieson, *The Antimafia: Italy's Fight against Organized Crime* (London: Macmillan, 1999); Deirdre Pirro, 'The Olive Tree of Peace: The Massacre in Via dei Georgofili', *The Florentine* 164 (24 May 2012).

5 Jamieson, 'Antimafia Efforts in Italy', p.258.

6 Gösta Gunnarsson, *Rapport av den särskilde utredaren för granskning av hotbilden mot och säkerhetsskyddet kring statsminister Olof Palme* (Stockholm: SOU 1989:1), pp.16–21.

7 George Grayson and Samuel Logan, *The Executioner's Men, Los Zetas, Rogue Soldiers, Criminal Entrepreneurs, and the Shadow State They Created* (New Brunswick, New Jersey: Transaction Publishers, 2012); Joel Hernández, 'Terrorism, Drug Trafficking, and the Globalization of Supply', *Perspectives on Terrorism* 7: 4 (2013), pp.41–61, on pp.46, 51–52.

8 Fredholm von Essen, 'Hybrid Threat Capability of the Afghan Taliban Movement', pp.313–346. For further details, see Fredholm von Essen, *Afghanistan Beyond the Fog of War.*

9 See, e.g., Michael Fredholm von Essen, *Afghanistan and Central Asian Security* (Stockholm: Stockholm University, Asian Cultures and Modernity 1, March 2002), p.16.

10 Antonio Giustozzi, 'Military Adaptation by the Taliban, 2002-2011', Theo Farrell, Frans Osinga, and James A. Russell (eds.), *Military Adaptation in Afghanistan* (Stanford: Stanford University Press, 2013), pp.242–262, on pp.246, 256, 259.

11 Sections 1 and 2, *Code of Conduct for the Mujahidin of the Islamic Emirate of Afghanistan*, 2nd edn of 29 May 2010 (Taliban Voice of Jihad Online in Pashto, 9 August 2010). The second edition included 14 sections and 85 articles. The first edition, which used very similar language, was published in the first half of 2009 and included 13 sections and 67 articles. The first edition in turn replaced the *Book of Rules for the Mujahidin*, first published in the holy month of Ramadan 2006.

12 Article 77, *Code of Conduct for the Mujahidin of the Islamic Emirate of Afghanistan*, 2nd edn of 29 May 2010.

13 Article 78, *Code of Conduct for the Mujahidin of the Islamic Emirate of Afghanistan*, 2nd edn of 29 May 2010. This article was also in the 2009 edition. However, it was not in the original 2006 *Book of Rules*.

14 See, e.g., the emphasis on statements such as 'The decisive terrain is the human terrain' and 'The people are the center of gravity', in *Counterinsurgency Guidance*, 1 August 2010, written by General David H. Petraeus, COMISAF/CDR USFOR-A.

15 Giustozzi, 'Military Adaptation by the Taliban', passim. The learning curve was also evident in the aforementioned updated and improved editions of the *Book of Rules* and *Code of Conduct*.

16 Ahmed Rashid, *Taliban: Islam, Oil and the New Great Game in Central Asia* (London: I. B. Tauris, 2000), pp.26–30, 125; William Maley (ed.), *Fundamentalism Reborn? Afghanistan and the Taliban* (New York: New York University Press, 1998), pp.71, 82. For full details on the Pakistani involvement in the establishment of the Afghan Taliban, which was noted by diplomats at the time, see Fredholm von Essen, *Afghanistan Beyond the Fog of War*, pp.192–202.

17 Pervez Musharraf, *In the Line of Fire: A Memoir* (London: Simon & Schuster, 2006), 202. See also Anthony Davis, 'How the Taliban Became a Military Force', Maley (ed.), *Fundamentalism Reborn?* pp.43–71, on p.71.

18 Rashid, *Taliban*, 125; Davis, 'How the Taliban Became a Military Force', p.71; Ahmed Rashid, 'Pakistan and the Taliban', Maley (ed.), *Fundamentalism Reborn?* pp.72–89, on p.82.

19 Musharraf, *In the Line of Fire*, p.203.

20 M. J. Gohari, *The Taliban: Ascent to Power* (Oxford: Oxford Logos Society, 1999), p.118.

21 Taliban web sites, www.taleban.com; www.afghan-ie.com (both now defunct).

22 Maley, *Fundamentalism Reborn*, pp.45–46, 49, 50.

23 Maley, *Fundamentalism Reborn*, p.12 n.25.

24 Jane's Sentinel Security Assessment: Afghanistan, Jane's Information Group, 30 August 2000; Ahmed Rashid, 'The Taliban: Exporting Extremism', *Foreign Affairs*, November/December 1999, pp.22–35; Rashid, *Taliban*, p.100; Anthony Davis, 'Struggle for Recognition', *Jane's Defence Weekly*, 4 October 2000, p.21; Anthony Davis, 'Foreign Fighters Step Up Activity in Afghan Civil War', *Jane's Intelligence Review* 13: 8 (August 2001), pp.14–17.

25 Davis, 'How the Taliban Became a Military Force', pp.68–71; Amin Saikal, 'The Rabbani Government, 1992-1996', Maley, *Fundamentalism Reborn*, pp.29–42, on p.39; Jane's Sentinel: Afghanistan, 30 August 2000; Davis, 'Struggle for Recognition', p.21; Davis, 'Foreign Fighters Step Up Activity, pp.14–17; Rashid, Taliban, p.49; Ahmed Rashid, *Jihad: The Rise of Militant Islam in Central Asia* (New Haven: Yale University Press, 2002), p.174; Human Rights Watch (HRW), *Fueling Afghanistan's War* (HRW Press Backgrounder, 2001).

26 U.S. Consulate (Peshawar), 'New Fighting and New Forces in Kandahar', Cable, 3 November 1994, Confidential. Declassified and available from the National Security Archive (http://nsarchive.gwu.edu/non-state actorEBB/non-state actorEBB97).

27 U.S. Embassy (Islamabad), 'The Taliban – Who Knows What the Movement Means?' Cable, 28 November 1994, Confidential. Declassified and available from the National Security Archive (http://nsarchive.gwu.edu/non-state actorEBB/non-state actorEBB97).

28 'Remembering Our Warriors: Babar "the Great", *Defence Journal* (Pakistan), April 2001.

29 U.S. Department of State, 'Developments in Afghanistan', Memorandum, 5 December 1994, Classification Unknown. Declassified and available from the National Security Archive (http://nsarchive.gwu.edu/non-state actorEBB/non-state actorEBB97).

30 U.S. Embassy (Islamabad), '[Excised] Believe Pakistan is Backing Taliban', Cable, 6 December 1994, Secret. Declassified and available from the National Security Archive (http://nsarchive.gwu.edu/non-state actorEBB/non-state actorEBB97).

31 U.S. Embassy (Islamabad), 'The Taliban: What We've Heard', Cable, 26 January 1995, Secret. Declassified and available from the National Security Archive (http://nsarchive.gwu.edu/non-state actorEBB/non-state actorEBB97).

32 U.S. Embassy (Islamabad), 'Eyewitness to the Fall of Herat Says Taliban are Winning Hearts and Minds – For Now', Cable, 18 September 1995, Confidential. Declassified and available from the National Security Archive (http://nsarchive.gwu.edu/non-state actorEBB/non-state actorEBB97).

33 U.S. Department of State, 'Afghanistan: Taliban Rep Won't Seek UN Seat For Now', Cable, 13 December 1996, Confidential. Declassified and available from the National Security Archive (http://nsarchive.gwu.edu/non-state actorEBB/non-state actorEBB97).

34 The Taliban representative's name is redacted in the declassified cable. However, his name is mentioned in U.S. Department of State, 'U.S. Engagement with the Taliban on Usama Bin Laden', Secret NODIS, circa 16 July 2001. Declassified and available from the National Security Archive (http://nsarchive.gwu.edu/non-state actorEBB/non-state actorEBB97/index3.htm).

35 Bette Dam, *Expeditie Uruzgan: De weg van Hamid Karzai naar het paleis* (Amsterdam: De Arbeiderspers, 2009), pp.43, 47–8.

36 Support from Pakistan: HRW, *Fueling Afghanistan's War;* Jane's Sentinel: Afghanistan, 17 October 2000; 30 August 2000; Jane's Sentinel: Afghanistan, 28 May 1999; Rashid, Taliban, pp.44–45, 72, 183–184; Ahmed Rashid, 'Heart of Darkness', *Far Eastern Economic Review*, 5 August 1999, pp.8–12; Ralph H. Magnus and Eden Naby, *Afghanistan: Mullah, Marx, and Mujahid* (Boulder, Colorado: Westview, 1998), p.190; Maley, *Fundamentalism Reborn*, p.69.

37 *New York Times*, 25 September 2001.

38 Rashid, *Taliban*, pp.35, 120, 123–124; Rashid, 'Heart of Darkness', pp.8–12. The Taliban in mid-2000 banned the cultivation of opium poppy. Some Western drug law enforcement officials claimed that this was merely a public-relations exercise, and that drugs were instead stockpiled in order to push up the price. Because of the 2001 downfall of the Taliban, we may never know their ultimate intentions. The Taliban certainly made substantial profits from the narcotics trade *before* they outlawed it. See, for instance, *Far Eastern Economic Review*, 28 December 2001. They also reportedly sold large quantities of the stockpiled drugs after the 11 September 2001 terrorist attacks on the United States in order to finance the expected war. Roland Jacquard, *Les archives secrètes d'Al-Qaida: Révélations sur les héritiers de Ben Laden* (Paris: Jean Picollec, 2002), p.62 n.4. According to Vladimir Fenopetov, Chief, Europe and West/Central Asia, UN Office on Drugs and Crime, the Taliban ban of opium production, which came into force in 2001, was merely a ruse to (1) make full use of an existing overproduction, and (2) increase the price of opium. Trafficking out of Afghanistan, according to United Nations statistics, in fact remained constant. Vladimir Fenopetov, 'Eurasia's Narcotics Situation', conference on 'New' Security Threats in Eurasia: Implications for the Euro-Atlantic Space, Central Asia-Caucasus Institute/Silk Road Studies Program, Stockholm, 20 May 2005.

39 Jacquard, *Archives secrètes*, p.24.

40 Ahmed Rashid, 'Pakistan and the Taliban', Maley, *Fundamentalism Reborn*, pp.72–89, on pp.84–85.

41 On 19 September 1998, the uncompromising Taliban leader Mullah Omar insulted Prince Turki and the Saudi royal family. Saudi Arabia then ceased its support for the Taliban, although the diplomatic recognition pushed through by Pakistan in May 1997 was not withdrawn. Perhaps significantly, from October 1998 the Taliban, who previously had generally been able to seize the initiative in any military offensive, began to lose ground to a Northern Alliance offensive that managed to maintain its momentum until the summer of 1999. Rashid, Taliban, pp.48, 72, 131, 138–139, 201–202, 227–233, 264 n.16.

42 Rashid, *Taliban*, pp.95–104, 220–221.

43 Jane's Sentinel: Afghanistan, 30 August 2000.

44 Jason Burke, 'Lies, Payoffs, Traps Are Allies' Weapons', *Observer* (London), as included in *Japan Times*, 10 November 2001.

45 Afghanistan was not on the United States list of states sponsoring terrorism, since the United States did not recognize the Taliban government.

46 Rashid, Taliban, pp.49–50, 73–74.

47 Jane's Sentinel: Afghanistan, 30 August 2000.

48 Rashid, *Taliban*, p.100.

49 Carl Hammer (pseud.), *Tide of Terror: America, Islamic Extremism, and the War on Terror* (Boulder, Colorado: Paladin Press, 2003), pp.223–287.

50 National Counterterrorism Center (NCTC), *Afghan Taliban* (NCTC web site, www.nctc.gov, 2013).

51 Giustozzi, 'Military Adaptation by the Taliban', p.244.

52 See, e.g., Michael Fredholm von Essen, 'The Need for New Policies in Afghanistan: A European's Perspective', *Himalayan and Central Asian Studies* 15: p.1–2 (2011), pp.54–75, on p.67. In time, the Taliban also began to receive some support from Iran. In 2010, at least three meetings between Iranian Islamic Revolutionary Guards Corps (IRGC, *Pasdaran-e Enghelab-e Islami*) officers and Taliban leaders took place. The Iranians reportedly had considerable success in offering patronage to individual Taliban commander. Giustozzi, 'Military Adaptation by the Taliban', pp.247, 257.

53 Antonio Giustozzi, *Turmoil within the Taliban: A Crisis of Growth?* (Central Asia Program, George Washington University: Central Asia Policy Brief 7, 2013); Antonio Giustozzi, *The Taliban and the 2014 Elections in Afghanistan* (Washington, DC: United States Institute of Peace, 2014), p.6.

54 Giustozzi, *Turmoil within the Taliban*; Ron Moreau, 'Taliban Forces Desperate to Hear from Their Absent Leader, Mullah Omar', *Daily Beast*, 1 May 2013.

55 The Leadership Council (Rahbari Shura) in Quetta was the main decision-making body of the Taliban and accordingly included several old Taliban leaders. Although of diminishing importance because of a

decline in revenue and power, as a collective force the Rahbari Shura still enjoyed a certain amount of prestige within the movement.

56 Abdul Qayyum Zakir's alliance within the Quetta Shura was based on Zakir's personal network but also included those of several other Taliban leaders. Zakir, a former Guantanamo detainee transferred to Afghan custody who following his 2007 release by Hamid Karzai's government returned to the insurgency and in 2009 was appointed head of the Quetta Military Commission, was supported by both the Pakistani government and the Peshawar Shura, thus enjoying his own sources of revenue. See, e.g., Giustozzi, *The Taliban and the 2014 Elections in Afghanistan*, p.17.

57 Akhtar Mansur's alliance within the Quetta Shura was based on Mansur's personal network, funded from sources inside Afghanistan and among the Afghan Diaspora, and also included the powerful Baradar and Dadullah networks (the latter revived in 2010–2011 after a period of disorder due to the death of its founder; Giustozzi, *Turmoil within the Taliban*, p.3) in common opposition to Abdul Qayyum Zakir. As head of the Quetta Political Commission, Mansur had considerable political influence.

58 The Peshawar Shura, which itself consisted of several smaller networks, some of which were of Pakistani jihadist origin, was reportedly more state- and university-educated than clerical as well as directly supported, and thus under a certain level of control, by the Pakistani government. See, e.g., Giustozzi, *Turmoil within the Taliban*, p.2; Giustozzi, *The Taliban and the 2014 Elections in Afghanistan*, p.17.

59 Don Rassler and Vahid Brown. *The Haqqani Nexus and the Evolution of Al-Qaida* (West Point: Harmony Program, Combating Terrorism Center, 2011).

60 Statement dated 25 April 2014, Voice of Jihad, Islamic Emirate of Afghanistan web site (http://shahamat-english.com).

61 Anand Gopal, Mansur Khan Mahsud, and Brian Fishman, *The Battle for Pakistan: Militancy and Conflict in North Waziristan* (Washington, DC: New America Foundation, 2010); Gretchen Peters, *Crime and Insurgency in the Tribal Areas of Afghanistan and Pakistan* (West Point: Harmony Program, Combating Terrorism Center, 2010); Rassler and Brown, *The Haqqani Nexus and the Evolution of Al-Qaida*.

62 Rassler and Brown, *The Haqqani Nexus and the Evolution of Al-Qaida*.

63 Institute for War and Peace Reporting (http://iwpr.net/), 27 March 2014.

64 GlobalSecurity.org, *Hizb-i-Islami* (www.globalsecurity.org, 15 August 2012).

65 Kenneth Katzman, *Afghanistan: Post-Taliban Governance, Security, and U.S. Policy* (Washington, DC: Congressional Research Service, 21 September 2012), p.48.

66 On that topic, see, e.g., Fredholm von Essen, *Afghanistan Beyond the Fog of War*.

67 See, e.g., Giustozzi, 'Military Adaptation by the Taliban', p.255.

68 For an example of the Taliban IED campaigns, see Carl Forsberg, *The Taliban's Campaign for Kandahar* (Washington, DC: Institute for the Study of War, 2009), p.29.

69 Giustozzi, 'Military Adaptation by the Taliban', pp.250, 251, 252.

70 Giustozzi, 'Military Adaptation by the Taliban', p.252.

71 Giustozzi, 'Military Adaptation by the Taliban', p.251.

72 Forsberg, *The Taliban's Campaign for Kandahar*, p.25.

73 Michael Fredholm von Essen, 'The New Face of Chechen Terrorism', *Central Asia – Caucasus Analyst*, September 2003 (Johns Hopkins University).

74 For this and other examples, see, e.g., Forsberg, *The Taliban's Campaign for Kandahar*, pp.40, 46.

75 Forsberg, *The Taliban's Campaign for Kandahar*, pp.25, 42.

76 Forsberg, *The Taliban's Campaign for Kandahar*, p.30.

77 See, e.g., BBC News, 15 June 2014.

78 See, e.g., the Textually.org web site (www.textually.org/textually/archives/2008/03/019260.htm); citing AP, 1 March 2008; Forsberg, *The Taliban's Campaign for Kandahar*, p.33.

79 See, e.g., Forsberg, *The Taliban's Campaign for Kandahar*, pp.44–46.

80 Thomas H. Johnson, 'The Taliban Insurgency and an Analysis of *Shabnamah* (Night Letters)', *Small Wars and Insurgencies* 18: 3 (September 2007), pp.317–344.

81 Reuters, 16 August 2010; *The Telegraph*, 27 January 2011 (www.telegraph.co.uk, with video).

82 Here we will disregard the question of the extent to which the Taliban movement funded its activities through Afghanistan's abundant opium production. The opium trade was fundamentally a means for funding, thus providing the means to fight, and not intended as a means for hybrid threat projection as such, even though one could argue that in the long term, drugs from Afghanistan would play its role in destabilizing some of the states which provided troops to ISAF.

83 Giustozzi, 'Military Adaptation by the Taliban', p.245.

84 AFP, 25 May 1997 (Pakistan, on 25 May); *The News International*, 27 May 1997 (Saudi Arabia, on 26 May); AFP, 28 May 1997 (UAE, last of the three). Incidentally, the Taliban government in turn recognized the separatist government in the Russian republic of Chechnya in January 2000, an act which caused the lasting enmity of Russia. Jane's Sentinel: Afghanistan, 1 June 2000.

85 Rashid, 'The Truth behind America's Taliban Talks'.

86 CNN, 5 October 2008.

87 Reuters, 14 August 2013.

88 *New York Times*, 4 February 2014.

89 Radio Sweden news program *Ekot*, 1 July 2010 (http://sverigesradio.se); Försvarsmakten (Armed Forces), Årsrapport Säkerhetstjänst 2011: Militära underrättelse- och säkerhetstjänsten, MUST (Försvarsmakten, 2012), p.18.

90 *New York Times*, 19 June 2004.

91 Joseph Fitsanakis, 'Analysis: Mullah Mansour's Killing Will Shape Future of Afghan War', *IntelNews*, 24 May 2016 (https://intelnews.org/2016/05/24/011907/).

92 *New York Times*, 22 June 2011.

93 Trinquier, *Modern Warfare*, p.83. Trinquier describes the enemy in both counterinsurgency and counterterrorism as an armed clandestine organization, engaged in clandestine warfare. The clandestine organization operates in one or both of two modes, that of partisan/guerrilla and terrorist, respectively. These two categories function in different ways since they operate in different types of terrain. In the partisan/guerrilla mode, an armed clandestine group will choose targets to establish a presence and gain territorial control through a display of power. The post-2001 Taliban movement operated in this mode in Afghanistan, and the same went on among jihadist insurgents in Pakistan, Yemen, Somalia, Mali, Syria, and fundamentally in any other place where armed clandestine groups operated. Having established a degree of territorial control (cf. Al-Qaida in Afghanistan prior to 2001), the group was, simultaneously with conducting local operations, free to engage, or not, in international terrorism as well. Ibid., p.16. Yet the importance of a local base is often forgotten in terrorism studies. Trinquier's experiences would have been particularly useful in post-2001 Afghanistan but were largely forgotten when operations were initiated.

94 Fredholm von Essen, 'Need for New Policies in Afghanistan'.

95 John Pike, www.globalsecurity.org, 2002.

96 Center for Defense Information (www.cdi.org), 2002.

97 Bill Roggio and Alexander Mayer, *Charting the Data for US Airstrikes in Pakistan, 2004-2014* (www.longwarjournal.org).

98 Patrick B. Johnston and Anoop K. Sarbahi, *The Impact of U.S. Drone Strikes on Terrorism in Pakistan and Afghanistan* (paper, RAND Corporation and Stanford University, 11 February 2014).

99 Johnston and Sarbahi, *Impact of U.S. Drone Strikes*, p.25.

100 See, e.g., Reuters, 20 May 2011, based on a U.S. diplomatic cable from 11 February 2008 exposed by WikiLeaks detailing discussions between Pakistan's chief of army staff General Ashfaq Kayani and Admiral William J. Fallon, then commander of U.S. Central Command.

ABOUT THE AUTHOR

Professor Michael Fredholm von Essen is an historian and former military analyst who has published extensively on the history of Eurasia, and lectured, during conferences or as visiting professor, around the world. He has published a large number of books, including *The Goths 1-2* (Society of Ancients, 2021-2022); *Afghanistan Beyond the Fog of War* (NIAS Press, 2018); *Transnational Organized Crime and Jihadist Terrorism: Russian-Speaking Networks in Western Europe* (Routledge, 2017); numerous articles in Slingshot, the journal of the Society of Ancients, and Arquebusier, the journal of the Pike and Shot Society; and many books for Helion and Company Publishing.